Practical Tools for Game Design Students

By

Zack Hiwiller

Table of Contents

Preface

Game design is an esoteric field. Whereas most members of a more traditional field (say electrical engineering) take the same classes in school, follow the same career paths and generally have the same skill sets, game designers are a much more mixed breed. We have degrees in: English, Cognitive Science, Art, Digital Media, Film, Philosophy, Math, Statistics and, (of course) Computer Science among others. My undergraduate degree was in Information Systems. Only recently has game design itself been deemed a worthy field of study and as such you are seeing more and more game design programs popping up all across the world.

The reason for this divergence is the nature of the field itself. Game design can encompass elements of all those fields listed above and more. Designers may use art skills to craft level geometry, English skills to write a document or to script dialogue, statistics to calculate probabilities and computer science to describe a behavior all in the same day. Modern game designers need to be renaissance men and women.

But each of these disciplines here in the present day also carry with it a number of software packages that assist the designer in pulling that esoterica into a final product. Some of these you may already be familiar with; very few students lack at least basic experience with a word processor. Some you may have seen in passing; Powerpoint is becoming more and more prevalent in secondary education. Some I would be very surprised to hear wide use of at the student level; students do not often use mind mapping software and bug trackers. In this book we will cover a variety of tools that the modern designer will use in industry.

This book is primarily for students either entering game design programs or for those looking for a broad exposure to tools used by game designers. When I say “game designer” in this book I generally refer to folks making digital games in a corporate environment. Of course, this is not the only kind of game designer. As I write this board games are enjoying a popular resurgence thanks to the fertile European market for advanced board games. I would be remiss not to note that many developers of digital games are independent coders/artists/designers who do not work in a corporate environment at all. Hopefully, this book holds something of use for these kinds of designers as well. The tools covered in this book will have applicability even if some of the "application" sections are not particularly appropriate for the indie workflow.

The philosophy of this book comes from the Design Tools class I teach at Full Sail University. The purpose of the class is to give students exposure to a wide variety of tools used in industry such as word processors, spreadsheets, mind mapping applications and more with special focus on how these tools are used specifically by professional game designers. The nature of Full Sail's classes (intensive one-month sprints) means I don't get enough face-to-face time with students to go as in-depth as I would like.

Hence this book.

In order to cover all the tools I cover in my class, I would need for the students to buy something like ten books while only covering a tenth of each. Instead, in this book readers get an introduction to all of these tools in one place. But more importantly, readers will get insight regarding how these tools are used in the game industry--something I have found in no other book.

The goal of many books that cover the technical is to be as deep as the format allows. Thus you see thousand-page Word references that cover every possible function in depth. This book will not do that. Instead, this book will highlight some of the most used and most useful functions in these software packages.

Why cover a large number of tools at all? Is not human history just a timeline of specialization? Perhaps. Counterintuitively, the purpose of this book is not to simply teach the tools themselves, but to **cultivate designers who know how to learn tools quickly and skillfully.** Any reference book of this type will become out-of-date quickly.

A designer "on the front lines" may be required to pick up a proprietary tool at a moment's notice. Say a level designer has to take a leave of absence. A designer familiar with UDK and familiar with picking up new and strange tools will be much more valuable than a designer who has to have his or her hand held.

At the very least, in times of peril, you can use this book to bludgeon invaders. The corner nearest the binding should be the strongest. Unless you are reading this as an e-book then sorry, I have got nothing for you.

A designer's education is never complete. Every year there are new techniques to learn, new software packages to familiarize with, new languages to learn, new games to play, new mistakes to make, and new genres and titles to experience. Every conference I go to—be it the spectacle of the annual Game Developer's Conference in San Francisco or the intensive workshopping at Project Horseshoe in Texas—designers gather and clamor to learn from each other.

Professional designers know that our learning is never and can be never truly complete. It is only by constant study and hard work that we can grow. Imagine the differences between the designers of a game from the 1980s - say, the text adventure phenomenon *Zork* - versus a designer of one of today's massive MMOs or Facebook games. The world changes fast.

It is almost a Sisyphean task. You learn software only for it to become obsolete in the next breath. But there is no alternative. Designers love to learn by nature. If you are familiar with nothing covered by this book, congratulations! You are getting the true education of a designer: the elation that comes with breaking new ground. If you think everyone else knows everything and you are just a poseur, congratulations! You echo the feelings of just about every designer humble enough to know their place.

This book is just a stepping-stone. The real education comes with practice. Only by actually designing can you learn design. When you are done with this book, put it away for a while and pick up something else that will bring your skills closer to where you want to be. Then make some games. Fail. Learn. Build. Fail again. Learn more. Build more. The cycle never ends and it is glorious.

Let's get out our tools.

Thanks

The first thanks goes to my ever-supportive and loving fiancée Gloriana. She knows how important she is to me, but seeing it in print probably can't hurt.

Thanks to my parents Jan and Dan Hiwiller who supported me even after I decided to chase video games after spending six figures on a college education. Of course, they bought me an Atari when I was young. So whose fault is it really?

Thanks to Jesse Schell who inspired me to become a game designer after I took his Game Design class just as a fun way to fill an elective. He sees hundreds of the best and brightest students in the world every year and yet still spent some time on guiding and inspiring this insufferable hack. His *Art of Game Design* is the one book I recommend to everyone in the industry.

Thanks to all the various mentors I have had so far in my career: Jon Dean, Jason Barnes, James Hawkins, Phil Frazier, and many others who may not even know what impact they had on me.

Thanks to my elite editing team especially Raza Ali, Matthew Gallant, and all of the folks who gave me handy advice. Additional thanks to my colleagues at Full Sail University who make teaching an enormous pleasure.

About the Author

Zack Hiwiller is a game designer and educator. He has worked on games on numerous platforms: Game Boy Advance, Nintendo DS, Sony Playstation 2, Microsoft Xbox, Nintendo GameCube, Microsoft Xbox 360, Sony Playstation 3, PC, Facebook, iPad and others. He currently teaches Design Tools at Full Sail University in Winter Park, FL. He also runs a game design blog at www.hiwiller.com and his articles have been reprinted on *Kotaku*, *GameSetWatch* and in magazines such as *Handshake* and *Hacker's Monthly*. Between his personal blog and his guest articles on other game design sites, he's served well over a million and a half readers. Follow him on Twitter at @zhiwiller.

Overview of Topics

By its very nature a book of game design tools must be incomplete. Not only are there too many tools to realistically put in a single book or even in a single collection of books, but the tools change so rapidly and so drastically that any book of its nature that aimed to be completely authoritative would be obsolete as it was being typed.

That said, there are evergreen topics that are of great importance to all designers, especially fledgling designers looking for their first formalized design work. This is what I endeavor to cover in this book.

First, I give a broad overview of who **"the industry"** is and what kinds of roles are available in the many diverse types of organizations. We will also cover the software development life cycle, since knowing how software is actually made is a prerequisite to understanding the best ways to make game software.

Next, we talk about **written communication**. The game design document is foremost in this discussion as it is the industry standard artifact used for designers to communicate within teams and externally. We will cover what a game design document is, whom it is for and best practices for how it is made.

We will cover Microsoft Word and some useful functions with regards to writing clear and concise game documentation. Wikis are growing in popularity as a design tool and will be briefly covered. We will also cover some secondary tools to assist your written communication via charts and images, notably Microsoft Visio, Cacoo, and Adobe Photoshop.

The third section is about **number crunching**. Excel is the most underrated software tool that designers have. We will discuss how Excel can be used for organizing data like schedules but also its flexible use as a simulation device. We will dive into the features that help you get the most of Excel as a game designer, along with some discussion of the theoretical base that will help you think abstractly to apply Excel simulations to real world examples.

Fourth, we will talk **ideas**. Ideas are the trade of designers. We will cover how designers pitch their ideas along with the most dangerous software tool out there: Microsoft Powerpoint. This section is a safety class, teaching you how not to hurt yourself with this sharpest of tools. We will cover some of the most important functions of Powerpoint, along with some ties to written documentation that goes hand-in-glove with the pitch: notably, pitch documents and feature overviews.

Next, we will discuss ways to **get your hands dirty**. Every year the number of books on game design grows. But no book can truly teach you how to design. You must make games to become a designer. And yes, at first they will be terrible. But there is no substitute for production and failure. In this section of the book, I will detail some of the tools out there to dive into making games.

Finally, we will talk about **personal promotion**. Game design is a hard field to break into and an impossible field to master. We will talk about ways to improve your skills and increase your visibility in the field. Game design is a field of constant study and improvement. There are software tools out there that can help you connect to be discovered and land that important first job.

The Out-Of-Date Disclaimer

This book covers a lot of current software, referencing specific methods to achieve certain results. Since software is constantly changing with upgrades moving or changing functionality, examples in this book may be out-of-date. Copy editing a book of a single piece of software is an endeavor enough, but one that features a dozen different software packages is a fool's errand I have undertaken. Errata will be kept on the book's website at http://www.hiwiller.com/designtools but if you do not see a problem addressed, please let me know via email (zack@hiwiller.com) and I will attempt to remedy the situation in the next edition.

The Personal Pronoun Disclaimer

Throughout this book, I endeavor to use a gender neutral "he or she" when using a third-person singular. At times, I may slip and use a "he". Normally, I am not one to make an issue out of this. The language is parsable with either. But the game industry has a homogeneity problem and it can even be seen in game education. There are vastly more men getting into this field than women. In creative fields, we need differing viewpoints and backgrounds. I am using this space to make a clear statement that any use of 'he' alone is not meant to be gender-exclusive but is done out of error or for brevity.

Part One – The Digital Games Industry

Any game design student would be remiss to not know at least an overview of the industry he or she is trying to break into. Surely you've heard the tales of how difficult it is to get your first "game job" but game-job-where? What will you do?

Often students have this fixed notion of what the industry is, that designers spit out ideas and someone does something mumble mumble and then a game is on the shelf. The digital games industry is not only a massively complex organism, but also its structure changes greatly from firm to firm. We will try to remove the mystery of the beast by going through how a game gets from idea to execution to final product and the different people that make that possible.

We will also discuss the software development life cycle. Creating software is a complicated endeavor and there are many competing theories on how to manage that complexity. We will discuss the two most popular methodologies that you will see in games and how that affects the final product.

The industry changes by leaps and bounds every year. It was only recently that the iPhone changed mobile development and a whole new genre and delivery system dropped with Facebook games. Five years from now the landscape will change again. Being able to understand how shifts affect the development cycle will keep you ready to take on the jobs of the future.

Chapter 1 - Digital Games Industry Overview

How does a console game get from an idea to a final product in front of millions of gamers worldwide? And why are they so damn expensive? And how do other genres such as MMOs or Facebook games differ? To answer these questions, you have to be aware of the long chain of stakeholders that deals with the game idea from inception to completion.

In the list below, you will see repeated uses of the words "many", "often" or "sometimes". Models of development vary wildly from place to place and I am trying to comment on common structures.

Many games start with a **developer**. A developer is a group of creators: designers, engineers, producers, artists, sound folks and so on that work together to make the actual code and art of the game. Examples of developers are: EA Tiburon, Sony Santa Monica, Naughty Dog, or Valve.

Developers often need to team up with a larger entity to get their game further through the process. These entities are called **publishers**. They serve as a point of contact and generally will handle the financing and marketing. Examples of publishers are: Electronic Arts, Activision-Blizzard, and Nexon. Sometimes publishers will own developers as in the case of Electronic Arts and EA Tiburon or Sony and Sony Santa Monica.

One of the elements that a publisher can help with is getting the attention of and financing the agreement with **licensors**. A licensor is any external person or group that owns a piece of intellectual property that a developer would like to use in a game.

One example of licensors involves sports games. Most sports games license the use of real players, teams and stadiums. Since the leagues and teams own these elements, developers need permission to use these, usually need to pay large sums of money and must abide by certain rules. Licensors are not just the major logos on the front but can be any element in the game. Games like *Forza Motorsport* license every real-life car found in the game. Games like *Grand Theft Auto 4* license music. In the *NCAA Football* series the Heisman Trophy needs to be licensed every year from the Downtown Athletic Club. Publishers have legal and business staff members experienced in drawing up the contracts that make these relationships possible.

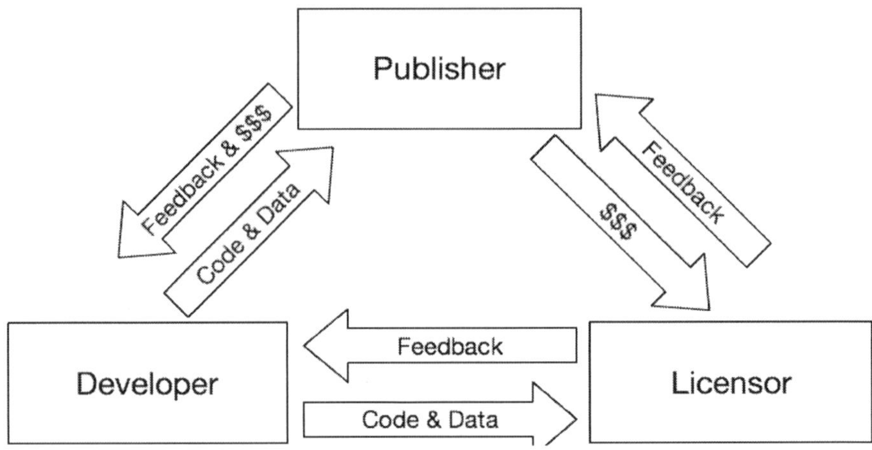

Figure 1.1 - Publishers, Licensors and Developers

If you understand all the different relationships the licensor needs to handle, you will also understand why many licensors choose to limit their intellectual property to one particular trusted partner.

Additionally, if you want to create a game on a console like the Playstation 3 or the iPhone, you need the platform manufacturer's seal of approval before doing so. Developers and publishers do this by interfacing with what is called a **console group**.

Why are these necessary? In the late 1970s, the industry was pretty homogenous. The hardware markers for home consoles also made all the games. A group of disgruntled Atari programmers broke off and formed Activision. Atari sued Activision claiming that it was illegal for them to develop games for Atari's system.

Once the legal suits were settled, anyone could reverse-engineer a cartridge and produce for an Atari system and many did. Even food companies like Purina were quickly throwing together games (*Chase the Chuck Wagon*) that flooded the market with poor titles. This, among other factors, almost destroyed the fledgling home console market in the early 1980s.

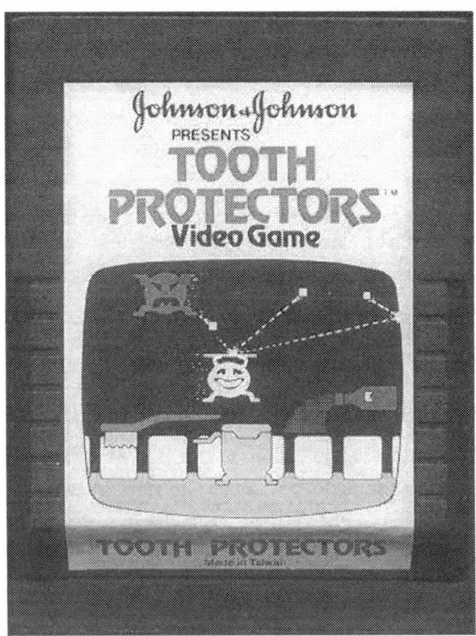

Figure 1.2 - For No Good Reason. © Johnson & Johnson

As a result, modern game console developers require software to be officially certified by their console groups. These games have to meet certain quality and formatting standards. Every game on modern consoles has to conform to each console group's unique standards. Additionally, from the console manufacturer's point of view, they make money on every software sale so no one can profit on their work without the console group first getting a cut.

The publisher generally acts as the point of communication between the console groups and developers. Many developers cannot even talk to console groups without already being signed on with an established publisher.

The Physical Process

If you are buying a console game, somehow that plastic package and disc had to get into your hands. How does that happen? Again, the publisher is the point of contact here.

The **manufacturer** prints the discs, cartridges, cases, booklets and whatever else will be shipped with the game. When a game has "gone gold", it usually means it has been sent to the manufacturer for printing. From there, the boxes of games go to a **distributor** who gets the games from a warehouse at the manufacturer and ships them to the millions of **retailers** who will sell you the final game.

While this part of the chain is not nearly as sexy as the creative side, it is extremely important to the process of actually getting the games in players' hands.

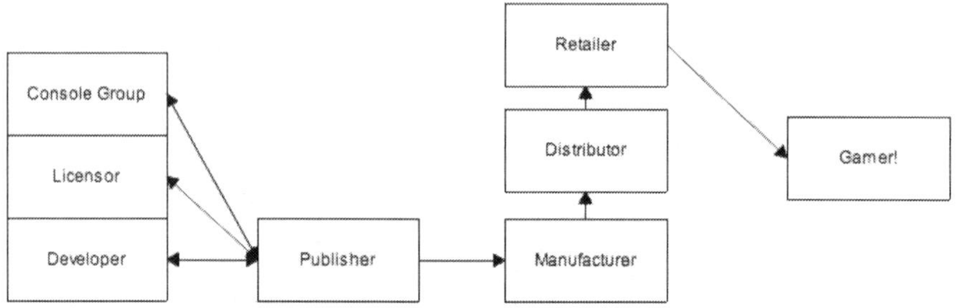

Figure 1.3 - The Publisher-Centric Model

Different Methods and Models

What we looked at above is just one possible model--the current status quo for developing and releasing a disc or cartridge for a major console. That is far from the only method. Take digital distribution of a game without licenses through a platform like Steam.

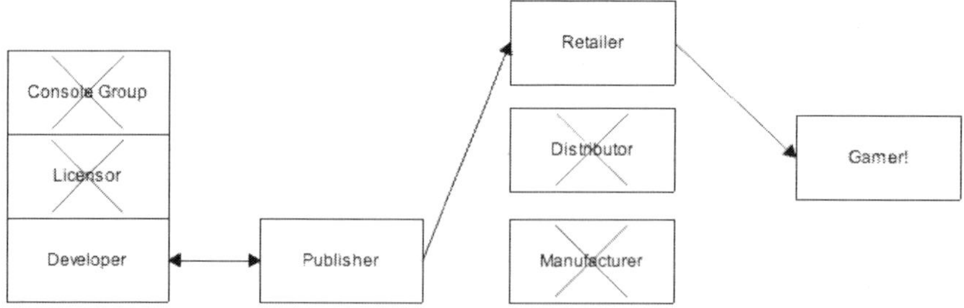

Figure 1.4 - An Unlicensed Steam-Distributed Game

You can instantly see what an attractive model this can be. Half of the entities have been eliminated! The extremely expensive licensors and console groups get the shaft (Steam games are mostly on PCs) and the act of getting a disc manufactured and shipped is not necessary.

Some developers are taking to self-publishing games on Apple's App Store. In that case, developers can gain an expensive console group, but can eschew pricey publishers and retail channels. Some App Store games do have a separate publisher that focuses on marketing and public relations.

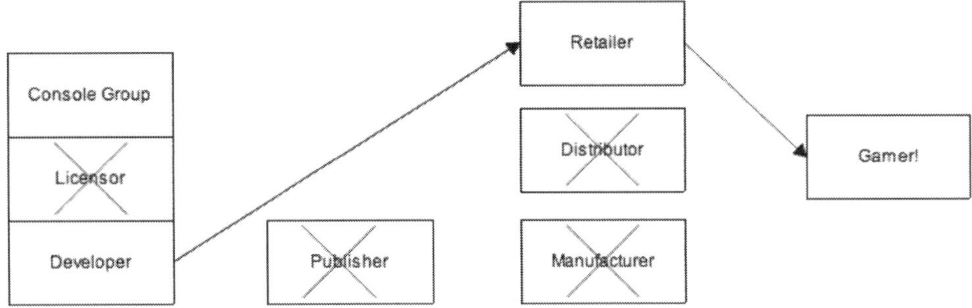

Figure 1.5 - App Store Distribution Channel

There are numerous models that fit games of all shapes and sizes. For instance, MMOs have a unique delivery and payment mechanism.

Other Entities

There are also some other groups that don't fit neatly into any particular box above.

Entertainment Software Ratings Board - This is an independent entity that rates and labels video games. While funded by publishers, they are wholly independent. Developers and publishers who want a rating submit a tape and/or final code to the ESRB. Often console groups, licensors or retailers will require specific ratings in order for the game to be sold. The ESRB only has jurisdiction in North America. Europe has a similar board called PEGI (Pan-European Game Information). Germany itself has a much stricter board called the USK (abbreviated from the much more verbose Unterhaltungssoftware Selbstkontrolle).

The **International Game Developer's Association** - The IGDA serves as an advocacy group for game developers worldwide. It has over ten thousand members and serves such diverse functions as organizing local get-togethers (the local groups are called "chapters") to publishing white papers and research. Chapter groups vary in activity, so it is best to check the group's website for local events. Certain cities like Boston and San Francisco have extremely active chapters. The cost is inexpensive for both students and professionals. The IGDA party at the Game Developer's Conference every year is a great place to meet like-minded individuals. We will cover the group more in a later chapter.

Middleware Companies - Middleware companies sell ready-packaged tools for developers to use so they can spend their time on elements unique to their game. Middleware is available for physics (Havok), engines (Unreal), bug-tracking (DevTrack), and even foliage generation (SpeedTree). Using middleware can save a large amount of time and money, but often has a steep learning curve and high initial investment.

Developer Types and Funding Types

Certain terms are thrown about with such frequency that it can often be neglected that everyone may not know the definitions. In the final section of this chapter, I would like to just highlight a few.

First Party Developers are development studios (see the developer boxes above) that are wholly owned by a console group and whose games are published internally The developer, publisher and console group are all three divisions of the same company. Examples of this are Nintendo's HAL Labs or Sony's Santa Monica studio.

Third Party Developers are the most common. These are different entities than the console manufacturers and may develop for multiple systems. These may or may not be owned by a publishing group. EA Tiburon is a third party developer that is owned by a publisher. Double Fine is a third party developer who publishes their titles through an external publisher.

Second Party Developer - I do these out of order because this term is almost never used. It technically refers to a developer who is not wholly owned by a console group but who develops exclusively for a particular manufacturer's platforms. Insomniac Games is an example of this, but more often they are simply referred to as a third-party developer.

Additionally, there can be stark differences in how a company is run based on how the company was funded.

A **publicly traded company** has shares listed on a stock exchange for anyone to purchase. These companies have to abide by complex government rules and report their earnings to shareholders quarterly. As a result, there is enormous pressure to consistently deliver earnings quarter after quarter. Video game companies often get a pass until the quarter containing the Christmas season, but the pressure to earn revenue regularly can result in ship dates being pushed forward. Examples of publicly owned game companies are your giants: Nintendo, Sony, Electronic Arts, Activision-Blizzard and so forth.

A **venture-funded company** is funded by a private group of investors. While they have less pressure than a publicly traded company to perform from quarter to quarter, these investors are generally looking for explosive growth. These companies generally have a lot more freedom to explore due to the cushion of their funding combined with the possibility of long-term focus in management. Many Silicon Valley companies are venture-funded like Telltale Games and Zynga.

A **personally owned company** is an organization where the owners are also employees of the company. If well capitalized, these kinds of companies have the broadest ability to create without any shareholder pressure. These companies also have no safety net for failure unless the owners themselves have deep pockets. These are the former garage developers that made it big. Valve is the most popular example, but many independent developers also fit this description.

Chapter 2 - Industry Roles

You want to be a game designer and you want to work at a development studio. But what does that mean? There are many roles one can fill in the industry.

If you break it down, there are three groups that are essential to game development: designers, artists and engineers. In every studio, you will see these three groups.

The primary misunderstanding new folks in the industry (and especially designers) make is that these groups are well defined and have a distinct set of responsibilities. The popular notion is that designers design, artists make assets and engineers do the code thing. In practice, this is usually not the case. The truth is that *everyone is a designer*. For the people with "designer" on their business cards, their job is to be caretaker of the design and communicate that design amongst the team.

Designers are in charge of **mechanics**. They figure out how the rules work, how the edge cases are affected, how players participate with the game.

Artists are in charge of **interface**. They affect how players interact with the game. Interface is any time the game meets the player. This ranges from the explicit user interface of the game (the menus, the heads-up display, the iconography) to the environments the game is played in to the sounds and other sensations produced directly by the game.

Engineers are in charge of **implementation**. All the elements in the game that make up the mechanics and the interface need to be put together in a way that players can use. In video games, this is writing and compiling code.

It is important to note that these three roles don't have to be shared by three unique people. A single person can take all three roles. In the early days, this was quite common: a single person designed, created the art and coded a game in the Atari days. Some indie games now even have all work consolidated to a single person. But it is important to know that all three roles are filled. These are different hats that people can wear. Someone who is a programmer can wear the design hat.

These three roles are found in all games. In a traditional video game like *World of Warcraft*, it is evident. Design decides what items drop, where quests are triggered and so forth. Art creates the world and the look and feel of the menus and HUD. Engineering handles the task of hooking all these things up so they work as intended.

Now examine a board game like *Monopoly*. There was a designer—Charles Darrow[1]—that decided how the game was played and the values of the properties. There were artists that designed the look and feel of the pieces of the board and of the rules. In board games, the role of implementation falls to the players themselves. The players ensure that the game is set up and played correctly.

How about a sport like basketball? Dr. James Naismith designed the game, but it has been since heavily revised by many different organizations. The interface to the game is the court, the ball and the basket. All three have been very deliberately created. Most of the implementation is handled by professional officials in sanctioned games and by the players themselves in pickup games.

Roles by Discipline

By the very fact that you are reading this book, I will assume that you are aspiring to be a designer. But what kind? There are many types of designers, even at the entry level. What kind of designer do you want to be?

A **level designer** creates mockups, places objects in levels and scripts them to do his or her bidding. The level designer is heavily involved in playtesting and storytelling and has positions from junior to lead in many studios. Level designers are not a part of all games. Sports games in particular have no level designers. Most Facebook games have no level designers. Level designers need to have a strong sense of aesthetics and may have at least a casual study of architecture in addition to the many other standard designer areas of expertise.

A **systems designer** is primarily focused on how the mechanics work together to create systems. For instance, a systems designer will craft the experience point progression or the game's economic mechanisms. Systems designers are generally employed on games with complex interactions,

[1] Darrow is popularly cited as the designer of the game, although there is overwhelming evidence that he was not the original designer.

often between human players. Systems designers need a grasp of economics and psychology well above the generalist designer. Systems designers also need an intuitive level of understanding of how complex systems behave and how to represent systems symbolically with math. Every systems designer needs a deep level of understanding with spreadsheets like Excel.

A **content designer** focuses on instances of content for games with a lot of diverse areas. For instance, an MMO may employ a content designer to craft quests or reuse content in new ways to create new interactions. Content designers are much like level designers except their focus is not primarily on the spatial layout of a level.

Someone with the title **game designer** can be any of these things. Smaller projects and more flexible projects often hire generalist game designers that can fill any of these roles. They may have expertise in storytelling, economics, psychology, algorithms, philosophy, human-computer interaction or any of the other dozens of fields useful for game designers. Often entry-level game designers will be tasked with managing documentation and other ancillary design issues before being entrusted with owning particular designs.

The design team tends to be headed by a **lead designer** on smaller projects or a **creative director** on large projects. Their job is largely to adjudicate issues between members of the team and act as the holder of the game's vision.

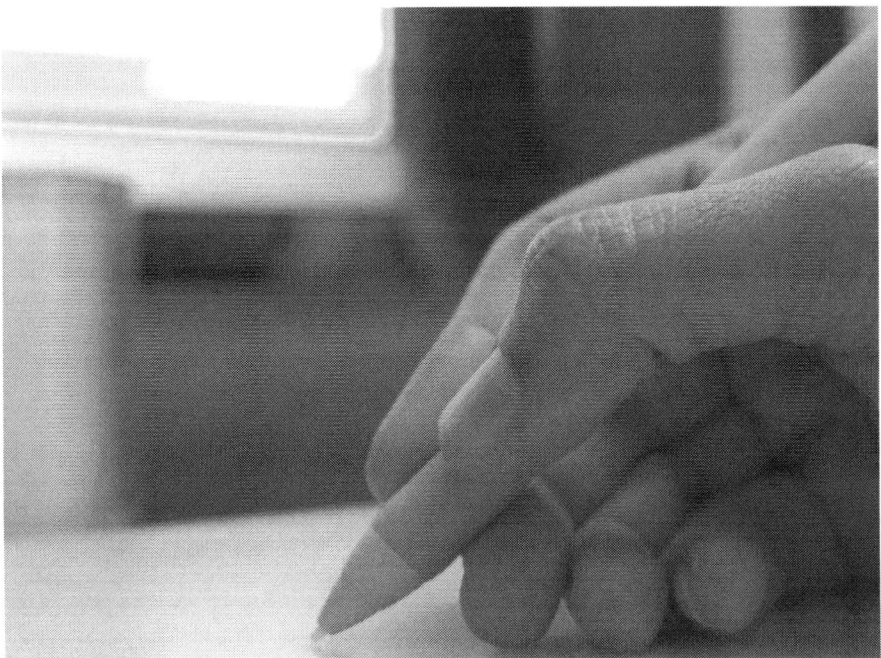

For as many ways as there are for players to interface with a game there are artist roles to fill the need. Generally, artists are organized by what they output even though they have similar roles. Starting in preproduction, **concept artists** are often painters who paint reference or inspirational work based on early concepts of the design. Later, **character artists**, **texture artists** and **environmental artists** will use these concept pieces to craft the look and feel of characters and level elements. **Animators** apply designed motion to characters and objects. **Modelers** shape 3D versions of characters and objects. **Lighters** position lighting sources. **Riggers** help set up models for animators to apply their sequences. Riggers and **technical artists** are often crosses of artists and programmers highly proficient in programming and aesthetics. Often forgotten are the **sound designers** who create the sounds used from foley to speech. Above all is the **art director** who serves as communication for the art team and decides the overall look and feel of assets.

Just as there are dozens of artist types, there are also dozens of engineer types who serve to implement different parts of the game. The generic entry-level job title is **software engineer**. These folks can touch any part of the code where they have expertise and are needed. Some engineers are **audio engineers** dedicated only to triggers and faithful reproduction of sounds in the game. **AI engineers** implement complex artificial intelligence algorithms so that enemies and characters act realistically or to specification. Network code is some of the most difficult code to write and test so specialized **network engineers** are deployed to craft robust network systems. **Test engineers** specifically focus on automating and easing the testing process, building code that goes not in the game itself but tests game functions. **Tools engineers** create and customize tools to help the development process. Leading this group is the **technical director** that needs to have expertise in all the areas of implementation and can herd together sometimes standoffish clans of software geeks.

Of course, there are other areas of game-related jobs that are not necessary in every game but become useful in certain projects or at certain team sizes. Producers, dedicated testers, usability experts, marketers, business developers and community managers are just a short list of other possible jobs. These all sit on top of the design, art and engineering pillars to help facilitate the other areas of production and business.

Entry-Level

Gaining entry in the industry can be a catch-22. You cannot get experience without having a job and you can't get a job without having had experience. However, you can qualify for many of the entry level positions by proving your experience outside of an official job. This is where your student and personal projects become super-important. We will cover this in a later section. Job titles to focus on when doing your search are generally prefixed with "Assistant" or "Associate", but read all listings. Some plain-jane Game Designer positions may not require industry experience.

Chapter 3 - Software Development Life Cycle

Software development can be a complex endeavor. In many cases it requires the coordinated effort of dozens of distinct egos that have to work together to fit moving parts together seamlessly. Needless to say, this can take a lot of organization.

We use models like the software development life cycle to wrap our heads around the various processes that go into creating a complex software process. We use the metaphor of the life cycle. This is a model of *order*: when do we do things and what steps follow what others?

There are many different formulations of the software development life cycle as the needs for various industries differ. I'll be talking about two models that most studios follow.

Waterfall Development

The simplest software development model is the waterfall method. Even though it is generally cited as a poor way to organize your software project, its simplicity, predictability and the fact that many publishers draw their contracts up based on this model leads to many studios still employing this method. It was first mentioned in the 1950s and takes its name from a waterfall in that it is nature's one-way street: water flows down never up.

Figure 3.1 - The Waterfall Method

The waterfall method starts with **ideation**. This is literally the generation of ideas. We will discuss idea generation in a later chapter. This is where the brainstorming, concept art and sometimes prototyping come together and the team gets an idea of what they are about to build.

In **specification**, the team gets down to specifics as to what they will build. Designers write game design documents (or GDDs), engineers write technical design documents (TDDs) and artists start creating base assets or media design documents (MDDs). These first two steps together are generally called **preproduction**.

Next, the team enters what is usually the longest phase: **production**. In this phase, the team actually constructs the things they laid out in their design documentation. The key aspect of the waterfall method is that work only flows in one direction. This means at this point, the team is strictly making what is on the design documents not revising and changing the requirements to adapt to new issues. Production is generally split into self-contained **milestones** where individual features are completed and then not touched again. This allows the team to schedule with a great amount of specificity.

The last two steps can be troublesome. In **test**, the team works together to eliminate any bugs and rough edges generated during production. This can be a laborious process since the nature of the waterfall method does not allow the team to go back and make changes that may result in fewer bugs and technical challenges. When the system is sufficiently bug-free, the product is **released** and the team starts over with a new project.

You may see various terms thrown about in game news like alpha, beta and gold. All of these terms are explanations of the portion of the test phase. **Alpha** is the state of the project when all the features have been completed and the testing stage begins. **Beta** is the state where the bug count has been reduced to zero, but bugs are still incoming. **Gold** is where the publisher or team decides the game is sufficiently bug free and is sent to the manufacturer (or released to partners) to be printed/distributed. These terms can vary from place to place. For instance, Google likes to label their products as Beta long after they've been released.

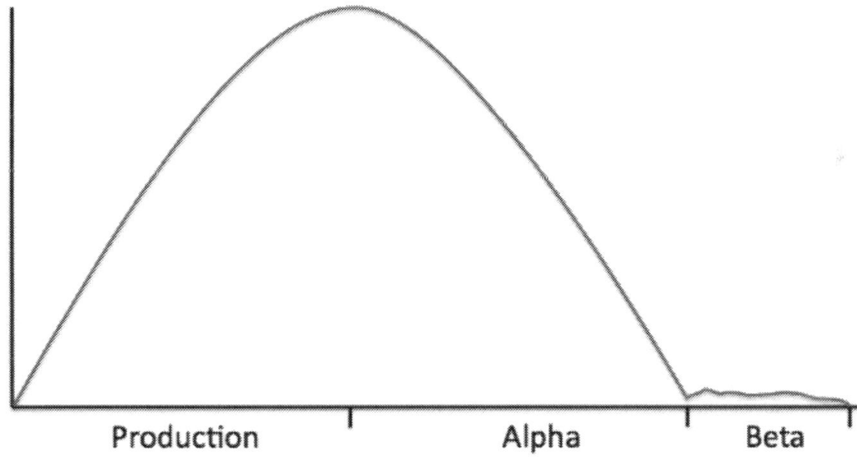

Figure 3.3 - Bug Count in an Ideal World

In the above diagram, the number of bugs in the project increases until the features are all complete. In alpha, the team tackles the bugs decreasing them (while some bugs are still being added as mistakes are made). In beta, the team bounces above zero as new bugs are added and tackled.

The waterfall method is very predictable. It can be broken down to tiny measurable tasks. The financiers can know exactly when the cycle will end and can plan the massive multimillion-dollar ad campaign around that release date.

But the drawback is that games are not straightforward. Regular software has an easy end state: did my document print? Did my source compile? Did my photo effect get applied? If yes, you are done. Games are different. Games involve challenge, mystery and learning. When you start making a game, you have no idea if your implementation will be fun *until it is made.* If you have no qualms about releasing an unfinished game, then maybe the waterfall method is for you.

Agile Development

Agile takes the waterfall method and transforms it into an iterative process. Instead of being tied to the lockstep of stage after stage, the process constantly repeats allowing teams to learn from mistakes and adjust to the uncertain process of game creation. If you've ever heard the phrase "find the fun", it is usually in reference to an agile development model.

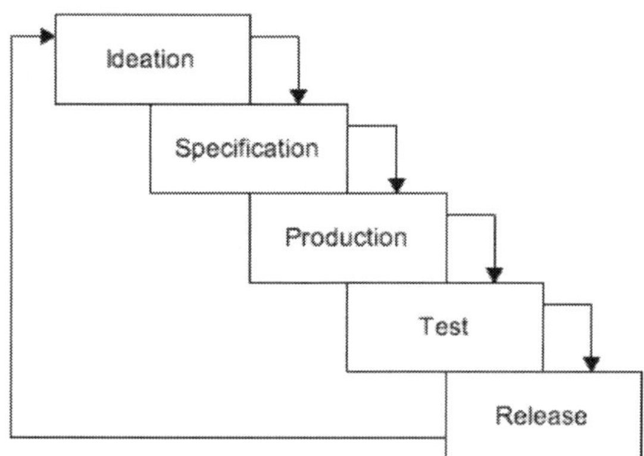

Figure 3.4 - The Agile Model

In the agile model you can repeat this loop twice, a dozen times or once a day. It is up to the team. If you want to go back to re-specifying a feature, the loop will begin again shortly. Teams will have builds to play with early and often and can evaluate them for fun. Incrementally, on every loop the team gets closer and closer and better and better.

There are different practices for agile development and the most popular is called "Scrum". Teaching Scrum fully is beyond the scope of the book. It involves setting up specific roles for various people including the "ScrumMaster" and the "Product Owner" and puts a focus on solving problems endemic to the software development process such as marathon meetings and outside interference.

One of the great metaphors in the Scrum literature is the story of the pigs and the chickens. The story goes thus: a pig and a chicken get together and decide to open a restaurant. The chicken suggests serving ham and eggs, but the pig balks. He says that the chicken is only *involved*, but the pig would be *committed*. The fable is a parallel to the two types of people involved in a project. Chickens are involved in the project and provide input or consultation but ultimately it is the pigs that need to make the big decisions because they are the ones fully committed. Keeping the metaphor alive puts the power of the project in the hands of those most instrumental to the project's success or failure.

Agile development is best for user testing as it results in testable versions of your software after every sprint or loop. Even with a set deadline, it can provide better implementations of software than waterfall simply due to the iteration of product when you inevitably meet successes and failures. For more information on the method, Schwaber and Beedle's "Agile Software Development with Scrum" is the primary literature.

Summary

- There's a long chain of stakeholders that stand between a designer's idea and it being in front of gamers worldwide.
- Digital distribution and other innovations remove middlemen from the chain and can result in cheaper games or more revenue for developers.
- There are a vast number of possible roles in the industry. Being aware of the skills needed allows you to find a great fit.
- Designers, artists and engineers are the three roles necessary in development.
- Agile development provides the flexibility to iterate that waterfall methods do not and is best suited for creating games.

Part Two - Written Communication

As we learned in part one, designers come in all shapes and sizes. The "traditional" designer role is the one seen at big studios: designers manage and communicate the vision for a large team, often crafting levels and features themselves, but just as often delegating to engineers and artists.

One thing is certain: in a large studio environment, you can't rely only on verbal communication. Documentation is key to ensure that ideas and issues are communicated without signal loss. What good is a designer whose concepts get lost in the shuffle?

Every designer thinks they communicate clearly, but not everyone can be above average. Only by study, reflection and work can you become better at the skills that are the bread and butter of successful designers.

In this part of the book, we will talk about the purpose and craft of the game design document and we will cover some best practices on how to create one using Word. We will briefly cover wikis as a design document alternative. We will also cover image and diagram creation using tools like Photoshop and Cacoo or Visio.

Chapter 4 - The Game Design Document

Oh, the Game Design Document! It is one of the most useful tools in a designer's toolbox for communication, but also one of the most misunderstood. Nearly every professional designer deals with game design documents (or GDDs). But what are they? Why are they so ubiquitous?

When a game development team is only three people (say a designer, artist and programmer), the team only has three channels of communication they need to keep open: designer-artist, designer-programmer and artist-programmer.

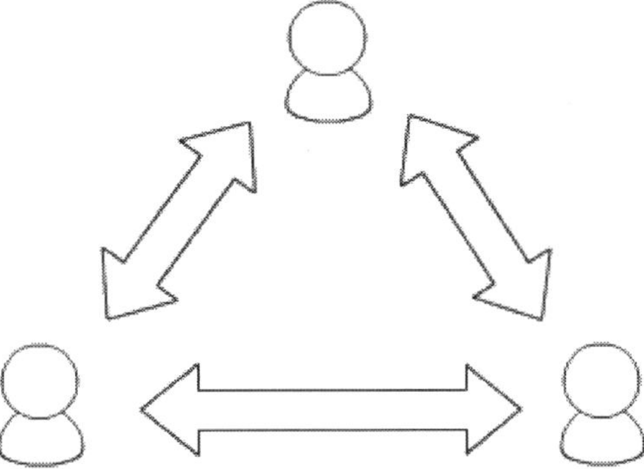

Figure 4.1 - Three Members and Three Communication Channels

But add just one more programmer and the number of lines of communication jumps from four to six:

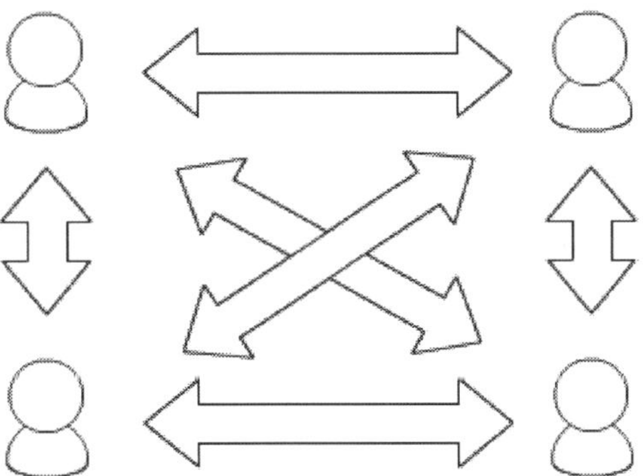

Figure 4.2 - Add One Member and Communication Lines Double

Professional game development can be a mammoth undertaking with team sizes that can top well over one hundred people. If everyone on a team of one hundred had to connect with every other team member, it would require four thousand, nine hundred and fifty connections. *World of Warcraft* is estimated to have over a hundred and forty people on the team.[2] If this is true, there are 9,730 connections between the team members that would need to be maintained if every team member needed to directly talk with each other[3].

This is too unwieldy. Real-world teams are not structured where every team member needs access to every other team member. Instead, larger teams are subdivided into groups by either discipline or project area. For instance, the artists may all talk to each other but route their communication with other disciplines through a producer. Or all of the team members working on the multiplayer portion work together while the single player teammates only communicate with their own.

This causes another problem: instead of team members being able to directly communicate with each other freely, communication has to be routed through gatekeepers such as producers or leads. If you ever played the childhood game *Telephone*, you know how multiple rebroadcasts can add noise to a channel:

Figure 4.3 - The Telephone Game

A fluid and, at times, highly vague concept like a game design can't be faithfully communicated in such a manner. Teams devise artifacts that can be digitally replicated to eliminate the signal loss of the "telephone" method above. The game design document (or documents) is a tool to solve this problem.

A game design document is any method of documentation that gives instructions for building a game or feature. It is important to note that from

---

[2] From the horse's mouth: http://www.computerandvideogames.com/193951/interviews/blizzards-rob-pardo

[3] If you are interested in the math behind this, see "On the Shortest Route Through a Network" by GB Dantzig (1960).

team to team and studio to studio, game design documents can take wildly different forms and be constructed from wildly different methods. There are also common misconceptions about the form and purpose of a game design document.

Common Misconceptions

Common Misconception #1: The Game Design Document is a repository of all information about a game or feature.

Game design documents are there to serve a primary purpose: to inform team members as to what they are to build. To this end, there are a number of stakeholders:

- Programmers. Because they need to build the thing.
- Artists. Because they need context to know what they are creating.
- Producers. Because they need to be able to gauge how long a feature will take.
- QA. Because they need to know what a feature looks like when it is working.
- Other designers. Because their systems need to work with the feature.
- Licensors. Because they need to ok use of their intellectual property.

To look like they are producing a lot of content, many designers fill a GDD with explanations of all of influences behind a system, backstory, design discussions or other ephemera. Here's the rule of thumb: **Unless it directly instructs a programmer or artist what exactly to make, leave it out of the GDD proper**. You may relegate it to an appendix (see below) or to another document.

In some cases, it is necessary to keep a second pseudo-GDD. In cases where you have external licensors or overly involved executives, they will want to get their hands in what the team is making. In these cases, the GDD will likely be too technical for what they need. For these situations, "Design

Overviews" or "Executive Summaries" are sometimes useful and are covered at the end of Part Four.

Common Misconception #2: The word in the GDD is law.

Aspiring designers who are just entering the field often hold this misconception. Game design is an iterative process: it requires experimentation and often-copious trial-and-error. Yet many game design documents are written and attitudes are hardened as if the game design document will never change. In the worst-case scenarios, programmers will print out the GDDs and build from a static conception of what the feature is.

The GDD is the formulation of an idea **at a given time**. The GDD's function is to foster communication throughout a team, not to be a dictate.

Often I have heard from programmers that they don't read game design documents. We will get into the cardinal sins that cause this attitude below but one of the reasons for this attitude is that GDDs are not kept up-to-date. If a programmer reads a GDD and then is told to make something contrary to what he or she read, she will wait to be told in the future instead of trusting that what the GDDs say. It is the designer's job to keep documents as up-to-date as possible, no matter how tedious a job that may be.

Remember the purpose of the GDD: Unless you personally want to communicate a change in design to every member of the team, you must keep the GDD aligned to the most current design.

Common Misconception #3: There is a template to how studios create design documentation.

Often students will ask to see sample design documentation. I will show some made-up examples later in this book. Why I am hesitant to show anything at all is that every studio has its own documentation processes. The purpose of a student asking me for a sample is to copy formatting. The formatting is the least important part!

The design documentation is written specific to a particular audience. Blizzard's design documentation for MMOs on hundred person teams is going to look quite different from Quantic Dream's narrative-heavy design process. Who are your programmers? What do they know implicitly[4]? You are going to write your documentation for a particular audience.

Some studios do, in fact, have massive templates for game design documentation. This can be a useful practice if there are needed sections that are commonly left out. The danger with templates, however, is that they are not updated as the team and the project change and are thus prone to overloading documentation with wasteful, empty categories. Empty sections that have to be scrolled through make it more difficult for programmers and other stakeholders to find the information they need. That is anathema to having formal game design documentation at all.

Clarity Über Alles

Given all the other things you have to deal with when writing your design document, keep clarity as the most important goal.

---

[4] For instance, designers at EA Tiburon (who are responsible for the American Football franchise *Madden*) don't need to spell out what a "first down" is every time they make a new yearly iteration. That knowledge is implicit to the team.

Chapter 5 - GDD Creation Process

Now we will go through an example together of creating a short, concise design document. Assume we are on a small team putting together a Fantasy RPG for Facebook. The lead designer comes to you and says you need to design a crafting system for the game. How would you go about creating the documentation?

Step One - Determine Purpose, Desired Scope, Locate Connected Systems

Designers usually have lead designers or creative directors above them. From one of these folks, you must clearly determine the goals of the designs. You must find out: the purpose of the design, the scope of the design and the systems that will necessarily connect with the design.

The purpose of the design: Without knowing the purpose of the system, all you can do is copy a similar crafting system from another game. Your lead designer says: "We need a system to use the items that players receive via gifts from other players. We want it to encourage creativity and social connections." That is a start. Interview. Ask probing questions. Really understand the motivations behind the assignment before you begin writing or prototyping.

The scope of the design: Designers have an awful tendency to over-design. What this means is that given an assignment, designers will come up with nuanced, complex systems. In isolation this is not a problem. But in aggregate, no project can sustain complexity in every system and still expect to ship on time and be understood by users. Great designers know which systems benefit from complexity and which benefit from simplicity. By identifying the scope of the feature, designers get an idea as to the depth of the system to create.

Possible Scope Levels of a Design:		
Present (Level 4)	The design is as bare bones as it can be while still satisfying the purpose of the design.	Example: Driving in *Alan Wake*
Market-Standard (Level 3)	The design is at the level that is expected from other titles in the market.	Example: Multiplayer Ranking in *Uncharted 2*
Market-Leading (Level 2)	The design is at the level of the top example of other titles of the market.	Example: Cover in *Gears of War*
Innovative (Level 1)	The design is beyond the level of other titles in the market and is something that has never been tried before.	Example: Creature Creator in *Spore*

In our example, the lead designer says: "We have a lot of art time for this, so you can make it broad, but the entire game is pretty casual so keep the complexity low." In this instance, I would probably choose to go with the "Market Standard" complexity. We will deal with the implications of this choice below.

The systems that will connect: Clearly, from the original proposal, this system will be interacting with the gifting system. In addition there may be an inventory system. Perhaps you will make salable items? What designer is in charge of the economy so you don't flood your game's market with free goods? Who do you need to contact?

Assure that none of these statements are contradictory. For instance, if the purpose of the design is to have a fully customizable character generator while the scope of the design is to be simple, then you will need to meet with your lead designer to find out what must give.

Step Two: Research

The scope level you come to in the previous step will help you to decide how much and what type of research you need to do. Having a wide breadth of exposure to other titles in the industry helps here. I remember working in a studio that only produced one genre of game. Many of the designers there never played games from other genres! How will you know about features that may eventually creep into your genre without exposure? What is going on in matchmaking for leagues in sports games may become relevant for real-time-strategy games.

I have often said that the best examples for growth in being a designer is to play bad games and endeavor to understand why they are bad. By identifying features that were unsuccessful, you can design around the pitfalls and mistakes of your industry brethren.

Of course, your research is not just limited to games.

Research Techniques Based On Scope	
Present (Level 4)	Play games that implement similar features and try to find what is common between all of them. Can anything else be taken away while still preserving the purpose of the feature? This requires design by subtraction.
Market-Standard (Level 3)	Play games that implement similar features. Which are the worst implementations? What can we do to avoid their pitfalls?
Market-Leading (Level 2)	Play games that implement similar features. Which are the best implementations? Why are they the best? How can we adapt their system to our game's requirements?
Innovative (Level 1)	Since, by definition, you are attempting to create something that has never been done before, you cannot take features from other games and apply them to yours. However, you do still need to know the best practices for that feature to determine whether yours exceeds the quality of the market leader. This step requires influences from beyond the world of games. You do read outside your design work, correct? From what fiction and nonfiction can you pull inspiration? From what non-game interactive systems (ATMs, Toys, Events) can you draw inspiration? Be thorough.

Step Three: Brainstorm

We are going to discuss brainstorming and its uses in a later chapter in depth. A brainstorm is a creative meeting where an individual or a group tries to create a quantity of solutions to a problem. Based on the research you completed in Step Two, you should be well equipped to envision a number of possible solutions. See the Idea generation chapter for the how-to of using this technique.

Step Four: Reduction

You will have a lot of possible directions to pursue after your brainstorming. It is best to sleep on them to have adequate time to think them over. When this is done, come back to the list of possible ideas. In Brainstorming, you don't discriminate against ideas. In the Reduction step, discrimination is all you do.

Eliminate ideas that are:

- Not in line with the chosen scope
- Impossible to create
- Not effective in researched titles
- Don't meet the purpose of the design
- Conflicts with another design in the project

Step Five: Write the Best Method Down

Now fire up a word processor and get this idea down on (digital) paper. You've been exposed to a large amount of research in Step Two and a large amount of ideas in Step Three. It would be easy to put your voluminous knowledge down to paper. Stop!

Remember your audience.

If you are writing for programmers (and it is likely that you are), remember that programmers will change your words into logical code. The closer the form your document is to how they think, the easier it will be for them to translate it into code that works for their system. Generally, they will like hierarchically formatted lists like:

- Player chooses a race (See RaceList.doc).
  - If player chooses elf, +2 speed.
  - If player chooses dwarf, + 2 strength.
  - If player chooses cow, +2 mooing.
- Player then chooses a class (See ClassList.doc).
  - If player chooses priest, starting skill is heal (see Skills.doc)
  - If player chooses paladin, starting skill is smite. If player chooses paladin, he/she cannot choose evil alignment later.
  - If player chooses critic, starting skill is annoy. If player chooses critic, he/she cannot choose good alignment later.

This, of course, is a generalization. There are many types of programmers and each like different styles, but I have found it to be helpful. When in doubt, *ask the programmers what they like to see*. They are just as afraid of you as you are of them. Generally they will tell you, "Something short and easy to read." No one has ever said "Something thirty pages long with lots of details."

Err on the side of brevity. Remember how I have told you that it is your duty to keep the design documents up-to-date? Which do you think is easier to update: short hierarchical bulleted-lists or vast walls of text? Always ask yourself: what can I do to make this document clearer and shorter?

References

Did you see the "See RaceList.doc" mentions in the above example? Those are *references* and are the most helpful technique to keep your document size small. If you find yourself copy and pasting information into multiple designs, consider separating that information out into a reference and add a hyperlink. In the above example, I could have spelled out all the races, their designs, attributes and locations in the character creation design, but is it relevant?

Appendices

What if there is some background information that is necessary or helpful to include? We don't just throw that out, right? Absolutely not. Jesse Schell points out in *The Art of Game Design* that game documentation is a cure for the frailty of human knowledge. But since the programmers won't be using that background information in scheming up how to create the feature, we don't want it cluttering up the design document proper. Therefore, all the "bonus" material should be put at the end of the document in a footnote section or in a linked "FAQ" document. Here you have little restrictions on brevity. Anything that needs to be remembered (design battles, reasoning for certain choices, sketches, etc.) can be added to the appendix section/document. If you find it painful to be brief in the design document, you can let loose in this section.

Step Six: Edit and Find Edge Cases

You've written down the most salient feature idea and condensed that idea down to a logical list form. Great! Now there are two things you must do and it helps to do them simultaneously. Send the design out to your fellow designers and folks implementing the feature. Ask them: is this clear? Are there mistakes? Where does it break down?

An *edge case* is a problem that occurs only under extreme conditions. While others are reviewing your documentation, try to find edge cases in your own design. Test the extremes to see if it breaks down.

For instance, here's a simple design:

"The player's jumping height is equal to his strength divided by the weight of items in his/her backpack."

Sounds reasonable. What if the weight of items in his/her backpack is zero? 18/0 means the player can jump an undefined height!

Here's another:

"Players can put items in the "bag" item, which has twenty storage slots."

Neat. What happens if a player puts a bag in a bag? What happens when a player tries to put a 21st item in a bag? What happens to the in-bag items when the player tries to sell the bag itself? These are all questions that will need to be answered. Since the bag-in-a-bag question is a little awkward, it would be an edge case. The others should have been thought out in the draft.

It is difficult to identify edge cases sometimes, at least more difficult than my simple examples above. The easiest way to check for edge cases is to make extreme examples of your players. What if a player has zero of something? What if he has everything? What if the maximum number of players all tried to stand on the same spot? What if a player did this action 20,000 times? What is the most illogical way the player could access the features in this design?

Figure 5.1 - A Dangerous Edge Case. From *Dead Rising 2* © Capcom.

Chapter 6 - Word Processors

Modern computing is dominated by the word processor. No other tool has been more influential in mass adoption of personal computing. Unfortunately for us, word processors are generally designed using the printed page as a metaphor. Game designers are not interested in creating printed pages; they are concerned with communication. But the ubiquity of word processors like Microsoft Word keeps us shoehorned into an old way.

In this section, we will look at Microsoft Word 2010 for Windows, but the lessons should be applicable to many other word processing tools. Only the location of the features should change. OpenOffice is a suite of free office software that is in popular use and looks to recreate some of the functionality of the Word juggernaut. Other alternatives are AbiWord, Apple's Pages application and the massively popular (and free) Google Docs. The fastest growing alternative to Word is not a word processor at all—we will talk about wikis in the following chapter.

To create a GDD, Word is still the top dog. Next, we will look at some tips and tricks to make the most of the software.

For these hands-on sections, it helps to follow along with the steps. If the exercise doesn't start with a blank document, the file you need will be on the book's website.

Create a Basic GDD

Get started by creating a very small and basic game design document. When you fire up Word, you are shown a blank document from which you can start your creative masterpiece. Is there anything more frightening than a blank page? Don't answer that. If you already have a document open, you can click on the "File" tab in the upper left and then "New" and then "Blank Document".

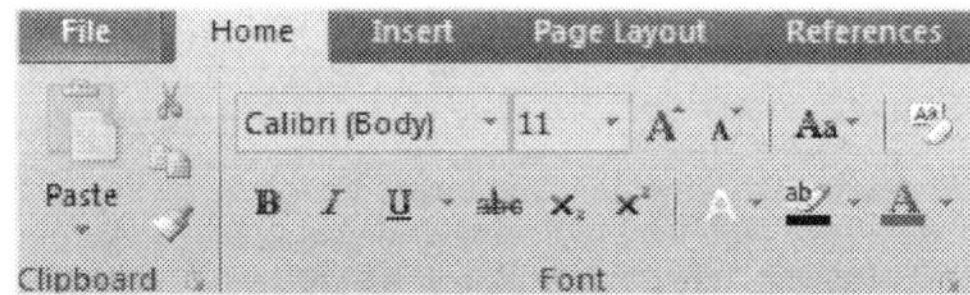

Figure 6.1 – The top left of the ribbon contains the "File" tab.

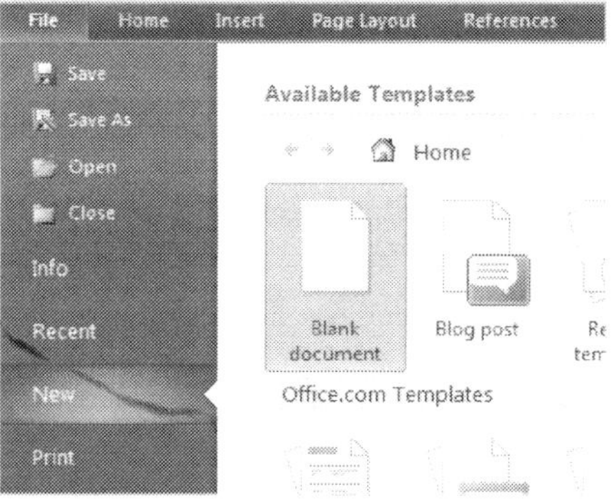

Figure 6.2 – In the file tab, select "New" and "Blank Document".

Before we start, I want to go over a part of Microsoft Office's interface that may be unfamiliar if you haven't used Office before, or if you used an earlier version than Office 2007. Along the top of the application is a bar called "the ribbon" which contains all of the relevant options for the task at hand. It is a little different than the File, Edit, et cetera menus of yore and can take a little getting used to if you are not familiar with them. I'll let you know which tab the features we discuss will be located.

Figure 6.3 – Our Friend the Ribbon.

Okay! Now you can start hammering out features for your GDD. Here's one I created that you can find on the book's companion website called "Chili Cookoff 1.docx". The feature is for a playable event of a Chili Cookoff in a MMO. Here's the basic snapshot:

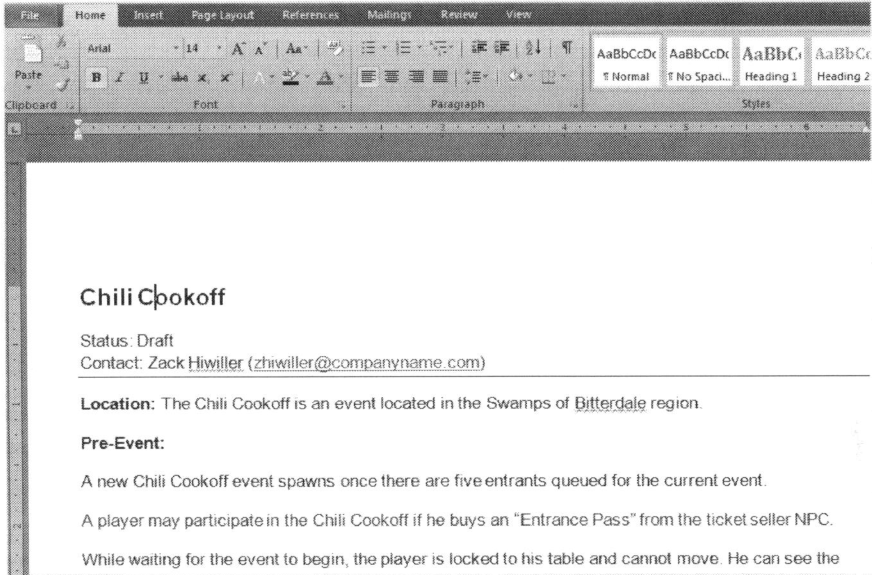

Figure 6.4 – The Greatest GDD in this Book (so far)

Now notice a few things about my (very basic) GDD:

Status – There is a status for the GDD at the top. Many things anger programmers, but starting work on an unfinished GDD and having everything change after he/she has worked on the feature a ton is up in the top tier. Not only is keeping a status a good thing to keep your programmers happy, but it also lets you know which documents need work, need to be approved or are ready for production.

Contact Information – Someone needs to be in charge of every single GDD. Even in the cases of collaborated efforts, there needs to be one and only one person in charge. Stakeholders need to be able to contact someone with questions and comments. If a list of people is put as the contact, there's a good chance for "response paralysis" where everyone assumes that someone else will answer.

Word will automatically (or perhaps auto-maniacally) turn something it thinks is an email address into a link. For this or any other AutoCorrect feature that you want to undo, hover over the offending AutoCorrected item and you will see a small blue underline to the bottom-left. Hover over it and click on the button that appears to open up the AutoCorrect menu.

Figure 6.5 – Notice the Blue Underline Under the 'zh'

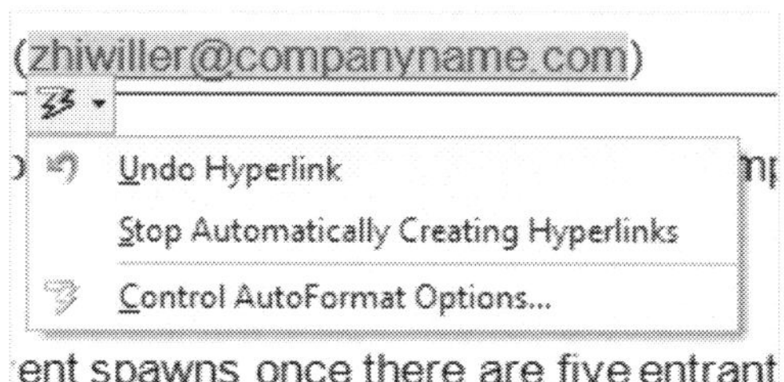

Figure 6.6 – The AutoCorrect Options Menu

The Horizontal Rule – Below the contact information is a solid horizontal line separating minutiae from content. You can do this easily in word by typing three hyphens (-) on an empty line and then pressing 'Enter'. Word will auto-correct that into a solid line. These lines are attached to paragraphs. You can further customize separating lines by highlighting a line or paragraph of text and then going to the Borders and Shading menu to add custom borders:

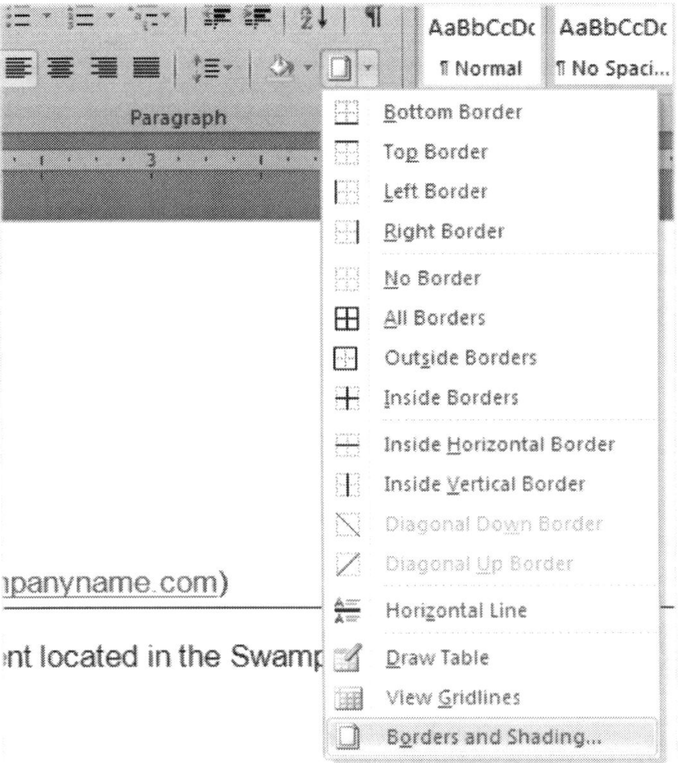

Figure 6.7 – Borders and Shading

Separation of Content into Logical Sections – Notice also how I have separated the content into location, pre-event, event and post-event sections. This is only one way these could be split up. Maybe your team needs it split into summary, interface, rewards and character. The same requirement returns: ask your team what they need.

Just the Facts – Also notice how concise I make the descriptions. Nothing is longer than it needs to be. Sentences are generally written in a consistent and simple structure. It makes the entire document easy to scan and parse. This first version is only a little over 400 words yet still contains the flow of the event from starting it to final rewards. It is missing things, for sure, but is a great draft to get in front of people to **iterate**.

Now you have a sort of okay draft of a game design document. In the next few sections, you will use some of Word's features to make it even better.

Tables

In our multitask-driven society, we no longer read from the start of an article to the end. Even you, in reading this book, probably dart around from topic to topic, image to image, looking to skip information you know and direct yourself towards information that is new. This is partially why our first design document (the Chili Cookoff) was broken up into sections with headers. Perhaps one developer will be doing the pre-event side while another will be doing the event itself.

We have a nice start to a game design document, but right now it is just a wall of text. We are going to break up the text with some tables.

Tables are extremely common methods to cordon off data from instructions. Why would you want to do that? Are not both instructions and data important? Yes, they are. But data changes quite often and is a cut-and-paste job while instructions require unique bits of code. Developers generally like to see code separated from content because the content can be anything as long as the code works.

In the Chili Cookoff GDD, there are two sections that jump right out as interspersing code with content: the scoring system and the rewards system.

Page Break

First, add a page break to separate the sections of the document. To do this, just position your cursor at the spot you want the page break and press Control+Enter. Breaking up your sections into their own individual pages helps break up the feel of the "wall of text". It does make your document physically longer, but if you are printing out the GDD then you are ignoring the iterative nature of the GDD. It changes all the time! Don't print out your GDDs!

Plan Your Table

Before you go dropping tables in willy-nilly, think ahead to what you want to do. In the table that explains scoring, we will want a row for each element that is scored (looking on the GDD, we see three of these). We will want a column for the title of each and a column for the value. In some tables you will want to budget an additional row for a header, but that is not needed in our small table.

Insert a Table

Position your cursor at the end of the section. Then go to the "Insert" tab in the ribbon. Slightly below that is section for Tables. Click on that.

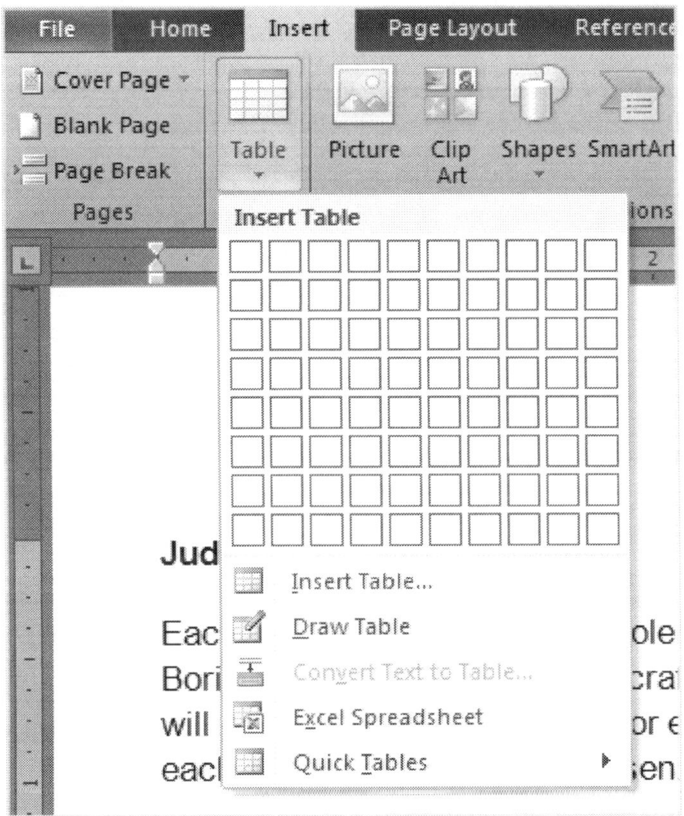

Figure 6.8 – The Tables Dialogue

You will see a large grid. Unfortunately, this is not for playing Battleship. If you want to create a table of a particular size, you can select the square that is a number of columns over from the top-left as the number of columns you want your table to be and a number of rows down from the top-left as you want rows in your table. That is okay but I prefer using the "Insert Table" menu item below that grid.

The Insert Table menu asks you for the number of rows and columns. It also asks you for your AutoFit preferences. If we set this to fit to the contents, the table will only be as wide as our widest row. Since we want this table to take up the length of the page, we will let it be.

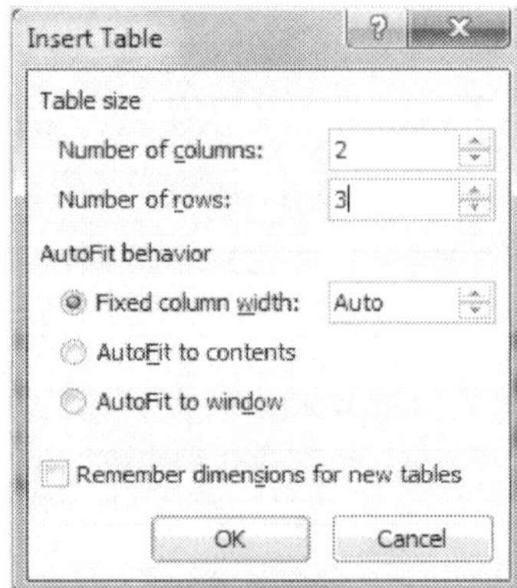

Figure 6.9 – The Insert Table Dialog

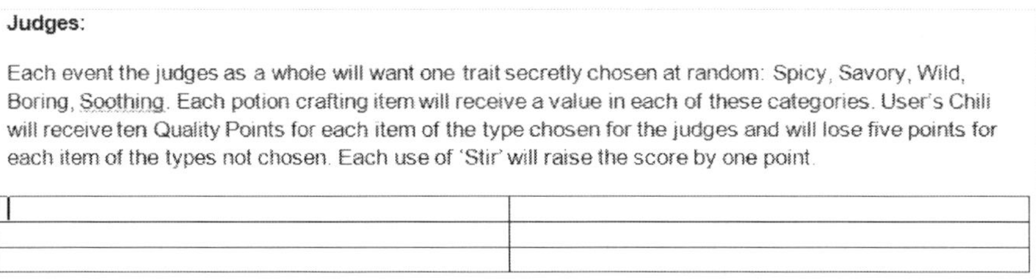

Judges:

Each event the judges as a whole will want one trait secretly chosen at random: Spicy, Savory, Wild, Boring, Soothing. Each potion crafting item will receive a value in each of these categories. User's Chili will receive ten Quality Points for each item of the type chosen for the judges and will lose five points for each item of the types not chosen. Each use of 'Stir' will raise the score by one point.

Figure 6.10 – A Beautiful, Empty 3x2 Table

Fill out the first column with the names of the conditions. Fill out the second column with the values of the conditions. Now go back in the text and delete the text descriptions of what we just put in the table. Now this section looks a lot cleaner:

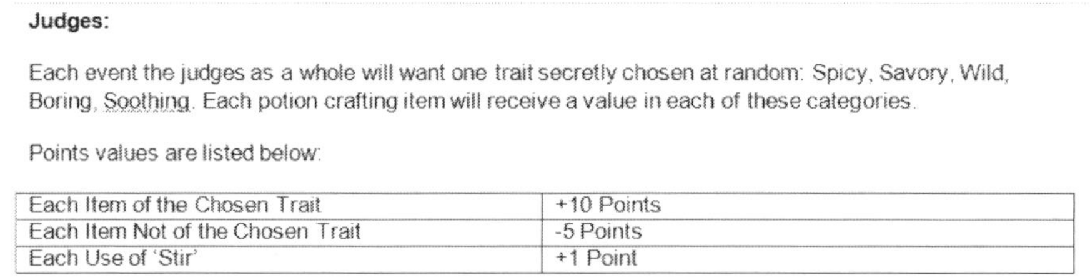

Judges:

Each event the judges as a whole will want one trait secretly chosen at random: Spicy, Savory, Wild, Boring, Soothing. Each potion crafting item will receive a value in each of these categories.

Points values are listed below:

Each Item of the Chosen Trait	+10 Points
Each Item Not of the Chosen Trait	-5 Points
Each Use of 'Stir'	+1 Point

Figure 6.11 – The New "Judges" Section

Add Rows

Say that feedback came back from sources (other designers, management, playtests) that suggest you need to add complexity to this system.[5] Say they want you to add at least three more conditions. You don't have to create a

[5] This never happens.

new table. Place your cursor in the bottom row, rightmost cell and hit the Tab key. A new row is created. Easy. Hold down Tab until you have three new rows. Now we will fill them with information.

Points values are listed below:

Each Item of the Chosen Trait	+10 Points
Each Item Not of the Chosen Trait	-5 Points
Each Use of 'Stir'	+1 Point
First Cook to Reach Five Ingredients	+5 Points
Use a Healing Potion	+5 Points
For Each Point of Charisma Above 20	+1 Point

Figure 6.12 – More Info in the Table

Remove Rows

Feedback came from above and they hate the Charisma bonus line. To remove a row, just right click on that row and select "Delete Cells". You will see a dialog box pop up.

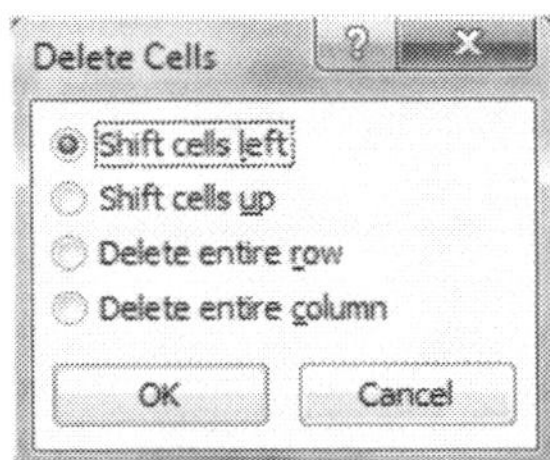

Figure 6.13 – Delete Cells Dialog Box

Select "Delete Entire Row." The first two options will only delete a single cell. Alternately, you can right click in the margin to the left of the row to be deleted and select "Delete Rows" from there. This is easier if you are deleting multiple connected rows.

Adjusting Cell Widths and Heights

This table takes up the entire width of the page while having very little data. If we want to shrink it down, we can either highlight the cell dividers (the lines in between the cells) and drag into new positions, or we do what we avoided earlier and turn on AutoFit.

Right click anywhere in the table and select "Autofit" and then select "Autofit to Contents". This will make the cell widths dynamic based on the width of the content in the cells.

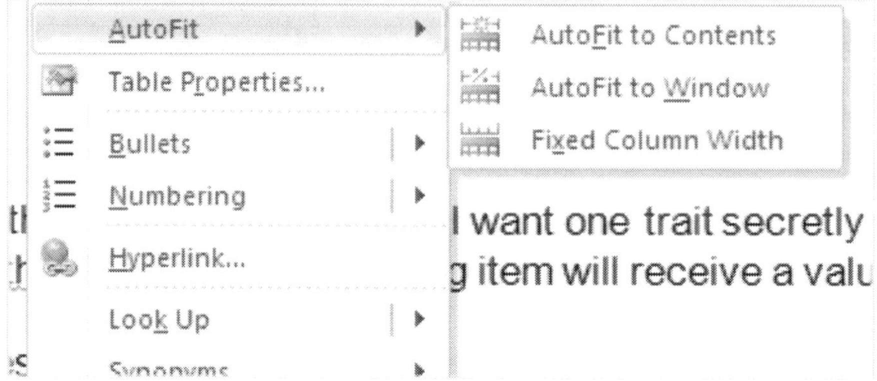

Figure 6.14 – Autofit

Select Entire Table

Often there are adjustments you want to make to the entire table. Say you want to change the font face or size, or maybe you want to cut the table and paste it somewhere else in your document. Right now, our document has a small table snug to the left margin. It would look nicer if it was centered.

When hovering your mouse cursor over the table, notice the little plus arrow that appears above the top-leftmost cell.

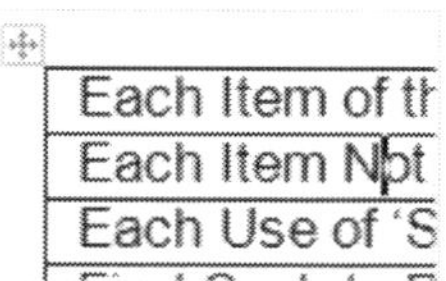

Figure 6.15 – Table Selection Icon

Click on that to select the entire table. You can now center the table by using the keyboard shortcut (Control+E or by clicking on the centering button on the Home tab of the ribbon, in the paragraph section.

Points values are listed below.

Each Item of the Chosen Trait	+10 Points
Each Item Not of the Chosen Trait	-5 Points
Each Use of 'Stir'	+1 Point
First Cook to Reach Five Ingredients	+5 Points
Use a Healing Potion	+5 Points
For Each Point of Charisma Above 20	+1 Point

Figure 6.16 – Centered and Looking Good

Adding/Removing Columns

Adding and removing additional columns is easy and straightforward.

To insert, right click on the table at the location you want to insert. Go up to the Insert menu item and there you can choose what (rows or columns) and where to insert (before the cursor or after).

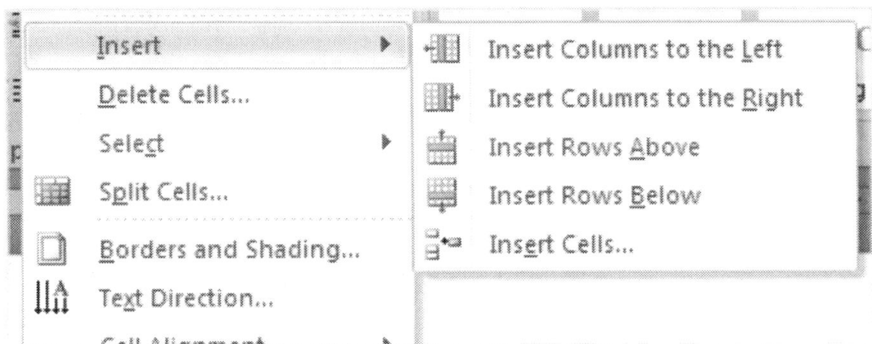

Figure 6.17 – Insert Menu Item

To delete a column, hover over the top border of the column you are looking to remove. Your cursor will change to a downward facing arrow. Right click and select the "Delete Column" menu item. You can delete multiple columns by dragging when the cursor changes and selecting multiple columns.

Formatting

Table cells can be formatted like any other piece of text in Word. You have your choice of coloring, font size, whatever. In a game design document, it is recommended to stick with a single sans serif font (unless you are writing code within a game design document for some reason, in which case use a mono-spaced font). Use color sparingly and only to highlight important information. Too much color can be distracting when your goal is clarity.

Pasting From Other Programs

Be careful when pasting tables from other programs (like Excel) or from web pages. Tables pasted from these sources often do not format correctly. If they are pasted correctly often they come with a heavy helping of extra formatting tags from Word that can render differently on different platforms and versions of Word. Unless you absolutely need to keep the formatting, there is an easy way to copy a web page table into a Word table.

Step 1 – Find the table you want. Count the rows and columns. Select the data and copy it to the clipboard. Here we will select the list of GDC Awards winners as found on Wikipedia.

GDC Game Developers Choice Awards [edit]

The Game Developers Choice Awards are chosen by registered game developers and unveiled at the Game Developers Conference (GDC) in San Francisco

Year	Game	Genre	Platform(s)	Developer(s)
2009	*Uncharted 2: Among Thieves*[70]	Action-Adventure: (Third-Person) Shooter	PlayStation 3	Naughty Dog Software
2008	*Fallout 3*[71]	RPG	PlayStation 3, PC, Xbox 360	Bethesda Softworks
2007	*Portal*[72]	(First-Person) Puzzle-Platformer	Windows, Mac OS X, Xbox 360, PlayStation 3	Valve Corporation
2006	*Gears of War*[73]	Tactical Shooter	Xbox 360, Windows	Epic Games
2005	*Shadow of the Colossus*[74]	Action-Adventure	PlayStation 2	Team Ico
2004	*Half-Life 2*[75]	(First-Person) Shooter	Windows, Xbox 360, Xbox, PlayStation 3	Valve Corporation
2003	*Star Wars: Knights of the Old Republic*[76]	RPG	Xbox, Windows	BioWare
2002	*Metroid Prime*[77]	(First-Person) Action-Adventure	GameCube	Retro Studios
2001	*Grand Theft Auto III*[78]	Open World Action	PlayStation 2, Windows, Xbox	Rockstar North
2000	*The Sims*[79]	Life simulation game	Windows, Mac OS	Maxis

Figure 6.18 - Wikipedia's Formatting

Now if we were to paste what we copied into Word, we would get this:

YearGameGenrePlatform(s)Developer(s)**2009***Uncharted 2: Among Thieves*[70]Action-Adventure: (Third-Person) ShooterPlayStation 3Naughty Dog Software**2008***Fallout 3*[71]RPGPlayStation 3, PC, Xbox 360Bethesda Softworks**2007***Portal*[72](First-Person) Puzzle-PlatformerWindows, Mac OS X, Xbox 360, PlayStation 3Valve Corporation**2006***Gears of War*[73]Tactical ShooterXbox 360, WindowsEpic Games**2005***Shadow of the Colossus*[74]Action-AdventurePlayStation 2Team Ico**2004***Half-Life 2*[75](First-Person) ShooterWindows, Xbox 360, Xbox, PlayStation 3Valve Corporation**2003***Star Wars: Knights of the Old Republic*[76]RPGXbox, WindowsBioWare**2002***Metroid Prime*[77](First-Person) Action-AdventureGameCubeRetro Studios**2001***Grand Theft Auto III*[78]Open World ActionPlayStation 2, Windows, XboxRockstar North**2000***The Sims*[79]Life simulation gameWindows, Mac OSMaxis

Figure 6.19 - Word's Mess

Gross. But we can fix it.

Step 2 – Open up Notepad or a simple text editor. Paste the text into there. It will look oddly formatted. This is because it strips the formatting and replaces each of the cell breaks with a tab character. This is called being "tab delimited" and will be important when importing files into Excel, which we will cover later. Select all the data in Notepad and Cut it to the clipboard.

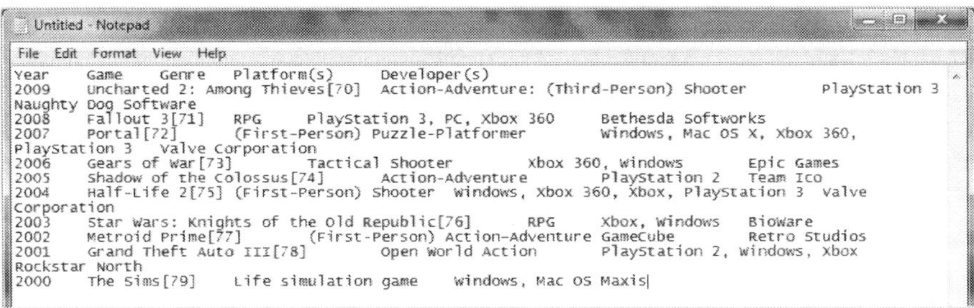

```
Year	Game	Genre	Platform(s)	Developer(s)
2009	Uncharted 2: Among Thieves[70]	Action-Adventure: (Third-Person) Shooter	PlayStation 3
Naughty Dog Software
2008	Fallout 3[71]	RPG	PlayStation 3, PC, Xbox 360	Bethesda Softworks
2007	Portal[72]	(First-Person) Puzzle-Platformer	Windows, Mac OS X, Xbox 360,
PlayStation 3	Valve Corporation
2006	Gears of War[73]	Tactical Shooter	Xbox 360, Windows	Epic Games
2005	Shadow of the Colossus[74]	Action-Adventure	PlayStation 2	Team Ico
2004	Half-Life 2[75] (First-Person) Shooter	Windows, Xbox 360, Xbox, PlayStation 3	Valve
Corporation
2003	Star Wars: Knights of the Old Republic[76]	RPG	Xbox, Windows	BioWare
2002	Metroid Prime[77]	(First-Person) Action-Adventure GameCube	Retro Studios
2001	Grand Theft Auto III[78]	Open World Action	PlayStation 2, Windows, Xbox
Rockstar North
2000	The Sims[79]	Life simulation game	Windows, Mac OS Maxis
```

Figure 6.20 - Notepad's Version

Step 3 – You counted the rows and columns in Step 1. Create a blank table with the right number of rows and columns.

Step 4 – Highlight the table and Paste your clipboard contents. Voila! They have copied correctly. Format the table as you see fit.

Year	Game	Genre	Platform(s)	Developer(s)
2009	Uncharted 2: Among Thieves[70]	Action-Adventure: (Third-Person) Shooter	PlayStation 3	Naughty Dog Software
2008	Fallout 3[71]	RPG	PlayStation 3, PC, Xbox 360	Bethesda Softworks
2007	Portal[72]	(First-Person) Puzzle-Platformer	Windows, Mac OS X, Xbox 360, PlayStation 3	Valve Corporation
2006	Gears of War[73]	Tactical Shooter	Xbox 360	Epic Games

Figure 6.21 - Fixed

Now you have some nice-looking tables. You've separated the code from the content and made your document easier to scan.

Footnotes and Appendices

Keep it simple.

Easy to scan.

Easy to read.

These are the rules you want to live by when creating GDDs. But what is *too* simple? Is not it possible to leave out too much?

Usually when you ask that, the answer is: no, it is not possible. Cut it.

Sometimes you truly do want to keep in that blob of backstory or a note of reminder to provide some sort of anthropological reasoning to the feature.

But you don't want to put these optional bits in-line or it will make the document harder to read and may be unnecessary for some readers. In these cases, you have two techniques: footnotes/endnotes and appendices.

In most viewing modes, footnotes appear in small text under a separator at the bottom of the page referenced by a small superscript number where that text belongs in-line. Endnotes are the cousin of footnotes. They look the same as footnotes except instead of appearing at the end of the page, endnotes occur at the end of the document.

The use of footnotes rarely occurs in the first draft. Instead, after the draft is completed and passed around, points of contention or confusion will cause the designer to add special case notes to the design.

Let us go back to the "Chili Cookoff" GDD. You sent the design around for approval and the location line was seen as too vague. Now in this GDD adding information to the location section inline is not a problem as the document is already sparse, but say we wanted to add detail about the location, but not alter the flow of the document. Here we can place a footnote.

First, position your cursor where you want the footnote to appear. Generally, these appear at the end of sentences to which the footnote refers. Put your cursor at the end of the sentence.

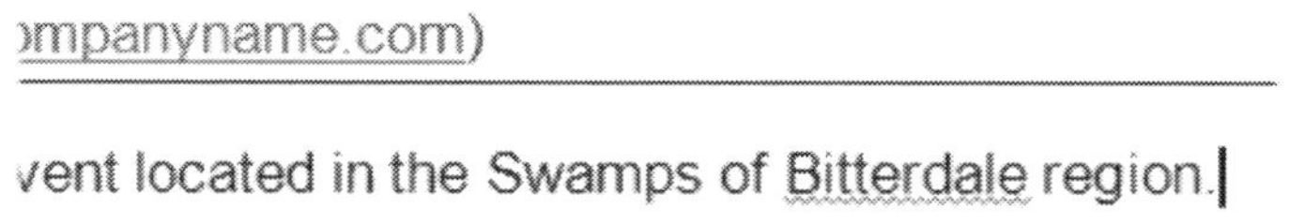

6.22 – Place Your Cursor Here

There are two ways to go about the next step. Either you can go to the Reference tab in the ribbon and then select "Insert Footnote" or you can use the keyboard command Ctrl+Alt+F.

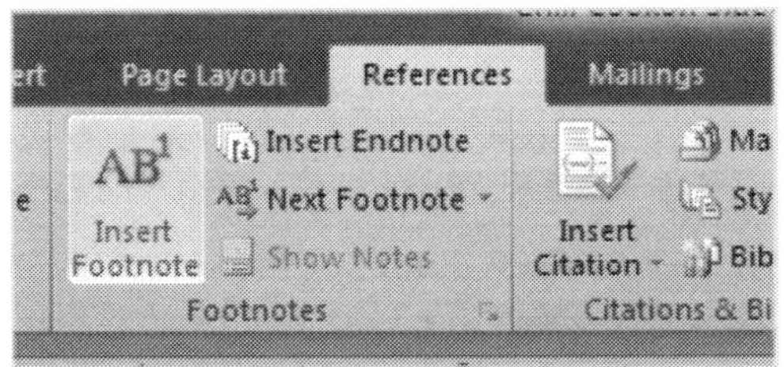

6.23 – The Insert Footnote Button in the Reference Tab

You will be taken to the bottom of the page where your reference number will be placed. Type away to start your footnote.

[1] The Swamps of Bitterdale Region is large. Check the latest map file for the location. The Chili Cookoff should be placed in the largest town in the region or in any traveling fairs (See the Travelling Fairs GDD).

6.24 – Your Beautiful Footnote

If you insert another footnote on this page, it will be referenced with a superscript 2 and the text will go directly below what you have typed here. If your footnote is referenced on another page, the numbering will stay the same but the footnote will appear at the bottom of the new page.

Moving/Deleting Footnotes

Even though footnotes are references to specific points, you can still move them or cut and paste them like any other element of your document. The footnote text will follow, placing itself at the bottom of whatever page has the reference.

Deleting a footnote is as easy as deleting the inline reference number. Delete the little '1' in your main document and all the text attached to the '1' goes flying into the void with it.

Appendices

Footnotes are nice, but they are largely more relevant for notes that belong inline but result in a cluttered look if left in the document proper. Game design is a messy field with a lot of opinion and arguing. Often squabbles end up with both sides claiming partial victories and demanding *something* of theirs be placed in the GDD. Appendices allow you to say "Oh, yeah, I put that in the GDD!" without actually putting that idea somewhere dangerous that a programmer might see. Appendices in documents are like appendices in the human body: easily ignorable unless you have a problem.

Appendices appear at the end of the document on a separate page and can sometimes take the form of an FAQ. Appendices can answer questions longer than what a footnote would afford. Often they serve as helpful reminders of discussions past ("Why did we limit the amount players can carry?" or "Why do we make objects disappear after they've been abandoned for 60 seconds?") Think about the questions the *other* stakeholders who are not actually implementing the system would ask. Place those in the appendix. You can do this in a more conversational style than the utilitarian method of the GDD proper.

One of the benefits of using wikis (see later chapter) versus a standard word processor is that every page comes with a "Talk" page. If you are familiar with wikis already, treat appendices as your "Talk" page.

Images

Pictures are generally a more effective delivery mechanism of information than text. As we will discuss further in our Powerpoint section, pictures beat the pants off of text when it comes to image retention. In "Brain Rules", John Medina lists off results from a number of studies that suggest the superiority of images. In one, adding images to an oral presentation increased retention sixfold.

It works just as well in game designs.

"Okay, smart guy," you say. "If images are so great, why does this book have so many words?"

Remember the capital rule: brevity. Which is better at quickly communicating an idea: a text description or an image? An image may, in fact, contain *too much* distracting information. It may not be concise at the point you are trying to drive home.

You are describing a level and you want to focus that it is crowded. If you put this image in the GDD to show that you want the level to feel like a crowded Asian marketplace:

Figure 6.25 - Stock Reference for a GDD

An artist constructing the level may be confused: Does the designer really want that many people on the street? Do they want that kind of architecture? Do they want that variety of people?

In this case it is better to use text to be as clear as possible:

- The street should be very busy, containing as many bystanders as possible.

But in many other cases, such as showing screenshots or diagrams, images provide the right amount of information in a form the brain is ready to process.

Inserting Images

Inserting images is quite simple. Position your cursor where you want the picture to go. Go to the Insert tab on the ribbon and then right beside the Table option is the Picture button that can be used to insert an image directly into the document. You will then be given a file dialog box. Find where you have saved your image file (when adding pictures from the Internet, save them on your hard drive first) and then select Insert to add it.

Figure 6.26 - Image Button

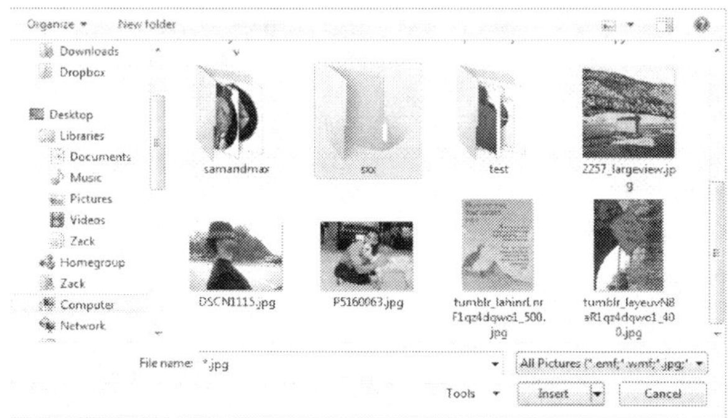

Figure 6.27 - Then Choose Your File

There is a bit of advanced functionality that is sometimes helpful. When you choose your file if you click the small arrow by the Insert button, an additional menu opens up where you can select "Link to File". If you do this, the image in the document will update every time the saved image updates. This can be useful for files that never move that are changed often. However, if your file ever moves or is deleted, the image will disappear from the document.

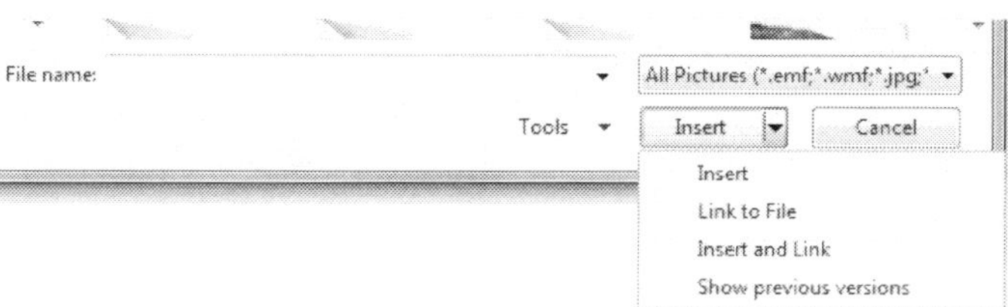

Figure 6.28 - Link to File

Formatting Images

Inserting the image is the easy part. Getting it to look how you would like is the hard(er) part.

First, pictures are generally larger than you would like them to be in your document. To open up the picture options, right-click on the image. Older versions of Word require you to enter a picture options menu after this, but Word 2010 puts many of the options available from a simple right-click.

Figure 6.29 - Right-click on an Image for Options

On top is a height and width adjuster. Alternatively, you can go to "Size and Position" to adjust these as well (which is what you must do in older versions). There is also a crop tool available (next to the width box) which lets you easily trim the image.

Word 2010 has many photo adjustment features that are new to this particular version. Since I am trying to keep the instruction for this book as backwards compatible as possible, I won't go into depth here, but experimentation will yield some interesting results.

One other feature to mention is Text Wrapping. Text wrapping can be found in the Size and Position menu. This feature adjusts how text is formatted around your picture. "In Line With Text" is the default that treats the picture as if it was a single character. This is the easiest to deal with conceptually, but if you place the picture in a paragraph of text, you will see odd-looking results.

Figure 6.30 - In Line with Text

"Square" and "Tight" wrap the text around the image and are best to yield a newspaper-like style. The problem with these is that editing other parts of the document can get the image to shift jumping around page breaks and other elements. The end result is that the image may not be next to the text it is describing.

Figure 6.31 - Square Looks Better, But Can Often Shift

My personal preference is to keep images "In Line with Text" but give them their own line. This way, text doesn't look lost on a line of its own and the image is always next to the text it describes.

A Warning Regarding Copy and Paste

Word does its best to preserve the formatting of things pasted into Word documents. If you paste an Excel spreadsheet into a Word document, Word will treat it exactly as an Excel spreadsheet. Sometimes, however, this results in more overhead than you need. Sometimes you need text or numbers or other data without embellishment.

One example of this is copying and pasting images from Adobe Photoshop. If you attempt to do this, or insert a picture that is a Photoshop specific format, when you try to format the image in many versions of Word, the program tries to take you to Photoshop to edit the image instead of using the internal formatting tools we talked about in this chapter. An image that cannot be resized without resizing the source material can be a pain.

One simple solution to this problem is to paste said image into a program of which Word doesn't have compatibility problems. When I am using Windows, that program is Microsoft Paint. The workflow is this:

1. Select Part of an Image in Photoshop
2. Copy the Selection
3. Paste into Paint
4. Select All in Paint
5. Copy
6. Paste into Word

This gives the desired results. Alternatively you can save the file in Photoshop as a JPG, BMP or some other cross-platform format and then use the Insert function in Word. Often these images are not of high enough consequence to keep around outside the document, so I paste the bitmap version from Paint. If you care about the file size of your document, this may result in a ballooning file size

Comments and Change Tracking

Most game development happens in a team setting. Often these teams can get huge (as we covered earlier). As such, you will need to keep track of the comments, notes and suggestions of numerous stakeholders on your documentation. Since the purpose of the document is to explain features with brevity, you don't want a bunch of suggestions crowding up the text. We can markup the text avoiding these problems with the Comments feature in Word. Comments are a lot like footnotes in that they are an inline reference to external text.

Adding Comments

Inserting a comment in Word is amazingly simple. Place your cursor at or highlight the area where you wish to make the comment. Click on the Review tab and then "New Comment".

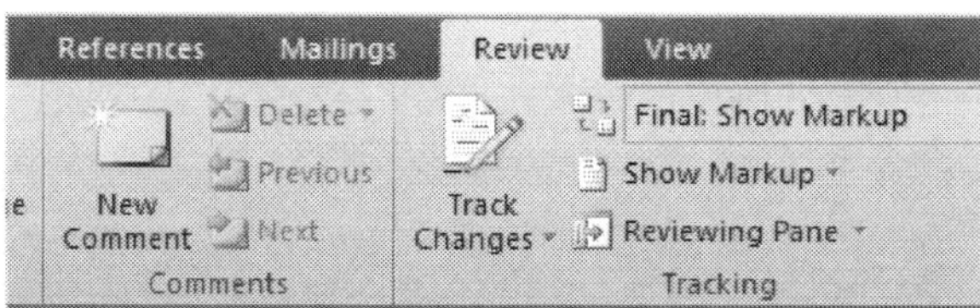

6.32 - The Review Tab and New Comment Button

A comment balloon will appear in the side margin. Type away. Click outside the comment balloon or press Esc when you are done.

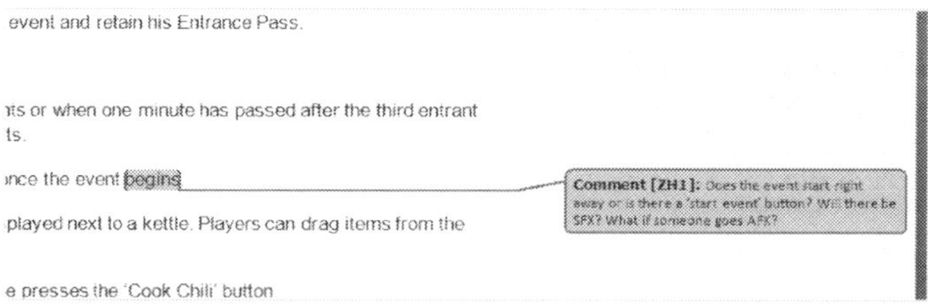

6.33 - A Comment

It can be very helpful to use the commenting tool to point out areas that need clarification or just don't make sense. For broader concerns about a feature or document, it is best to place these highlighted at the start or end of a document or raise these concerns personally outside the document.

Change Tracking

Many design documents are truly collaborative efforts where multiple designers are in charge of making changes. In these situations, it can be very helpful to see what has been changed in a particular version. On the Review tab in the ribbon is the "Track Changes" button. When this is engaged, Word will keep track of all additions, modifications and deletions. The default mode when tracking changes is "Final: Show Markup". Switching the dropdown next to "Final: Show Markup" to "Final" will remove the annotations of tracked changes and will show what it is would look like to someone printing the document (not that you would ever print the document) or to folks not enabling tracking. "Original Show Markup" and "Original" will show the document before the changes were made.

In areas where the text has been changed, word will add a black vertical line to the left margin to note that this was a changed area. This line will be removed in Final markup.

A nice feature Word includes is that each unique user will have a different color associated to their changes.

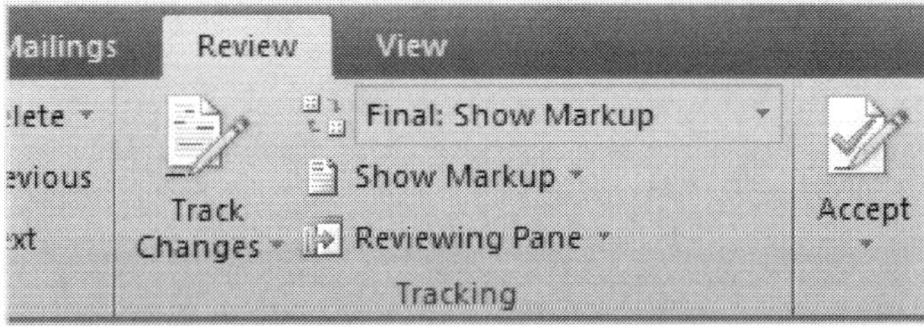

6.34 - The Tracking Area of the Review Pane

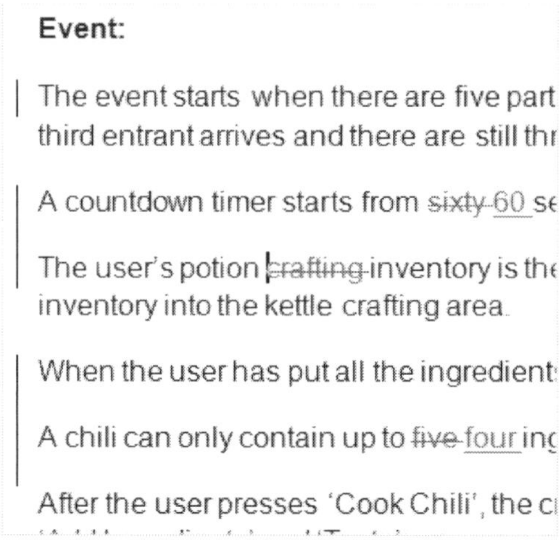

Event:

The event starts when there are five part
third entrant arrives and there are still thr

A countdown timer starts from ~~sixty~~ 60 se

The user's potion ~~crafting~~ inventory is the
inventory into the kettle crafting area.

When the user has put all the ingredient

A chili can only contain up to ~~five~~ four ing

After the user presses 'Cook Chili', the c

6.35 - Additions/Modifications/Deletions in Track Changes Mode

Removing Comments

Generally, you don't need to keep the comments for all time. For instance, if your wording is odd in a particular line and you fix it, you can delete the comment asking for clarification.

For more sustentative comments, you may want to make notes on them in the Appendix (see the previous section). In that case, remove the comment.

To remove a comment, right click on the comment balloon and select "Delete Comment". It is best to do this one at a time as you implement whatever changes need to be made regarding that comment.

If the document is going to production and you no longer need the comments anymore (think about this long and hard before acting), you can delete all of the comments by going to Comments in the Review pane, clicking the arrow below "Delete" and then "Delete All Comments in Document".

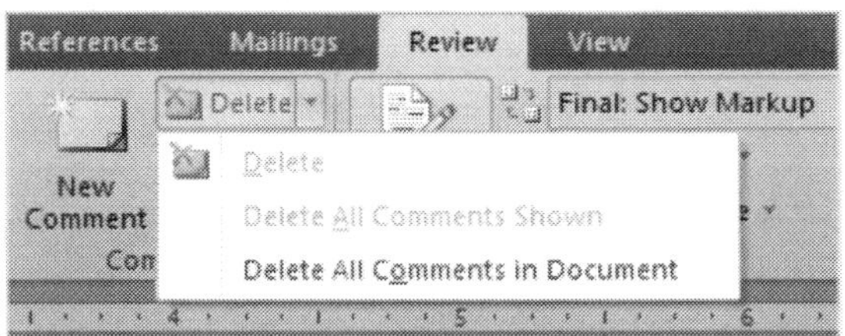

6.36 - Delete All Comments

Versioning / Comparing Documents

Every studio has a different way of tracking versions of documents. Some use dedicated versioning software like Subversion. Some use more manual methods. A method I always used is to save multiple versions of the document. For instance, my first version of Chili Cookoff would be called ChiliCookoff_01.docx. Then when I know I have to make changes, perhaps I have gone through an entire round of comments, I make the changes and save a new version called ChiliCookoff_02.docx.

This is an old-fashioned method of version control and can have some issues, but it is one of the simplest methods. Perhaps you use this method and you need to figure out what changes exactly you made between ChiliCookoff_03 and ChiliCookoff_04. Word can help you in this.

To compare documents, go to the Review pane and then click on "Compare". You'll see a dialog box that prompts you for the two files to compare. Choose the two documents (In our example, this would be ChiliCookoff_03.docx and ChiliCookoff_04.docx) and then below, choose the types of changes you want to track. Having all of these checked can be overwhelming.

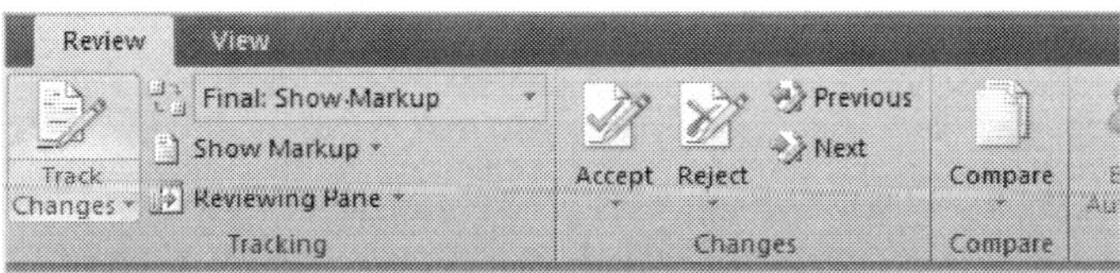

6.37 - Compare in Review Pane

6.38 - Compare Documents Dialog Box

You are then presented with a busy view of three documents - the original, the revised and the comparison.

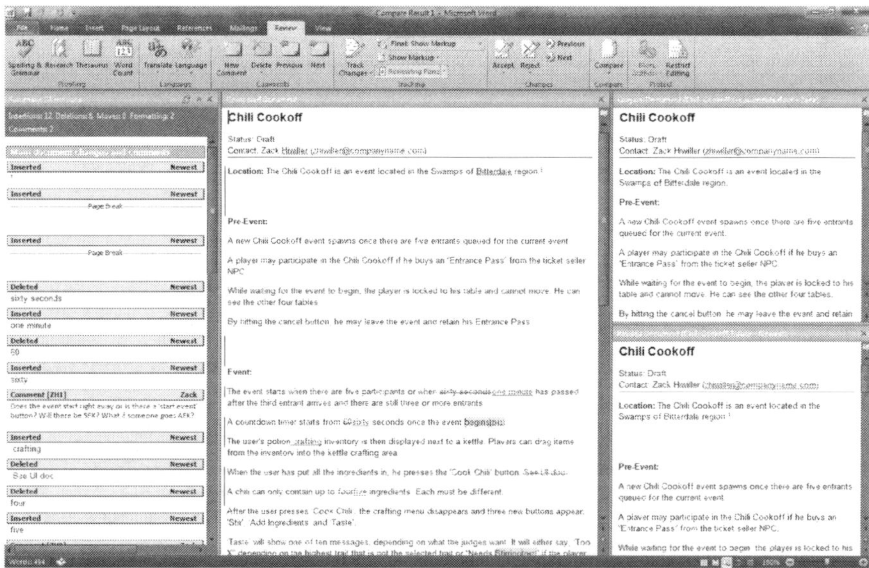

6.39 - Compared Documents

There are many ways to collaborate using Word and/or other software tools. The important part is not the steps in the collaboration but the communication between team members. No software tool can defend against reticent collaborators, inattention, laziness or passive-aggressive responses to criticism. Your job is not only to be keeper of the document, but also to be keeper of the idea - a subtle distinction that requires much more ownership.

Headers, Footers and Tables of Contents

There is one section of GDD writing that doesn't seem to eschew the artifacts of the printed word and that is the inclusion of headers and footers.

Creating a header or footer is easy: double click on the top or bottom margin to create a header or footer respectively.

Finding something meaningful to place in a header or footer is another issue. Many studios like to put their logo, the document title, the page number, the word "CONFIDENTIAL" and other ephemera on every page. This is easy to do, but hardly effective and counter to the purpose of the GDD. It adds visual clutter for the engineer to sift through to find his or her information.

While it is generally advised to not print out game design documents due to their always-changing nature, I have found that adding a page number is helpful in larger documents to help track down the location of certain items.

Adding a Page Number

First, how to add the page number:

Double click on the bottom margin of your page. The footer editor will appear.

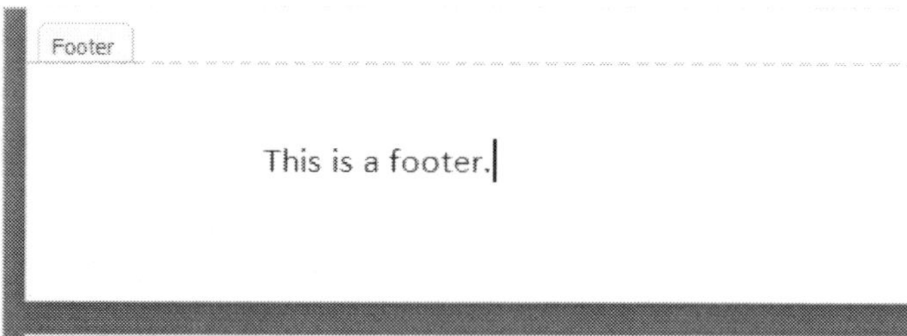

Figure 6.40 - The Footer Editor

Change your text to align right by either clicking on the right alignment button or by pressing Control+R. On the Header & Footer Tools Design tab there are many options. You may want to have a different first page or change the location of the footer. You can do all of these from this tab.

Click the Page Number button near the left side, then highlight "Current Position", then select "Plain Number". Word offers numerous pre-formatted ways to place the page number, but I have found that the simple method allows for the best control.

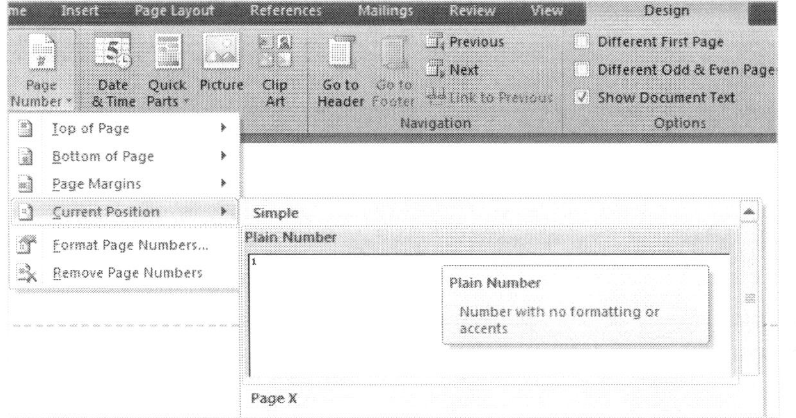

Figure 6.41 - The Page Number Menus

Now your beautiful page number is sitting down there in the lower-right corner.

Table of Contents

But simply having a page number is no good if it is not a reference to something. How else will the engineer know that the invite system starts on page 19 unless he either has a table of contents or reads through the first eighteen pages? The latter is a definite waste of time. Since we are all about optimizing our engineer buddies' time, create a Table of Contents.

Tables of Contents (or TOCs) require a little bit of legwork to implement properly. To drop in, Word needs to know what lines are section headers and what lines are simple text. In order to make a dynamic table of contents, you will need to go to every section header in your document and let Word know that it should also be a TOC header.

TOCs can have subsections. Just as this book has a "Written Communication" part with a "Word Processors" chapter and this "Headers,

Footers and Tables of Contents" section, so too can you have this sort of hierarchy.

Create a document that has eleven lines like so:

Title

Section 1

Text

Section 2

Text

Subsection 2.1

Text

Section 3

Text

Subsection 3.1

Text

Now, we will format this letting Word know which lines are section headers and which are not. Highlight "Section 1" (don't highlight the "Text" below it) then go to Styles in the Home tab of the ribbon. Click on "Heading 1".

Figure 6.42 - Styles in the Home Tab

In the default theme, this will change the font and color of the text. Don't worry, you can alter it later as you see fit like any other text. Do the same to the text marked "Section 2" and "Section 3".

When you highlight "Subsection 2.1" and "Subsection 3.1", click on "Heading 2" in the Styles pane.

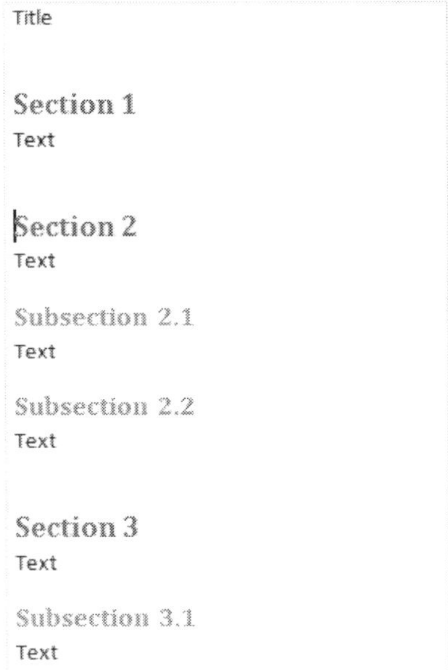

Figure 6.43 - Our Marked-Up Text

Now that Word knows what is heading and what is regular text, drop in a table of contents. Position your cursor in the space between "Title" and "Section 1". Then go to the References Pane and click on the leftmost button: Table of Contents.

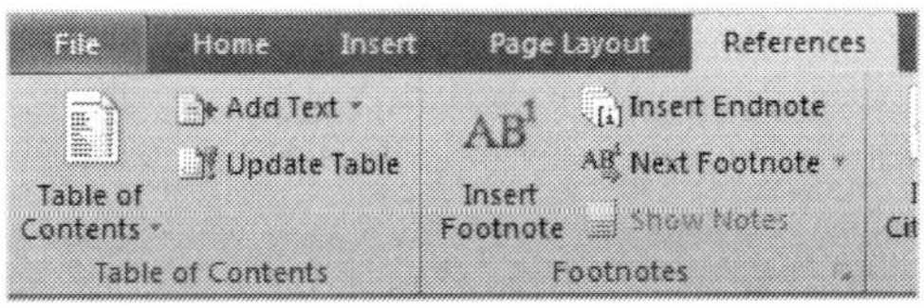

Figure 6.44 - TOC in the References Tab

There are some pre-formatted ones, but we prefer to do our own formatting, so go down to "Insert Table of Contents". This brings up the Table of Contents window where you can modify the look and feel of our TOC. I prefer to not use internal hyperlinks,[6] so I unclick the "Use hyperlinks instead of page numbers" preference to the right. Once you are satisfied, click "Ok".

[6] But if you like them, go ahead and use them. I know many that swear by them. It is a matter of personal preference.

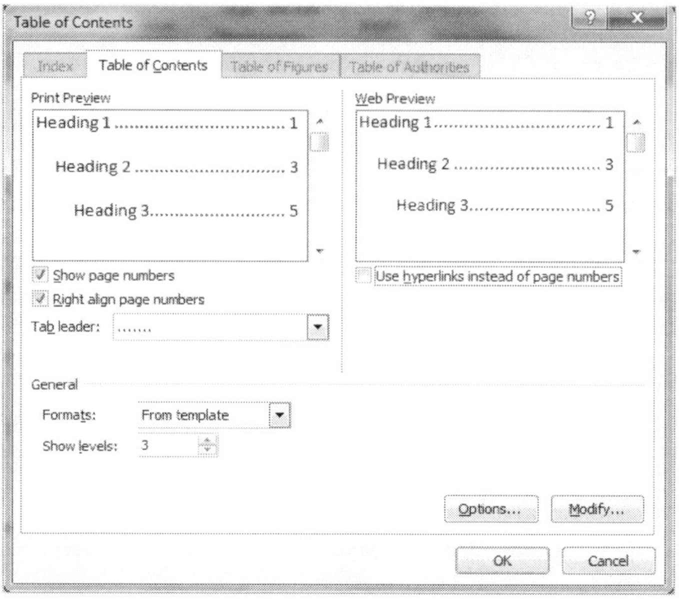

Figure 6.45 - Table of Contents Menu

The TOC is inserted at your cursor position. Ours is pretty boring since all of the sections start on page one, but notice how the subsections are indented. This is of great use on large game design documents and allows the engineers to quickly and easily locate what they are looking for. In a ten-plus page document, TOCs are absolutely essential. In a thirty-plus page GDD, it would be criminal to not include a table of contents.

Figure 6.46 - Our Table of Contents

There you go. You've learned some great tips and tricks for conquering the most popular word processor out there. Now we will shift gears and talk briefly about a written communication tool that is quite unlike Word and its brethren.

Chapter 7 - Wikis

Wikis are becoming a larger force in game design creation for a simple reason. Whereas word processors are built around the single-writer-leads-to-printed-page paradigm, wiki software has been built around the idea of multiple users with constantly changing documents in a digitally literate realm. Multiple users, changing documentation, digital literacy... sounds a lot like game development.

If you've used Wikipedia, you've used a wiki. Wikipedia is powered by the open-source MediaWiki software. MediaWiki can be installed on any server that has PHP and a compatible database backend. Editing wikis is as easy as browsing a website, making a wiki-based design document system significantly cheaper than a system where every user needs to have Microsoft Word.

Wikis are vastly different than the current Word hegemony that exists in industry, but are being widely adopted by teams looking for an alternative. As wiki technology specializes, you will see more and more studios adopting it as the de facto document production standard. Word worked in studios where design documentation was highly walled - where designers would write documents and "throw it over the wall" to be implemented. As more and more studios wake up to the need for collaborative iteration, new tools are adopted that better serve the needs of developers.

Benefits of Wikis

Internal Version Control - Wikis easily allow users to compare previous versions of a document. As you can see from the kludgy suggestion I gave in the Comments and Tracking section, easy viewing of changes is a significant boon. Need to roll back to the version before the Big Design Change? That's just a few clicks.

```
Line 284:
  |-
  ! height="25px" | Fabricate [[Buffalo Steak Sandvich]]
- | "1" x {{Icon weapon|weapon=Crit-a-Cola|icon-size=40x40px}} + "1" x {{Icon weapon|weapon=Sandvich|icon-size=40x40px}}
  | "1" x {{Icon weapon|weapon=Buffalo Steak Sandvich|icon-size=40x40px}}
- |"2 weapons"
  |-
  ! height="25px" | Fabricate [[Fists of Steel]]
- | "2" x [[Image:Backpack_Scrap_Metal.png|40px|Scrap Metal]] + "1" x {{Icon weapon|weapon=GRU|icon-size=40x40px}}
  | "1" x {{Icon weapon|weapon=Fists of Steel|icon-size=40x40px}}
- |"5 weapons"
  |-
  ! rowspan="2" class="subheader" style="text-align: center;" | {{Icon class|class=Engineer|icon-size=30px|link=Engineer}}<br/>Engineer
Line 301:
  ! height="25px" | Fabricate [[Jag]]
```

```
Line 314:
  |-
  ! height="25px" | Fabricate [[Buffalo Steak Sandvich]]
+ | "1" x [[Image:Backpack_Reclaimed_Metal.png|40px|Reclaimed Metal]] + "1" x {{Icon weapon|weapon=Sandvich|icon-size=40x40px}}
  | "1" x {{Icon weapon|weapon=Buffalo Steak Sandvich|icon-size=40x40px}}
+ |"7 weapons"
  |-
  ! height="25px" | Fabricate [[Fists of Steel]]
+ | "1" x [[Image:Backpack_Reclaimed_Metal.png|40px|Reclaimed Metal]] + "1" x {{Icon weapon|weapon=GRU|icon-size=40x40px}}
  | "1" x {{Icon weapon|weapon=Fists of Steel|icon-size=40x40px}}
+ |"7 weapons"
  |-
  ! rowspan="2" class="subheader" style="text-align: center;" | {{Icon class|class=Engineer|icon-size=30px|link=Engineer}}<br/>Engineer
Line 331:
  ! height="25px" | Fabricate [[Jag]]
```

Figure 7.1 - Differences on a Wiki Site

Pure Visibility - Many wikis show a "recent changes" section that displays what were the last documents to be changed. This allows anyone on the team to view the newest changes to the design without tons of pinging emails to the team.

Sharability - To share a design document with someone in the office, you can email a link to a private intranet drive. If you are sending to an external publisher or licensor though, you will generally have to zip the design document and email it. If you use a lot of images and references, this can be a cumbersome process and a large file. It is not guaranteed that the recipient will even see the same formatting if he or she uses a different version of the word processor. Using a wiki, you can set up an account for an external partner and email the link.

Ease of Collaboration - Wikis were designed to be collaborative. Word processors have had this functionality pasted-on. It is trivial to collaborate on a wiki. In Word, you have to manually track changes and enact a versioning policy.

Talk Pages - MediaWiki pages automatically come with a "Talk" page. This page allows the discussion of the topic to be separate from the design. This is created automatically and is a forceful separation of discussion and design.

Internal Search - Wikis come with a search function built in. Individual Word documents have this feature, but do not allow one search for every document in the system.

Links are Fair Game - In a Word document, links are nice, but they require the user to access a different application to explore. Web users can open links in new tabs to be viewed later, a much more natural workflow. This affords the designer to put more web resources in the appendices to his design documents. Anything that can be put on the web is fair game: images, text, video, even Flash games.

Most wiki software even imports images and stores them within the directory structure of the wiki, meaning you don't have to create separate directories of images and designs.

Cost to Quality - While there are open-source word processors that are viable alternatives to Word such as Google Docs and OpenOffice, the undisputed leader is still Microsoft Word that is not cheap. Wikis provide such a drastic difference in features and workflow that users will not note the dissimilarities to Word as they would using OpenOffice or similar competitors. This allows a (mostly) free solution to an expensive alternative.

Automatic Tables of Contents - MediaWiki and others will automatically generate a table of contents if you format the document using headings.

Drawbacks of Wikis

Formatting - This is the big one. One area that office applications have the edge in is in formatting. Because of its legacy in making printable documents, word processors come bundled with many drawing and positioning tools. Wikis, built from HTML markup, have considerably less of a focus on formatting.

Non-Linear Structure[7] - You cannot read a wiki from beginning to end, meaning some documents may get lost in the shuffle.

Printing - Some dinosaurs will still want a printed version of your design documentation. In a wiki, you will need to go to each article, print it and collate it. And it will still not look as nice as a document made in Word.

Learning the Markup Language - Wikis are getting more and more fully featured what-you-see-is-what-you-get (WYSIWYG) editors to make them feel like word processors. However, often times you need to learn some measure of wiki markup to quickly create in the new environment. For instance, in MediaWiki, to make something italic, you surround it with two

[7] Of course to many this is not a drawback at all.

quotes ''like this''. To make something bold, you surround it with three quotes '''like this'''. These are easy and generally have shortcuts available. However, when placing a table, users have to dig deeper into the markup language.

This will look foreign to folks unfamiliar with markup languages. Here's what a simple table would look like:

```
{|
! Item
! Amount
! Cost
|-
|Sword
|1
|7.00
|-
|Shield
|1
|3.00
|-
|Food
|10
|5.00
|-
!Total
|
|15.00
|}
```

Weighing Your Options

Unless you are independent or a design director, you will probably have little input as to which you use: a standard word processor or wikis. But it is important to know both as Word dominates and wikis gain in popularity.

Chapter 8 - Diagram Creation

In this book, you will see me reiterate time and again the power of pictures. There is a simple reason for that: they work! Our brains are naturally wired to interpret pictures. In fact, the cognitive process of us reading text is essentially breaking down letters into individual pictures and then reassembling them to generate meaning.

Dan Roam's popular book "The Back of the Napkin" champions the use of sketches to communicate ideas. His thesis is that not only can you present ideas better with sketches, but also that you can solve problems better when you draw pictures.

Yet so often we stick with text: in emails, in design documents, in pitches. These are places that simple diagrams and sketches can help.

"But I'm Not an Artist!"

The most cited reason people use to avoid using sketches is a perceived lack of artistic talent. This makes no sense. Most people are not Hemingway either, but that doesn't stop them from using text. Fear is not a requisite talent for designers.

Lose your fear that you will be judged on account of your chicken scratch. Some of the best designers I know are the worst artists. Your job is not to create art for the game necessarily—your job is to communicate ideas. Use every tool at your disposal.

Some designers think that they have to be as detailed as their artists for their image to have any measure of respectability. This is backwards. In fact, simple drawings are more useful for communicating ideas. Respected comics writer Scott McCloud calls this "amplification through simplification".

Simple diagrams and pictures allow audiences to "fill in the blanks". A sketch of the Mona Lisa doesn't adequately communicate its beauty because that idea needs to be communicated at high fidelity. Since your ideas are flexible and will change before they get to be a final product, the need for visual fidelity is low and your audience (artists and engineers) can create the high fidelity version in their minds.

In my opinion, the best tools for digital sketch and diagram creation are the simplest and quickest. Many designers, myself included, use Microsoft Paint for sketches (!) as it is simple and effective.

Open up Paint and create a quick diagram and sketch for our Chili Cookoff doc. We were pretty vague about the interface used in our Chili Cookoff event. Assume that there are no standard UI elements in your game that you could reference and that the interface will need to be created from scratch. What should it look like?

Here's what I created:

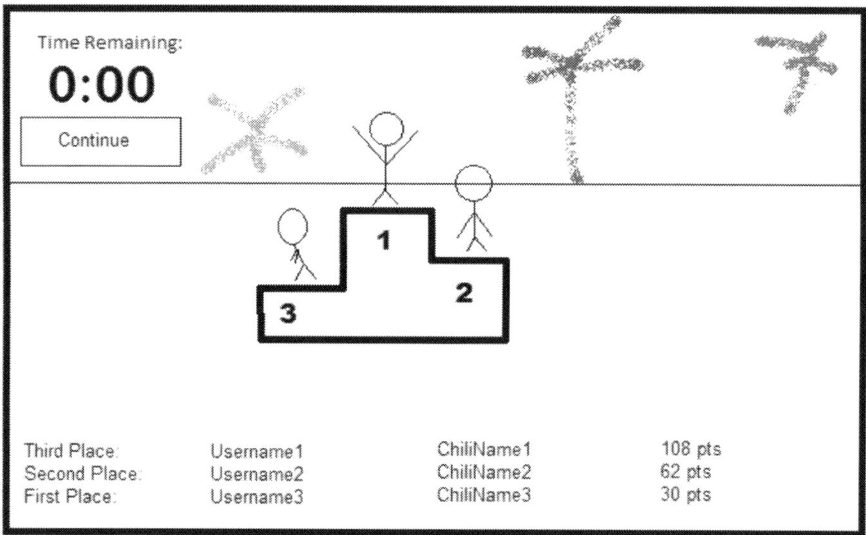

Figure 8.1 - Looks Ridiculous, Right?

Think how much time you would have wasted making finely crafted interface elements that match the visual style of your game? You have trained UI artists (likely) that are much better and quicker at this! They will look at this chicken scratch and in their minds fill it in with what the final product they create will be (after they are done laughing at it).

It answers all the questions without waste on artistic cruft: what elements need to be on screen and where? Which elements are static and which are dynamic?

Microsoft Paint has all you need to make these simple drawings. Going any deeper would be a waste of time since it is so drop dead simple.

If you are using a Mac, there are a bunch of free alternatives, but none are built in. The consensus best replacement is called Paintbrush.

Diagrams and Drawings in Word/Powerpoint

If you are using Paint, you can use the rectangular selector to copy your drawing and paste it into a Word document with little fuss. If you want to draw directly in Word, there's a method for that as well. It is called the Drawing Canvas.

From the Insert tab, click on Shapes. You can drop in a predefined shape from here. Or you can go to the bottom and click on "New Drawing Canvas." The drawing canvas gives you a defined space in which to draw your sketch.

I am personally not a fan of Word's built-in drawing tools. I find formatting within Word to be particularly cumbersome versus cutting and pasting sketches and drawings from other programs. You know when you cut and paste from an external program that your drawing will always look like what you created. Within Word, it can be difficult to keep objects sized and aligned appropriately, since Word likes to be "helpful" with its own formatting.

Of course, sketching is not the only means to quickly generate pictures. Sometimes some boxes and arrows are enough. In Powerpoint, it is simple to layout an image. Powerpoint contains all of the pre-baked shape types that you see in the Shapes menu in Word. By creating your image layout in Powerpoint and then cutting and pasting into Paint *and then* cutting and pasting back into Word, you create a round trip that locks your image elements into place in a single bitmap while taking advantage of Office's shape tools.

Microsoft Visio

Microsoft has a specialized program designed from the start with diagramming in mind. That software is called Visio. Unfortunately Visio is not free and not included in the standard Office distribution, but it is a very popular piece of software you may find preinstalled on many work computers. I show an alternative in a later section.

Visio is popular largely due to its versatility and ease of use. Elements of your diagrams can be moved around and connecting arrows stay attached and position themselves automatically. Visio supports a number of complicated use cases: data links, macros, browser operability, et cetera. Designers rarely have use for these advanced features. Most often, we just want to construct an attractive and useful diagram.

Flow Diagram

One of the most common diagrams designers are tasked with making are called *flow diagrams*. These images describe visually the behavior of system. Perhaps your UI engineers want to understand the designer's vision for the "front end" or the menu system that players first see. This could be described in a big wall of text or a designer can create a flow diagram.

Which is more readable?

First, the user is presented with the Nintendo boot screen. This lasts three seconds. Then the publisher's splash screen is shown for five seconds with the standard animation. Then, the licensor's legal screen is shown for three seconds with the ESRB logo. Next, we show the Press Start screen that leads to the main menu, which has five options: New Game, Continue Game, Online Game, Settings and Credits. Pressing New Game leads the user to the Character Select screen... (I can go on, but the image below will encapsulate this and more in a much smaller space.)

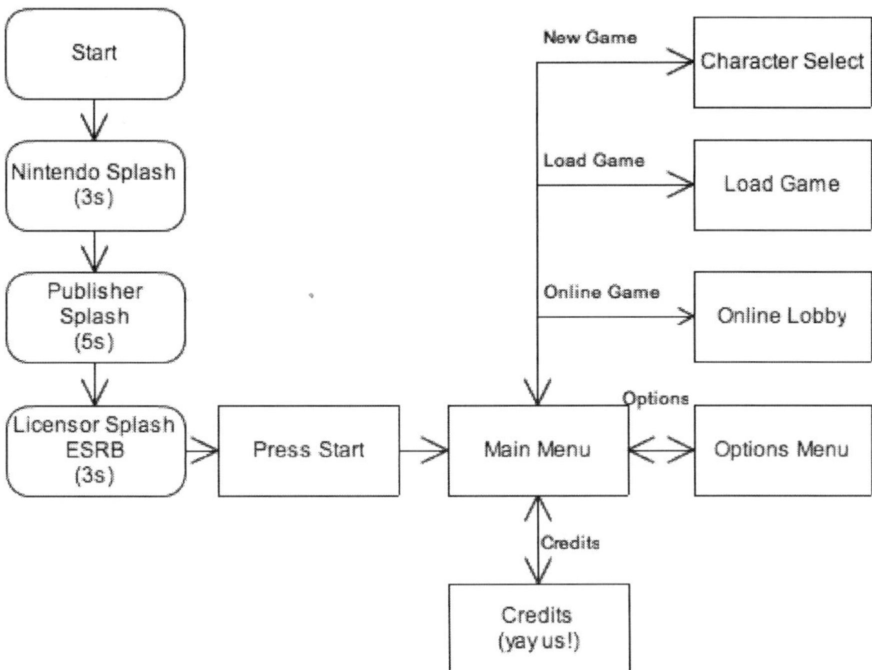

Figure 8.2 - A Sample Flow

Notice the additional information this diagram provides in less than a half page of area (with tons of white space) particularly direction of flow (I can get back to the Main Menu from Character Select, but I cannot get back to Press Start from Main Menu) and type of screen (in here, screens that require user input are rectangular where screens that transition automatically are rounded.) Note also how easy it is to count the number of screens in this diagram versus the wall of text. UI artists can more easily make estimates on this feature when reading it in diagram form versus in text form.

Even if you don't have to hand this off to another developer, flow diagrams can help you understand if there is a piece missing at a glance. Should the user be able to get to the options screen from places other than the main menu? In the diagram you can simply search for an arrow. In a wall of text, you have to digest the entire thing.

Planning Your Diagram

A large diagram can easily become as unreadable as a wall of text if it is not planned appropriately. The ease of moving elements in Visio or its alternatives allows diagram creators to crowd their screen with elements leaving spaghetti trails of arrows swooping around the screen.

Instead, have a plan when creating diagrams. In the diagram above, I had a section for the boot sequence (the top left) and then I expanded the diagram to the right so that when the diagram fanned out for the main menu there would be plenty of room. If my diagram was of larger scope, I would have to create more room. The "Online Lobby" part for instance may contain a dozen screens that would have to be crammed in had I not allocated space.

Only by planning ahead can you save yourself the choice of spending the time to move sets of screen elements around or have a visually cluttered and unreadable diagram.

Alternatives

Visio and Powerpoint are popular software packages for making diagrams, but recently new completely free competitors have threatened their domination. Cacoo is a diagramming application from Nulab that is particularly slick.

Cacoo (a take on the Japanese word for 'draw') rises head and shoulders above for game designers because of its ease of use and because it allows real-time collaboration within teams. Invited team members can view, chat, draw, and add text to diagrams. This can be incredibly helpful in remote development situations where the entire design team is not present. This feature can be more helpful when we get to brainstorming later, but in initial document creation it can be helpful as well. Many of the diagrams in this book were created with Cacoo.

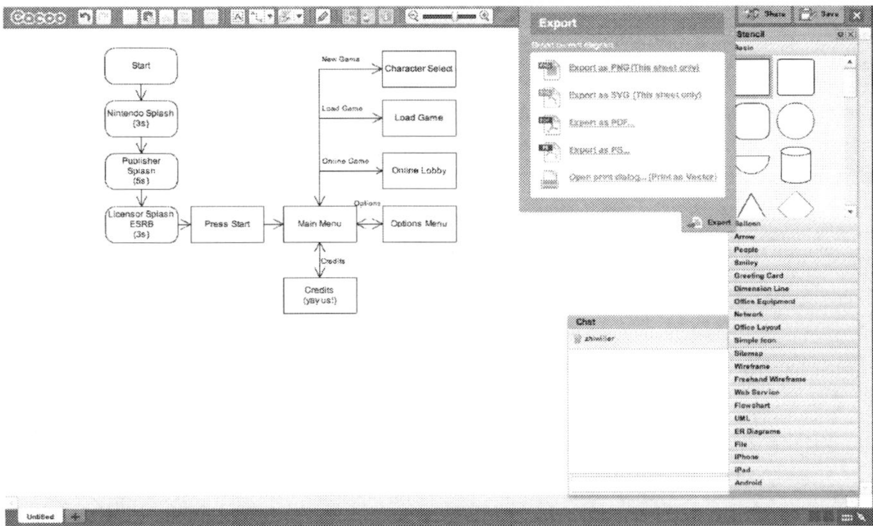

Figure 8.3 - Behold Cacoo in All Its Splendor

There are other applications that perform similar functions: Balsamiq Mockups, OmniGraffle, Dia, Gliffy, and Creately are all popular and range from completely free to requiring paid licenses. Experiment and choose the best for you.

Chapter 9 - Adobe Photoshop / 2D Image Manipulation

Many of you, when seeing a chapter on Photoshop likely shudder in fear. The "I'm not an artist!" reflex kicks in and you shut you shut your brain off. That's not necessary!

While Photoshop is indeed an extremely comprehensive tool, just knowing some of the basics of the tool can be very helpful to you as you design. Remember the power of images! With the vast resources of the Internet at your disposal, you don't need to be able to craft your own images by hand, but instead need to be able to manage the images you can find and use them to your own ends.

Photoshop has been around for over two decades and it is the de facto image manipulation tool for professionals. Much like Google's search engine, Photoshop is so popular that it has itself become a verb. To photoshop something is to use digital means to manipulate an image. Photographs that seem unlikely are often decried 'Photoshopped!' No matter how afraid you are of creating images, gaining a passing knowledge of the program is a wise endeavor to partake.

Transparent Images

Often when you find an image online that you want to use in a presentation, you copy it and paste it into Word or Powerpoint only to find that the white background is hard-coded into the image and looks awful in your document or on your slide background. How can we fix that?

Figure 9.1 - Awful Clip Art with No Transparency

Open the image in Photoshop. The image needs to be in a format that has what is called an **alpha channel**. Alpha represents transparency. Some popular file formats like JPEG do not support alpha channels. Formats like GIF and PNG do.

Copy the image to the clipboard. It can be helpful to start with a new image that has an alpha channel[8]. Go to File, then New and create a new image but be sure to set the Background Color as transparent. Since your old image is on the clipboard, Photoshop will helpfully fill in the correct dimensions.

Paste your image into the new canvas. Now behind the image will be the alpha channel, which is represented by a grey checkerboard pattern. What we want to do is remove the white parts around our image to make the checkerboard shine through.

Select the "Magic Wand" tool from the toolbar.

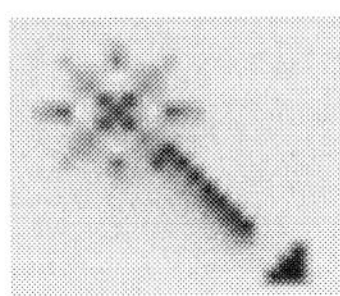

Figure 9.2 - The Magic Wand Tool Icon

The Magic Wand will select a range of pixels that, to the best of its knowledge, are connected. Any drastic change of color serves as a boundary. This allows you to select large contiguous pieces irregular in shape without the difficulty posed by cutting them out with the Lasso tool.

At the top of the screen, you should see a text box indicating "Tolerance". A higher tolerance will select more of the image, ignoring smaller changes in color. A low tolerance will exclude any color that is not extremely close to where the wand tool first selected. For each image, you will likely have to experiment with the tolerance number to get your desired results.

For this example, we are using a tolerance of 4. This means the magic wand will only create a border at sharp changes of color from the original selection. When each section you want to delete is selected, hit the Delete key or go to Clear in the Edit menu.

The guesses of the Magic Wand are not perfect. Often, you will need to touch up a selection by using the Eraser tool afterwards to eliminate some spaces that were not selected by the Magic Wand.

---

[8] In another popular photo manipulation program called GiMP, you must manually add the alpha channel. If you are using this, add an alpha channel by finding "Transparency" in the Layer menu and then selecting "Add Alpha Channel."

Figure 9.3 - A Selection (Dashed) of the Magic Wand

Figure 9.4 - After Deletion, Checkerboard Sections Are Now Transparent

When you are done, save the image with a file type that includes transparency (I usually use PNG) and make sure that transparency is enabled on the "Save for Web" menu if you choose to export that way.

Now you can import the file you saved into Word or Powerpoint and the background will be visible through the empty parts of the image. If you see odd noise, (little clumps of pixels that didn't get deleted) go back into

Photoshop and delete these marks with the eraser tool. If it helps, create a new layer behind the main image and fill that layer with white using the Paint Bucket tool. This will help you see the bits that you may have missed. When you are ready to export again, delete the white layer and the transparency will still be behind it.

Figure 9.5 - Successful Transparency

Cropping/Transforming

One of the most basic tasks a designer will use Photoshop for is to format images in a specific way for presentation in documents or slides. Learning some of these basic techniques will go a long way in improving how you use images in your documents.

Cropping Using the Crop Tool

Cropping is the act of cutting away unnecessary portions of an image to help focus on an important part of an image or to change the aspect ratio of the image. Cropping removes information and reduces the pixel size of your image. To retain the original pixel resolution and aspect ratio, you will have to stretch your image (see Free Transform below).

One of the methods of cropping is to use the Crop tool in the standard tool bar. Select the Crop Tool and then drag the area you want to keep. The rest of the image will darken. You can then drag the corners or sides of the image to adjust the crop area. When you are satisfied with your selection, hit Enter and the darkened area will vanish.

Figure 9.6 - Crop Tool Icon

Figure 9.7 - Crop Tool in Action

Cropping Using the Rectangular Selection Tool

A quicker way of cropping involved using the Rectangular Marquee tool. Just select the area you want to keep and then select Crop from the image menu. This is the method I tend to use since it is so much faster.

Using Content-Aware Fill

Sometimes you will have an image and there will be something right smack in the middle of it that makes it inconvenient. Say you have this picture that you want to use for a slide:

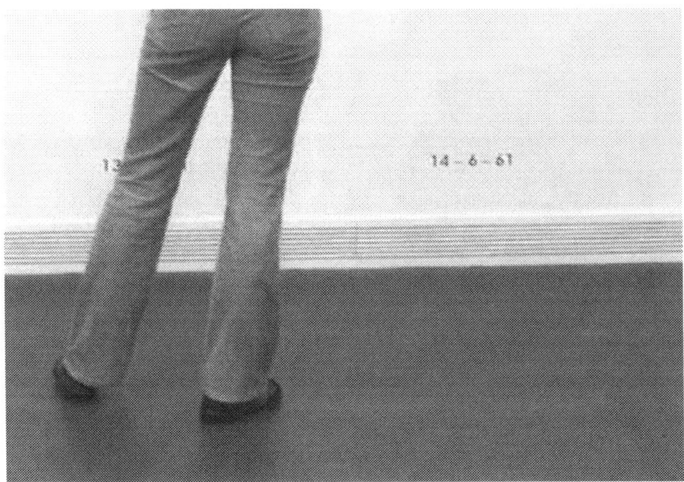

Figure 9.8 - Before Content-Aware Fill

And say you want to remove the legs from it. You could go in and erase the woman out, but there would be a large hole where you erased her. You could then try to paint over the area in a reasonable way, but that would take a lot of time. If you have a copy of Photoshop CS4 or newer, there is a feature that will pretty much look like black magic to you the first time you use it. It is the Content-Aware Fill.

Select the woman using the rectangular marquee and then go to Edit and then Fill. In the "Contents" section of the Fill dialog box, select "Content Aware". Hit Enter. Photoshop will likely think for a moment or two as this is a processor-heavy operation. What Photoshop will do is take samples from all around the selection and make best guesses as to what should be in the selection based on its surroundings. It is really quite clever.

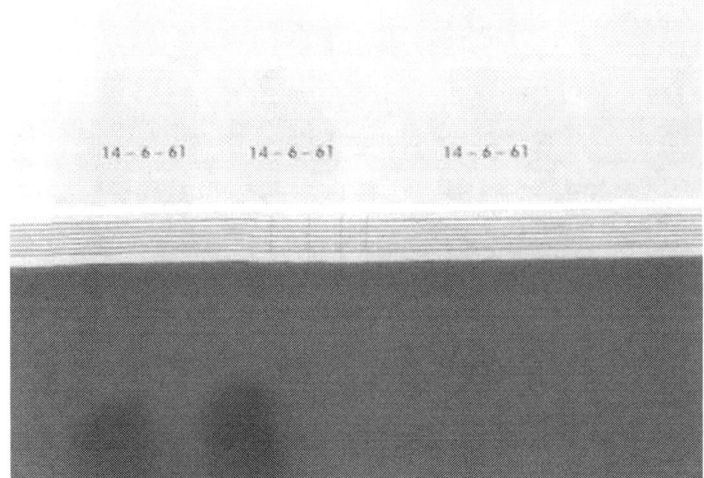

Figure 9.9 - After Content-Aware Fill

Not bad! Her shadow remains and the numbers were repeated, but that is nothing a little touching up with the Blur or Smudge tools or another content-aware fill cannot fix.

Content-Aware Fill does not work in all situations. It works best in areas where it is surrounded by repeating patterns or textures (like grass or clouds) and it works poorly in areas with well-understood edges - don't try to content-aware fill the edge of someone's face unless you want to see what they would look like at the edge of a black hole! Actually, playing with this feature and seeing where it works and where it breaks down can be quite entertaining.

Increasing the Dimensions of a Canvas (Without Stretching)

Often you will want to increase the size of your canvas without stretching your image. If you use the Image Size menu located under the Image menu, your image will stretch. This can be okay if you are making small nudges to the size of your image, but for more drastic changes you should use the Canvas Size menu option instead.

In the Canvas Size menu, there is an odd 3x3 grid with arrows labeled 'Anchor'. This tells Photoshop from which direction it needs to cut or add. If the center is selected (which it is by default) then the additional canvas size will be added to or subtracted from all of the edges evenly. Choosing a corner will tell Photoshop to crop from or add to the corner (or side) *opposite* the chosen square. Thus, if you want to keep the upper-left portion intact and add to (or crop from the lower-right, you would choose the top-left square.

Cropping is much easier with the two tools I selected above, but this method is best for getting your canvas to the exact size needed.

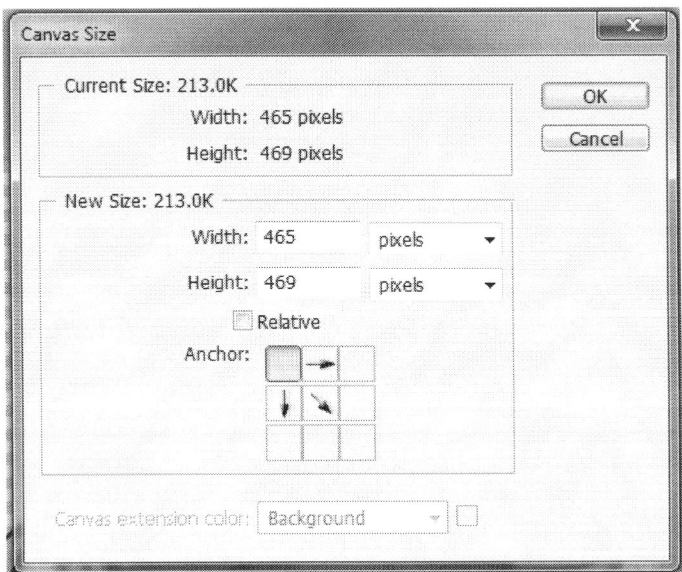

Figure 9.10 - Canvas Size Menu

Content-Aware Scale

When we used the content-aware fill, we used it to fill in a square on top of the hi-res image we already had. Photoshop can also use the content-aware algorithms to guess what are important and non-important picture elements when increasing or decreasing the size of the canvas without stretching the image. Say you have the following image in a low resolution that is not large enough to fill a slide without horizontal stretching:

Figure 9.11 - Image To Stretch

Increase the canvas size using the above method to the resolution you want the final image to have. Select the parts of your image you want to sample with the rectangular marquee tool and in the Edit menu choose "Content-Aware Scale". Your original image will gain a border. Drag the side edge of the border until it fills up the new canvas. Instead of stretching the canvas, Photoshop will try to sample to guess what should fill in the blanks.

Figure 9.12 - Stretched the Waves with Content-Aware Scale

You can even use this to reduce the size of the image. Photoshop will make its best guess as to which areas are important and which are not, deleting empty space before objects. Experiment with the feature to obtain the best results.

Free Transform

The last technique I want to mention is the Free Transform. Free Transform allows you to move, stretch, skew or rotate any selected image. Highlight the section or image you want to select with the Marquee Tool and then either press Control and T or select Free Transform from the Edit menu. You can change the scale of the selection by dragging the corners. The cursor changes to a rounded arrow when you hover near the corners, clicking and dragging will cause the image to rotate.

Scaling, moving and rotating are the three most useful Transform methods. You can select others (such as Distort) by going to the Edit menu and selecting Transform.

Actions & Batch Editing

I had used Photoshop for a number of years before coming upon this great feature that likely would have saved me man-days of labor had I known about it sooner.

Often you will find yourself faced with a monumentally repetitive image task. Perhaps you need to resize all of the portraits in your game from 320x240 to 160x120. Maybe you need to put a border around all of your images or change them all to grayscale or save them all as PNGs instead of GIFs. If you have a lot of images, this can be extremely time-consuming.

Luckily, Photoshop allows you to automate actions and save the workflow for later. An action set is a list of commands that can be recorded and played back like a tape. First, open the actions palette by either pressing F9 or going to the Windows menu and then selecting Actions. There will be a bunch of default actions that come shipped with Photoshop. I have cleared them all. You can keep or clear yours.

The action set we are going to create will put a small black border around your images and resize them all to a standard 200 pixel width.

We are going to start from the end, just to be difficult. Here's what the actions pane will look like when you are done:

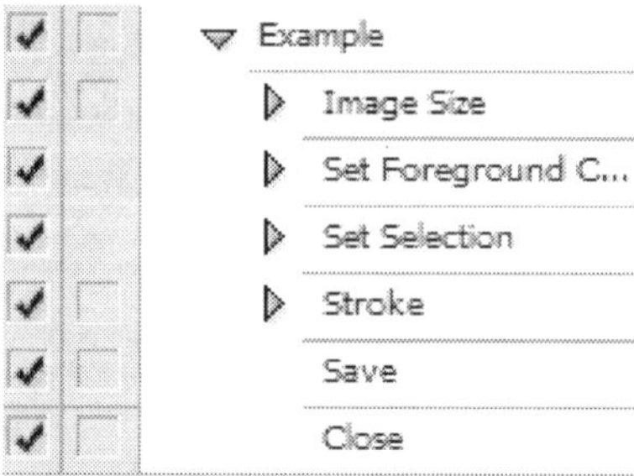

Figure 9.13 - Action Pane

The check mark selects whether or not the action will be done when you hit the Play button. Each step (command) gets a line. When the play button is pressed, the steps will be played out on whatever image is open.

First, open up one of your images that you want to edit. Go to "New Action" on the action panel, which is represented by a small page icon. Name the action "Example". You will be recording by default. While this is going, **every action you take** will be recorded for your automated action set. So don't do anything you don't want to be a part of your action. If you want to break out of the record, press the square stop button. You can press the circular record button to start it up again.

While you are recording, do the actions you want to be part of your action set:

- Go to Image and then Image Size and change the width to 200px.
- Then change your palette's foreground color to black.
- Then Select All (Control+A works) and go to Edit and then Stroke to add a five pixel black inside stroke around the image.

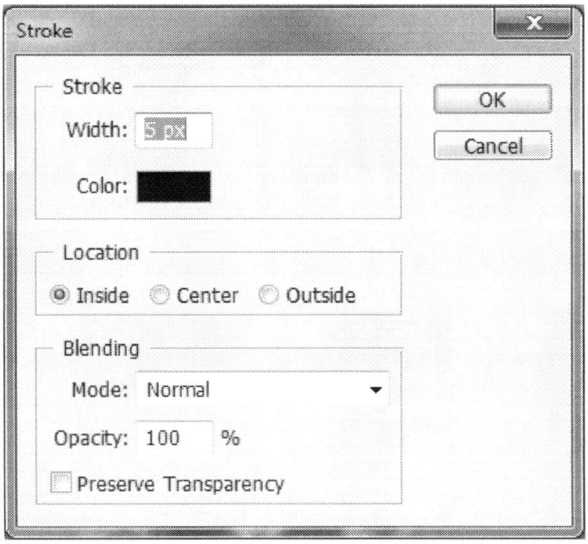

Figure 9.14 - Stroke Menu

- Now, save the image and close it.

Then press the square Stop Recording button. If you do not add the save and close steps then when you do this as a batch action, you will have to save each image individually and at the end all images will be open and eating up precious memory. Keep in mind if you choose to just save and close as I did here that your original files would be overwritten.

Now that you've completed the action, you can run it on any image you have open by pressing the Play (right triangle) button with the action selected in the action pane.

Figure 9.15 - Image Completed—Resized and Bordered

If we want to do the stroke part but not the resize part, we can uncheck the checkbox called Image Resize and press the play button. Photoshop will execute only the checked steps on the open image.

This saves time, of course. But it would save more time if we didn't have to open every image individually to run the Play command.

Luckily, we don't.

Hidden in the File menu is the Automate menu item. Select that and then "Batch".

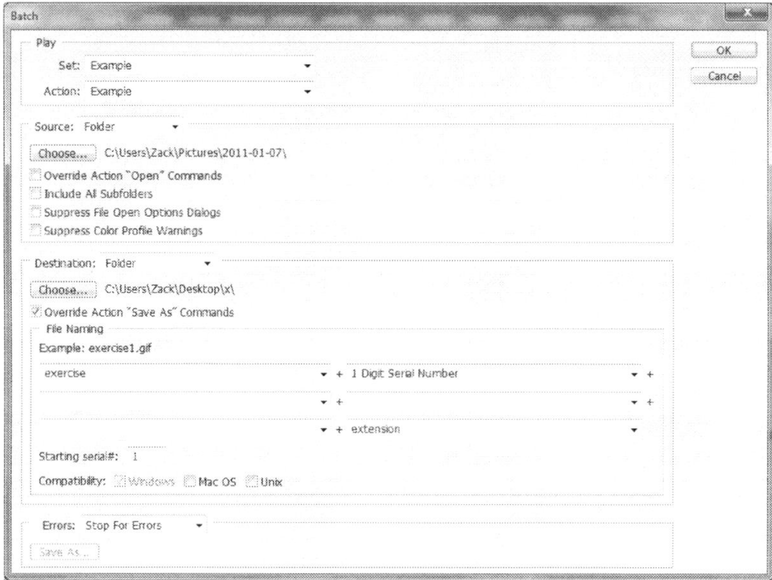

Figure 9.16 - Batch Menu

The set and action are found in the Action Palette. If you named your set "Example", then that is what you would select. Below, you select the folder you are drawing the images from (source) and the directory the images should end up in (destination). Under Destination you can specify to rename the files if you wish.

On the website, there is a zip file for this chapter called Chapter9Example.zip. In it contains a number of free stock images. You can run the Example action on the images in this collection. Extract the images to a folder and choose that folder as the source. I am going to use some random images from my PC.

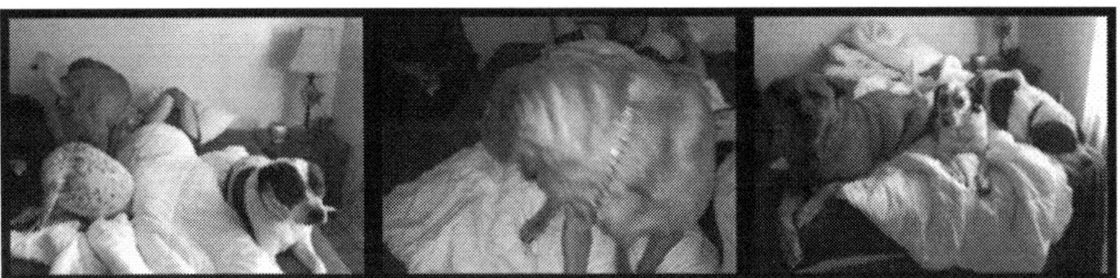

Figure 9.17 - Images After Batch Transformation

Automating actions that you do often can save a lot of time and heartache, but always keep the originals separate, create a backup first and check your results. Sometimes the results are not as you would have intended and you will need to either change the action or modify the image by hand. Regardless, this can be very useful for standardizing a large number of images for web or print.

Alternatives

At the risk of using a double negative, Photoshop is not inexpensive. Legit copies can cost hundreds of dollars. While Photoshop serves its niche well, there are other image generation areas it does not cover at all. There is a market for alternatives. Here are some of the most popular:

GiMP is an open-source image-editing program that attempts to mimic many of the main features of Photoshop. While it has suffered in the past from serious usability issues, newer releases have been more palatable. GiMP's main benefit when comparing to Photoshop is that it is free. Additionally, if you are part of the subset that uses Linux, it is one of your only options. Support for GiMP is also burgeoning. There are a number of books on GiMP available.

Illustrator is another software package from Adobe that focuses on vector-based drawings. Like Photoshop, it is not inexpensive, but is extremely popular for those who want to draw rather than edit already created images.

Paint.NET is another free image editing package similar to GiMP. It is not completely open-source, but is perpetually free-of-cost. It is only supported on Windows as it was originally designed to be a replacement to the default Paint application that comes with Windows. Both are appropriate for doing quick sketches for design documentation or for illustrating a point, but neither would be used (generally) for final assets.

Chapter 10 - GDDs for Indies, Students and Solo Teams

In this book I have written for a particular audience: students who want to land design jobs in the corporate world on medium to large teams where you are not always communicating with folks you know and are at your caste level.

But there is a whole other realm of development: smaller, more independent teams. Students, "garage" developers and hobbyists don't generally need the overhead of complex communication tools and persuasive imagery. This is true. But that does not mean that designers on smaller teams need to give up GDDs and documentation altogether.

Jesse Schell, in *Art of Game Design* describes two major uses for design documentation. One, communication, was what we focused on almost solely up to this point. The other main function is organizational memory. We are simply awful at remembering things. Documentation helps us not make the same mistakes over and over again while preserving out good ideas that we haven't had time to yet implement.

Many students and small independent developers use this workflow:

1. Open up a code editor

2. Code things

3. Throw out what doesn't work

4. Return to step two

They do this because it is fun to make things and this workflow is the quickest route to the "making things" step.

While that is a wonderful iterative process, it often contains more iterations than necessary due to lack of planning. Design documentation can help you figure out your edge cases and "holes" in design before you ever fire up your editor. Design documentation allows you a way of testing before building. You can put your design documentation in front of trusted teammates in order to suss out edge-cases. This is something you cannot do if you go code-first.

Consider slowing down a minute and using the six-step process listed earlier to craft some design documentation, not because you need to show it to a producer, licensor, or teacher but because it will save you time in the long run. Yes, it will take you a little longer before you can open up that editor and hack, but what is your goal: having fun hacking or creating a final product you can be proud of?

Exercises

1. Add the table for post-event rewards in the appropriate section of the Chili Cookoff GDD.

2. Go to Wikipedia and find a large table. Use the above process to recreate that table with simple formatting in Word.

3. Describe a feature of one of your favorite games in the form of a design document. That feature should have both "instructional" bits and "content" bits. Put the content bits in a table.

4. Take a review of a popular game from a website that focuses heavily on the mechanics of the game being reviewed. Separate the review into "code bits" that are instructional and "discussion bits".

5. Trade GDDs from Exercise 4 with another student. Use the comments feature to add comments to areas that you find confusing. Use the comments you receive to make a GDD that makes more sense.

6. Create a table of contents for your GDD. Include page numbers in the header or footer of your document.

7. Use a diagram creation tool like Visio or Cacoo to diagram the startup sequence of a video game you own. Include which screens require user input and which do not and directional arrows to control flow.

8. Use a diagram creation tool like Visio or Cacoo to diagram a user's behavior when buying an item from an online store. Choose any store you wish. Map the possible choices from the product's page until the user completes' the process.

9. Use Microsoft Paint or an alternative to create a sketch of a screen's HUD elements (health bar, experience bar, weapon selected, etc.) from a popular game. There should be at least ten elements to your sketch. How long did the sketch take you? How long would the sketch taken you had you attempted to create it in a higher fidelity?

Summary

- A game design document is not a "bible" of everything game related, but a focused set of instructions to help the team create the game.
- Like everything else in the game, the design process is iterative. It cannot be written and forgotten, but must be kept up-to-date with the current designs.
- Word can be used to streamline the time between a developer opening up your document and finding what he/she needs. Add tables of contents and separate instruction from content to help developers find what they need quickly.
- Images can be more helpful than text if done correctly. It doesn't matter that you are not an artist. A simple diagram or sketch can do wonders versus a wall of text.
- Wikis are a new alternative to word processors for crafting and maintaining design documents. There are pros and cons for wikis, but either can be used effectively.

Part Three - Number Crunching

Computers are capable of amazing things. Frankly, just being able to move a mouse around on a screen and interact with different objects requires the complicity of dozens of different systems. Yet somehow we still resort to heuristics to guess at problems when we have perfectly good number crunching machines in front of us.

Microsoft's Excel is one of the most powerful pieces of software routinely ignored by designers across the globe. Not only does it allow for easy compartmentalization of data, but also its internal function language makes simple simulation something you don't need to write a program to accomplish.

In this section, we will examine how to use Excel for the forces of good when it comes to the black magic realm of simple simulation. Much like in our section on word processors, there are other tools that can be used for this purpose. When it comes to Excel, OpenOffice Calc, Google Spreadsheets and Apple's Numbers are all similar to Excel. In this book, we will examine Excel 2010 but other alternatives should behave similarly.

If you have never used a spreadsheet program before, Excel can be a bit intimidating. With a program like Word, at least you have familiarity with the printed page. How we will tackle this is by jumping right in and discussing features and follow it up with practical applications.

After our brief tour of Excel, we will talk about ways to use it in the industry along with some theoretical tools that will help you visualize complex topics.

Chapter 11 - Excel Crash Course

Excel provides a solution to ordering and manipulating data. Most of the features we talk about in this chapter will allow you to enter or perform functions on data. Thus, appropriate applications of Excel are items with changing data that has to have some computational analysis provided with it. Schedules for instance are often done in Excel to do operations on people and tasks such as calculating productivity and assigning subteams. Excel is used to run simulations of simple data, like an experiment as to how much time it will take a player to defeat some number of players or how often certain complicated dice rolls reach a specific result. We will first discuss the features of Excel and then use them to create some dynamic applications.

Consider this your Excel Crash Course.

Entering Values and Filling Series

Each rectangle in Excel is called a "cell" and each cell holds a discrete piece of data like a name or a number. By placing like cells next to each other, we can relate cells together. Generally, a row of cells describes some instance (such as task, customer, or feature) and columns describe elements of that instance. Take the figure below. We are creating an Excel table of customers. One row is a customer. Each column is a feature of that customer.

LastName	FirstName	Address	City	OrderTotal
Doe	Alphonse	123 Fake Street	Springfield	$21.13

Figure 11.1 - Describing a Single Customer

Often, we don't have a unique identifier for every row, like we do in the above example. Sometimes we have to supply that ourselves. In database language, this is called a *primary key*. It is an identifier for every row that is unique. For instance, names are considered not to be candidates for primary keys because two people can have the same name (e.g., which John Smith did you mean?) so it is common to give a unique number to every row.

Say you just pasted a thousand values from some other source into your spreadsheet. Below I have a database of the GameRankings average for every game up until early 2011.

Date	Studio	Game	Platform	Rating	NumReviews
1/1/2011	BioWare	Mass Effect 2	PS3	92.97%	31
1/1/2011	Media Molecule	LittleBigPlanet 2	PS3	92.26%	51
1/1/2011	Visceral Games	Dead Space 2	X360	89.40%	43
1/1/2011	Visceral Games	Dead Space 2	PS3	89.24%	42
1/1/2011	Capcom	Ghost Trick: Phantom Detective	DS	84.77%	30
1/1/2011	Southend Interactive	ilomilo	X360	81.52%	26
1/1/2011	Hudson Soft	Lost in Shadow	WII	69.88%	25
1/1/2011	Square Enix	Kingdom Hearts Re:coded	DS	69.64%	29
1/1/2011	Reality Pump	Two Worlds II	X360	69.16%	22
1/1/2011	Atomic Games	Breach	X360	60.38%	24
1/1/2010	Nintendo	Super Mario Galaxy 2	WII	97.12%	54
1/1/2010	BioWare	Mass Effect 2	X360	95.66%	73
1/1/2010	Rockstar San Diego	Red Dead Redemption	PS3	94.76%	50
1/1/2010	BioWare	Mass Effect 2	PC	94.48%	30
1/1/2010	Rockstar San Diego	Red Dead Redemption	X360	94.18%	71
1/1/2010	Harmonix Music Systems	Rock Band 3	X360	92.38%	46
1/1/2010	Blizzard Entertainment	Starcraft II: Wings of Liberty	PC	92.34%	53
1/1/2010	Namco Bandai Games America	Pac-Man Championship Edition DX	X360	92.17%	29
1/1/2010	SCE Santa Monica	God of War III	PS3	92.04%	71
1/1/2010	Bungie Software	Halo: Reach	X360	91.59%	68

Figure 11.2 - Database Without Keys

We can just assume every game has a unique title and leave it at that. That would be wrong. Quickly looking through the data shows that remakes and different editions have the same title despite being different games. *Max Payne* for the PC (2001) is a different game than *Max Payne* for the Game Boy Advance from 2003. We must add a unique number to each row.

There are over five thousand rows in my database. Adding these numbers by hand would be tedious, take a long time and be prone to mistakes. In Excel, there is a better way.

First, we will add an empty column to place the numbers. Right-click on the "A" above the first column and select "Insert Column". Now that we have a place for them, type "1", "2", and "3" in the first three rows.

Key	Date	Studio	Game	Platform	Rating	NumReviews
1	1/1/2011	BioWare	Mass Effect 2	PS3	92.97%	31
2	1/1/2011	Media Molecule	LittleBigPlanet 2	PS3	92.26%	51
3	1/1/2011	Visceral Games	Dead Space 2	X360	89.40%	43
	1/1/2011	Visceral Games	Dead Space 2	PS3	89.24%	42
	1/1/2011	Capcom	Ghost Trick: Phantom Detective	DS	84.77%	30
	1/1/2011	Southend Interactive	ilomilo	X360	81.52%	26
	1/1/2011	Hudson Soft	Lost in Shadow	WII	69.88%	25

Figure 11.3 - Setting Up The Series

If you direct it to, Excel will try to figure out the pattern you are aiming for and fill in all of the appropriate spaces until the neighboring column runs out of data. When your series is 1,2,3, this is pretty easy. But Excel can also do 2011, 2010, 2009 or 3,6,9. It is not a remarkably detailed solution generator, but for the simple series like this, it does its job.

To direct Excel to do this, highlight the series elements you have already filled in (not just the last cell) and hover over the bottom-right portion of the last cell you filled in. There should be a small dot in this corner of the selected cell. Your cursor will change to a plus sign. If you have a short list, you can drag this plus down to the place you want the series to fill. If you have a long list like I do, you can double-click on this to have Excel fill in where it thinks everything should go.

	A	B	C	D	E	F	G
1	Key	Date	Studio	Game	Platform	Rating	NumReviews
2	1	1/1/2011	BioWare	Mass Effect 2	PS3	92.97%	31
3	2	1/1/2011	Media Molecule	LittleBigPlanet 2	PS3	92.26%	51
4	3	1/1/2011	Visceral Games	Dead Space 2	X360	89.40%	43
5	4	1/1/2011	Visceral Games	Dead Space 2	PS3	89.24%	42
6	5	1/1/2011	Capcom	Ghost Trick: Phantom Detective	DS	84.77%	30
7	6	1/1/2011	Southend Interactive	ilomilo	X360	81.52%	26
8	7	1/1/2011	Hudson Soft	Lost in Shadow	Wii	69.88%	25
9	8	1/1/2011	Square Enix	Kingdom Hearts Re:coded	DS	69.64%	29
10	9	1/1/2011	Reality Pump	Two Worlds II	X360	69.16%	22
11	10	1/1/2011	Atomic Games	Breach	X360	60.38%	24
12	11	1/1/2010	Nintendo	Super Mario Galaxy 2	Wii	97.12%	54
13	12	1/1/2010	BioWare	Mass Effect 2	X360	95.66%	73
14	13	1/1/2010	Rockstar San Diego	Red Dead Redemption	PS3	94.76%	50

Figure 11.4 - Our Series in A Few Seconds

You will find out that this is incredibly useful when using formulas.

Formulas

Formulas are the most powerful aspect of Excel. Formulas allow you to ask Excel to evaluate a statement: what's the average of all these items? How many times does this statement show up? What is a random number between one and one hundred?

Most formulas refer to a cell by name. For instance, the top-leftmost cell is A1. Columns to the right are alphabetic, while rows below are numeric. So the second row and the second column meet at cell B2. This is very elementary, but important to understand when talking about cells.

Formula Operator

Take the simplest possible formula: one that echoes the value of a cell. In cell A1 type the number 14. In cell B1 type =A1. The equals sign is the flag that tells Excel this is a formula. What follows the equals sign is what is to be evaluated. In this example, we tell Excel: "In this cell, put whatever is in cell A1. When you hit enter, you will see that B1 is also 14. Change A1 and B1 will reflect that.

Basic Math

Clear all the cells. Type three numbers in cells A1, A2 and A3. In cell A4, type =A1+A2+A3. When you hit enter, Excel will evaluate the function, adding all three cells together. You can even chain these together. Change A3 to =A1+A2. A4 will still sum all of the cells above it! This chaining is part of what makes simulating in Excel so simple and powerful.

=SUM(Range), =PRODUCT(Range)

You can use any of the basic operators in functions: + - * / ^. You can use parentheses to control the order of operations. If, however, you have a list of items you want to add or multiply that is very large, you won't want to spend the time typing =A1+A2+A3+A4+A5… Instead you can use the SUM function over a range.

A range is a collection of adjacent cells and is defined by a starting point followed by a colon followed by the ending point. If I wanted to sum cells A1, A2, A3 down to A100, I could type =SUM(A1:A100). Easy.

Likewise if I wanted to multiply those cells, I just change the function name: =PRODUCT(A1:A100).

=MAX(Range), =MIN(Range)

There are other operations that are particularly useful when discussing ranges. The MAX function returns the largest number in a range. The MIN function returns the smallest number in a range. Say you had a spreadsheet with 100 student grades in cells B2 to B101. To find the best grade, you would type =MAX(B2:B101). To find the worst: =MIN(B2:B101).

=AVERAGE(Range), =MEDIAN(Range), =MODE(Range)

Statistical functions are available. If I wanted the average grade in the aforementioned list, I would type =AVERAGE(B2:B101). These are very simple. MEDIAN provides the middle element when the list is sorted numerically. MODE provides the most common element in the list.

=RANK(Cell, Range), =PERCENTRANK(Range, Cell), =PERCENTILE(Range, Number)

Now we are getting into the more interesting functions. In each cell next to a student's grade, I wanted to put that student's rank in the class. In this case I am going to need to supply two arguments to the function separated by a comma. The first is the number I am examining. In the above example, when I am in C2, the number I am examining is in B2. The second argument is the array of numbers I am using to calculate my rank. To get the rank then, I would type: =RANK(B2,B2:B101). I would get returned a number from 1 to 100 where cell B2 fell. If it was the highest grade, the function would return a 1.

Absolute ranking is sometimes useful, but if you want to see a cell's rank as a percentage of the population, use PERCENTRANK. For some reason,

PERCENTRANK wants the array first and then the number being examined, completely reversed from the RANK function. =PERCENTRANK(B2:B101,B2) would give a number 0 to 1 where the cell ranked as a percentage. If the cell fell right in the middle, the function would return a 0.5. By using the formatting tools (explained in a later section) you can format this as a proper percentage.

PERCENTILE is the inverse of PERCENTRANK. You can give it a number and it will tell you where it would fall as a PERCENTRANK in that array. For instance, say that B2:B502 was a list of all SAT scores for a particular school. You want to know where a 1400 would rank among all of the students. =PERCENTILE(B2:B502,1400) would tell you that.

=ROUND(Number), =TRUNC(Number)

Often Excel will return a function with too much precision for what you are looking for. Go back to the grade example. Perhaps your institution only accepts integer grades. A 69.9 should be reported as a 70. But you don't want to go through and manually nudge all of the results to their proper place. You can use the ROUND function to round to the nearest integer or TRUNC to truncate the number (removing the decimal place part).

Another element that makes Excel statements so powerful is the ability to *nest* statements together. This means that in one cell, we can put multiple statements and functions inside each other.

Take the PERCENTRANK from the previous example. It will give a number between 0 and 1 as to the student's class rank. Say we wanted this in integer form. Perhaps the class is curved and the worst performing student gets a zero and the best gets a 100. First, we would have to multiply the PERCENTRANK by 100 to get the number to fall in the 0 to 100 range. But then we are left with pesky decimal places, so we can wrap a function around the PERCENTRANK function. Functions are evaluated from inside to outside so the PERCENTRANK happens first. Here's what it would look like:

=ROUND(100*PERCENTRANK(B2:B101,B2))

Both functions need opening and closing parentheses. This is why the statement ends with two end parentheses.

=RAND(), =RANDBETWEEN(Bound, Bound)

You are starting to get good at functions, so I'll introduce the pièce de résistance, the central functions that underlay all of simulation in Excel: the random number generator.

RAND takes no arguments. (It won't get an argument from me, har har). It returns a random number between 0 and 1[9].

There's an important note about Excel to bring up at this point. Every time you change a cell, Excel recalculates all the functions in every cell. This means that every time you change a cell, Excel will generate a different random number for each randomizer function in your workbook. This is the default behavior. If you want to change it so that functions calculate only when you say to, go to Excel's preferences and look for the Calculation options where you can switch this to "Manual". In that case, it will only recalculate when you hit F9 (or Cmd+= on Macs).

So you have a very precise decimal, but that is not often useful. Random numbers are great for generating die rolls, but when you roll a die, you don't get 0.20351 as a result. You get some integer between 1 and 6. There are two ways to fix this. In most programming languages, you must multiply the random 0-1 number by the largest number in your range and add one. Then you truncate the result. In Excel, I have already gone over the tools to do this. A die roll from 1 to 6 would look like this:

=TRUNC(6*RAND())+1

That's ugly though, so Excel gives you a function to simplify the process called RANDBETWEEN. It requires two arguments, a lower bound and an upper bound. Your 1 to 6 die roll becomes:

=RANDBETWEEN(1,6)

Much easier.

=CONCATENATE(Cells)

Concatenate is what is called a *string function* because it evaluates text which programmers call "strings". Concatenate takes two strings (bits of

---

[9] RAND returns in the range [0,1) which means it can return 0 at its lowest but 0.999 repeating at the highest.

text) and shoves them together. If you have last names in column A and first names in column B and want to put them together in column C with a space between, you would do this:

=CONCATENATE(A1, " ", B1)

Concatenate can take as many strings as you wish to supply it. You may be wondering what the second argument is. It is telling Excel to put a single space between the first and last name. If you only did =CONCATENATE(A1,A2), you would get results like JohnDoe, JaneDoe instead of John Doe, Jane Doe.

=VLOOKUP(Value, Range, Column, Approx.)

When you have a function like MAX above, often you want to know more about the row from which the return comes. If I am using my game reviews database from earlier, maybe I want to know what the highest rated game is. If I were to just do =MAX(F2:F5027), this would only tell me the highest rating, not which game that rating belonged to. With lookup functions, we can find out more.

VLOOKUP and its brother HLOOKUP are a little complicated, so we will break them down step by step.

The first argument VLOOKUP needs is the value it is looking for. Remember that we can *nest* functions meaning put functions inside of functions. So in our above example we are looking for the max value cell. The first argument will be a function in itself. One common error to note here is that the lookup value must be the leftmost column in the table array. You may have to do some rejiggering of how your table is formatted to get this to work. In this example, I am copying the scores into the A column.

The next argument tells VLOOKUP where it is looking. Here you have to put the top left-most cell and the bottom-right most cell to let the function know the bounds of where it should search.

The next to last argument tells VLOOKUP what you want to return. In here, we put a column number. In the table given to the function in the last argument, which column do you want back? In our previous example, we want to return the fourth column, the name.

The last argument is whether or not you want an approximate or exact match. Since we want an exact match, we set this to FALSE.

The form of a VLOOKUP statement is:

=VLOOKUP(Value, Range, Column, Approximate)

Putting these together we get:

=VLOOKUP(MAX(A2:A5027), A2:G5027, 4, FALSE)

And it returns "The Legend of Zelda: Ocarina of Time".

HLOOKUP works the same only it searches rows for a value instead of columns and then returns values from the column instead of the row.

=IF(Condition, Return True, Return False)

I have buried this a bit under the scads of other functions, but IF is the most important function of all. It is a *logical* function, which means it can evaluate between true and false statements. We use it in simulation to evaluate random results and we use it in conditionals like scheduling to make sure elements are scheduled efficiently.

The form of the IF statement is simple and contains three parts. The first part is the logical test itself, which must always return true or false. What are you evaluating? Perhaps you want to know if the cell is greater than the cell below it. In this case your logical test would be something like A2>B2. If the logical test returns true, then the whole IF function returns the second argument. If it returns false, it returns the third argument. These arguments can just be text strings like so:

=IF(A2>B2,"Greater","Not Greater")

Thus if A2 is greater than B2, this cell with have the word "Greater" as its data. Otherwise, it will have "Not Greater" as its data. Until you experiment with this, and we will later in the section, you may not realize how powerful the function actually is.

=COUNTIF(Range, Condition), =SUMIF(Range, Condition)

COUNTIF is a clever function that counts the number of cells that meet a logical test. For instance, in our game reviews database, how many of the reviews are above 70%?

=COUNTIF(F2:F5027,">70%")

This returns 3,497.

Note that the logical operation is only the second half of the equation. COUNTIF will fill in the left side of the equation of each cell in the range with the cell reference, so you only need to supply the comparison. You must include the quotation marks.

As a bonus, let me tell you about the COUNT function, which is limited in that it returns the number of cells that have numbers in them. (COUNTA is the name of the function that counts if anything is in the cell.) But when we combine it with COUNTIF or other functions, it becomes useful. Knowing that 3,497 reviews are about 70% doesn't help us. Out of how many is this?

=COUNTIF(F2:F5027,">70%")/COUNT(F2:F5027)

This returns 69.57%. This means that approximately 70% of games are a 7.0 (70%) or higher. If we were to create gaps in the data, deleting rows at will, this statement would still reflect the right proportion even with the gaps.

There is also a COUNTIFS function that allows you to chain COUNTIFs together in a single function.

SUMIF is similar to COUNTIF except that instead of identifying cells, it takes whatever is in that cell and adds it to every other cell it identifies.

Say we wanted to count the number of reviews in that database for each individual system. The platform is in column D and the number of reviews is in column G. If we wanted to count the number of reviews for the PS2:

=SUMIF(D2:D5027, "=PS2", G2:G5027)

The first argument is the range we are checking, the second argument is the criteria we are checking and the third argument is what we are looking to sum if the second argument is true. You can leave this third argument out if the first and third arguments will be the same.

Finding More Functions

We have gone over a bunch of functions but have only examined the tip of the iceberg. The official Excel documentation contains many, many more[10]. The link in the footnote sorts the functions by category so you can narrow down your search to the type of function you are looking for. If you think t can be done in Excel, it probably can.

Common Formula Errors

There are a number of common mistakes made when using formulas in Excel. Unfortunately, Excel is not particularly helpful with its error messages.

#NAME - One of the most common errors is #NAME. Excel cannot find the function you are trying to use. What likely happened is that you misspelled the function name. Maybe you typed CONUTIF instead of COUNTIF. Or you have a syntax error somewhere else. Are you missing quotes? A comma? A colon? (Better get that checked out.) Another reason this can show up is if you are referring to an advanced function that is not loaded in your version of Excel. This happens with older versions of Excel and functions from Add-In packs.

#DIV/0 - Despite your desires, Excel will not divide by zero. Somewhere you have two cells dividing (sounds like Biology) and one of them can be a zero. The quickest way to sniff this one out is to look for division symbols and then find the denominator cells. Then try to figure out under what conditions those can be zeros.

#VALUE - Something is wrong with your arguments. A function expects a logical operation and you put a string. Or it expects numbers and you put strings. Or perhaps you've left out a required argument in a function.

---

[10] http://office.microsoft.com/en-us/excel-help/list-of-excel-functions-by-category-HP005204211.aspx

#NUM - This is usually an easy fix. A formula expects a number but is getting text that is not a number. Or you are returning a number that is larger than Excel can handle. If you are using a function like IRR that guesses and checks, you will get this error if the function goes too long without finding an answer. To fix that particular problem, check to make sure your problem has an answer and provide a better starting guess.

#REF - This one is annoying. Excel is trying to find a cell that does not exist.

#N/A - This one is the most annoying of all because it is a "catch-all" error message that doesn't mean anything. It is likely you are using a function in the wrong way, supplying bad arguments or violating some assumption of the function (like VLOOKUP assumes the lookup column is the left-most column.) It is also returned when you are using a searching function that cannot zero in on a value.

######## - If you see a cell full of pound symbols, don't despair! This just means that your cell is not wide enough to display the proper value. This is not actually an error at all. Just drag the cell width larger and you should eventually see the correct value.

Anchors

Say you have a table in a spreadsheet like the following:

	A	B	C	D	E	F
1					Fudge Factor	1.25
2						
3			Points Given	Cumulative Point	Time for Action	Time Elapsed
4		User Clicks a Cow	1	1	0:01	0:01
5		User Invites a User	100		1:22	
6		User Opens a Treasure Ch	23		0:54	
7		User Stomps a Monster	17		0:32	
8		User Scores a Touchdown	7		1:29	
9		User Clicks Another Cow	1		0:02	

Figure 11.5 - A Time Journal

You have a list of tasks the player will do in a run-through along with experience points gained from each action. This is an extremely simplified version of the kind of analysis commonly done to determine when a player will hit certain game states.

You could go through each of the cells in the cumulative experience column and put the formula = Above Cell + Left Cell in each, but there is an easier way. Much like how you can drag a series and have Excel fill in the blanks, you can do this with formulas as well. And Excel is smart enough to know that when the cell moves down one row to change the formulas so that the inputs go down one row.

Create the first cell at D5 and fill it with the formula =D4+C5. This will add whatever is above it (the cumulative before this row) to what is beside it (the entry for this row). Now highlight the lower-right corner of D4 and drag down to D9 or just double-click the bottom of D9. Notice how Excel does the work for you! This is very nice with large spreadsheets with tons of rows or columns.

	A	B	C	D	E	F
1					Fudge Factor	1.25
2						
3			Points Given	Cumulative Points	Time for Action	Time Elapsed
4		User Clicks a Cow	1	1	0:01	0:01
5		User Invites a User	100	101	1:22	
6		User Opens a Treasure Ch	23	124	0:54	
7		User Stomps a Monster	17	141	0:32	
8		User Scores a Touchdown	7	148	1:29	
9		User Clicks Another Cow	1	149	0:02	
10						

Figure 11.6 - Drag Down Formula Fill-In

Now try it for the time estimate column. A common practice in time estimates is to include a "fudge factor" or a margin of error to factor in unforeseen events. Here, we will use 25% as a fudge factor. That is the function of the cell at F1. In cell F5 we will do this: =(F1*E5)+F4. This will multiply the fudge factor by the value to the left and then add the value above.

SUM | =(F1*E5)+F4

	A	B	C	D	E	F
1					Fudge Factor	1.25
2						
3			Points Given	Cumulative Points	Time for Action	Time Elapsed
4		User Clicks a Cow	1	1	0:01	0:01
5		User Invites a User	100	101	1:22	=(F1*E5)+F4
6		User Opens a Treasure Ch	23	124	0:54	
7		User Stomps a Monster	17	141	0:32	
8		User Scores a Touchdown	7	148	1:29	
9		User Clicks Another Cow	1	149	0:02	

Figure 11.7 - Non-Adjacent Formula

Now try dragging this down. You end up with some not great results:

	A	B	C	D	E	F
1					Fudge Factor	1.25
2						
3			Points Given	Cumulative Points	Time for Action	Time Elapsed
4		User Clicks a Cow	1	1	0:01	0:01
5		User Invites a User	100	101	1:22	1:43
6		User Opens a Treasure Ch	23	124	0:54	1:43
7		User Stomps a Monster	17	141	0:32	#VALUE!
8		User Scores a Touchdown	7	148	1:29	#VALUE!
9		User Clicks Another Cow	1	149	0:02	#VALUE!
10						

Figure 11.8 - Cell Errors

This is because when you drag it down, Excel is not only moving the reference to the left-hand cell but also our fudge factor cell. Click on cell F6. The formula there should be =(F2*E6)+F5, but F2 is empty.

What we need is a way to tell Excel which cell references to hold still and which to move when we drag formulas around. Excel has a simple solution to this and it is called an *anchor*.

Putting a dollar sign before either the row number, the column name or both will anchor them in place to never move when the cell containing the formula moves. In our case above, here is the correct way to write the formula: =(F$1*E5)+F4. This anchors the row number of F1 in place. No matter where we drag the cell to, the row number referenced here will be 1. If we want a little more security, we can anchor the column too: =(F1*E5)+F4. Now that cell reference will always be F1.

Remove the incorrect entries, add the fix above and drag down the formula. Success! Toy with the fudge factor to see how it affects the total.

F5 =(F1*E5)+F4

	A	B	C	D	E	F
1					Fudge Factor	1.25
2						
3			Points Given	Cumulative Points	Time for Action	Time Elapsed
4		User Clicks a Cow	1	1	0:01	0:01
5		User Invites a User	100	101	1:22	1:43
6		User Opens a Treasure Ch	23	124	0:54	2:51
7		User Stomps a Monster	17	141	0:32	3:31
8		User Scores a Touchdown	7	148	1:29	5:22
9		User Clicks Another Cow	1	149	0:02	5:24
10						

Figure 11.9 - Fixed with an Anchor

Cutting and Copying

Standard word processing functions like cut, copy and paste are available to you in Excel, but there are some notes to make regarding how cell references act when you try this.

When you **cut** a cell and then paste it somewhere else, the cell reference should stay exactly the same. Say I cut a cell containing =B10 from E1 to E2. It should still paste as B10. But if you **copy** the cell, Excel will attempt to move the cell references as if you were dragging the file. In this case, if it is not desirable, you would want to stick to the anchoring methods listed above.

Other odd behaviors regarding pasting with Excel are that Excel likes to try to preserve formatting and that Excel assumes where spaces in the text such as the separation between first and last name should really be a cell break.

To avoid pasting cells into a space and then having to redo the formatting, you can use the Paste Special command located in the clipboard section of the Home tab. Click on the Paste button's downward pointing arrow and then on Paste Special. When you use this, you get a dialog box and can choose from there to only paste the values, keeping the style of the cells unchanged.

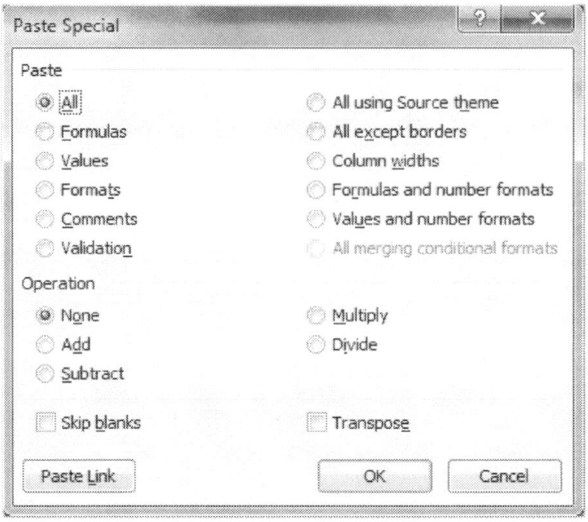

Figure 11.10 - Paste Special Menu

When copying text from a website or other source that was in a table, Excel often gets confused as to the location of cell breaks. But when you paste into Notepad or many other *plain text* editors, the text editor replaces cell breaks with a standardized character: the tab. (Note: the *plain text* part is important because it strips any unnecessary markup that you don't want to carry over.) If your text is still aligned poorly, you can easily go into the text editor and add tabs using your tab key or delete tabs in places where cell breaks need to occur. Then cut the text from the text editor and paste it in Excel and it should be formatted correctly.

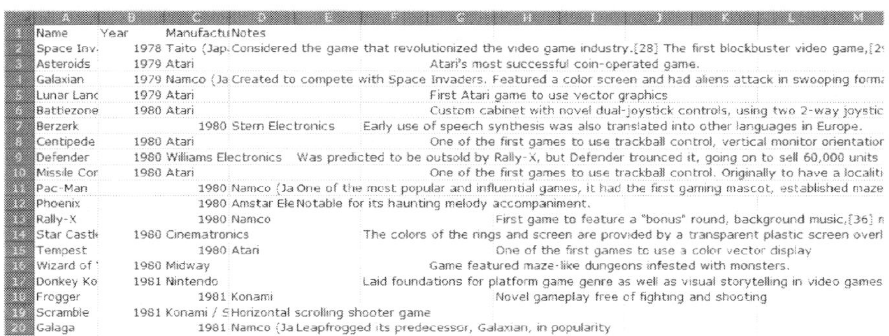

Figure 11.11 - Poorly Formatted Text

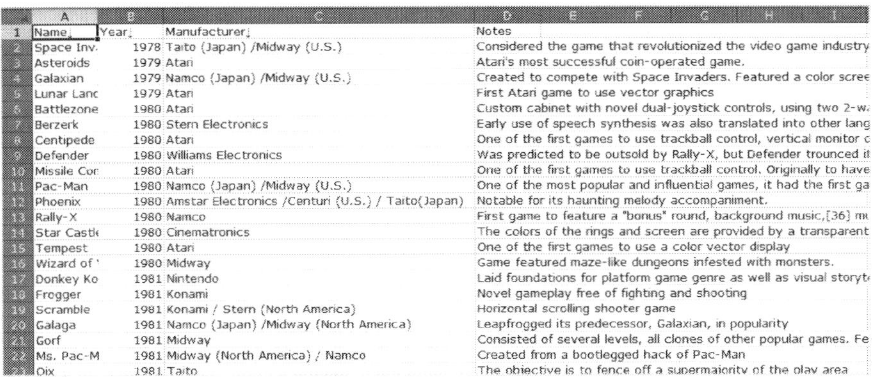

	A	B	C	D
1	Name	Year	Manufacturer	Notes
2	Space Inv.	1978	Taito (Japan) /Midway (U.S.)	Considered the game that revolutionized the video game industry
3	Asteroids	1979	Atari	Atari's most successful coin-operated game.
4	Galaxian	1979	Namco (Japan) /Midway (U.S.)	Created to compete with Space Invaders. Featured a color scree
5	Lunar Lanc	1979	Atari	First Atari game to use vector graphics
6	Battlezone	1980	Atari	Custom cabinet with novel dual-joystick controls, using two 2-w
7	Berzerk	1980	Stern Electronics	Early use of speech synthesis was also translated into other lang
8	Centipede	1980	Atari	One of the first games to use trackball control, vertical monitor c
9	Defender	1980	Williams Electronics	Was predicted to be outsold by Rally-X, but Defender trounced it
10	Missile Cor	1980	Atari	One of the first games to use trackball control. Originally to have
11	Pac-Man	1980	Namco (Japan) /Midway (U.S.)	One of the most popular and influential games, it had the first ga
12	Phoenix	1980	Amstar Electronics /Centuri (U.S.) / Taito(Japan)	Notable for its haunting melody accompaniment.
13	Rally-X	1980	Namco	First game to feature a "bonus" round, background music,[36] mu
14	Star Castle	1980	Cinematronics	The colors of the rings and screen are provided by a transparent
15	Tempest	1980	Atari	One of the first games to use a color vector display
16	Wizard of '	1980	Midway	Game featured maze-like dungeons infested with monsters.
17	Donkey Ko	1981	Nintendo	Laid foundations for platform game genre as well as visual storyte
18	Frogger	1981	Konami	Novel gameplay free of fighting and shooting
19	Scramble	1981	Konami / Stern (North America)	Horizontal scrolling shooter game
20	Galaga	1981	Namco (Japan) /Midway (North America)	Leapfrogged its predecessor, Galaxian, in popularity
21	Gorf	1981	Midway	Consisted of several levels, all clones of other popular games. Fe
22	Ms. Pac-M	1981	Midway (North America) / Namco	Created from a bootlegged hack of Pac-Man
23	Qix	1981	Taito	The objective is to fence off a supermajority of the play area

Figure 11.12 - Tab-Formatted Correctly

It is unfortunate, but sometimes you have to be very careful with your cell references and formatting to get the layout you desire. Luckily, the power of Excel's formula processing and other features makes the initial setup time worth it in the end.

Formatting Data

Strange Excel spreadsheets can be a confusing place. It is almost assured that in your first days in the industry you will be emailed or linked to a spreadsheet with thousands of rows and dozens of columns. In my experience these awful, nasty spreadsheets mostly have to do with audio assets. But they don't have to be eye-gougingly awful if you format your data in a pleasing way.

There are many different kinds of data that Excel can handle. There are standard numbers, percentages, currencies, dates and strings, among others. One of the first techniques you need to know is how to let Excel know what kind of data it is looking at so it can format it appropriately.

Here is a bunch of ugly looking data. It is ugly because the number of digits after the decimal point varies and is mostly more than we need to see. At least I gave the data bold headings! Often you won't even get that.

Name	**Grade**
Aaron A	92.33333
Bobby B	95.85714
Cory C	84.23529
David D	100
Emily E	78.78261
Farrah F	82.5
Greg G	94.8
Harry H	64.51613

Figure 11.13 - Some Uggo Data

Highlight the data you want to change. In large spreadsheets, you can click a column name to highlight the entire column and then while holding down the Control key (Command on Mac) click on the column header cell to exclude it. Then, in the Home tab in the Number section, click the dropdown menu to see all of the different formatting types you can apply to this data. The newest versions of Excel provide a preview under the name of the data type. This will show what your first cell of selected data will look like when you apply the formatting. Note that even those these are grades and are thus percentages, if we select percentage that first element will read as 9233.33%. To format something as an actual percentage, it has to be less than 1. So my 92.33 score would have to be written as 0.9233.

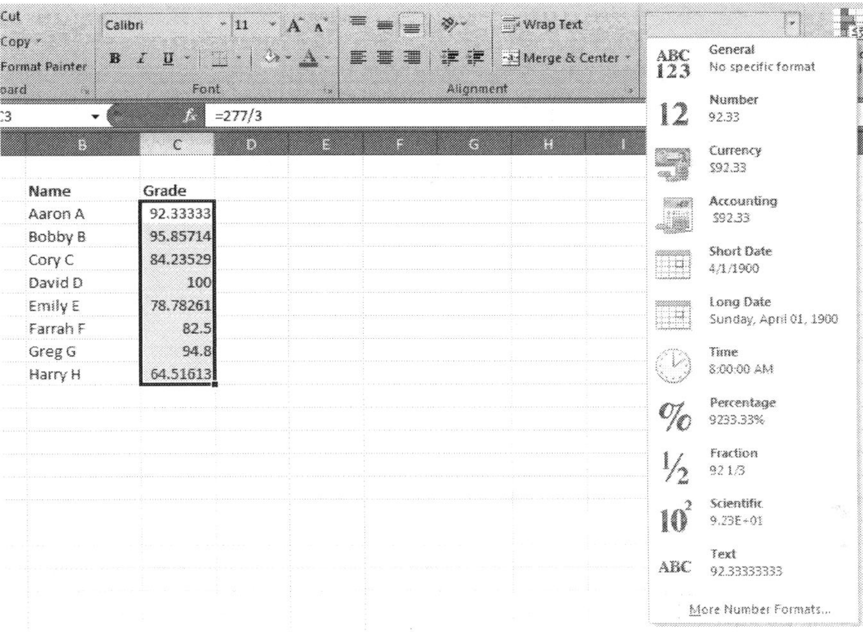

Figure 11.14 - Formatting Selections

Go ahead and choose "Number". This will format the data as a normal number with two digits. That looks a lot better, but what if we only want one digit after the decimal point? Look under the dropdown and find the button with the zeroes and the arrows. These will add or subtract digits after the decimal point. Click the one with the right hand arrow and reduce the selection to one digit after the decimal point.

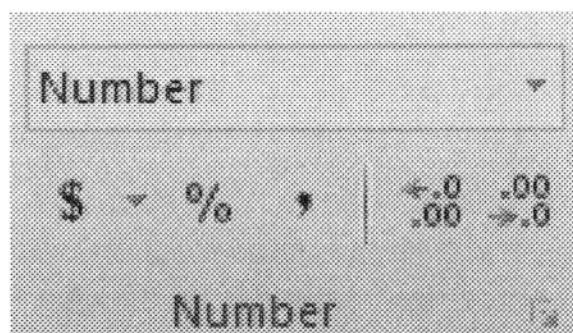

Figure 11.15 - Reducing Decimal Points

Name	Grade
Aaron A	92.3
Bobby B	95.9
Cory C	84.2
David D	100.0
Emily E	78.8
Farrah F	82.5
Greg G	94.8
Harry H	64.5

Figure 11.16 - Some Fine-Looking Data

Sorting

Getting data to be readable is often about presenting it in a way that makes the salient data be the most visible. There are two ways of doing that and we will cover both now. The first is to present the most important data first and Excel makes this easy to do. Select *both* columns from the previous example. If you only select the grades, you will only sort the grades and the names those grades are attached to will scatter.

Then look in the upper right on the Home tab to see the Sort & Filter button. If we were sorting alphabetical data, the Sort A to Z or (strangely) Sort Z to A buttons are right there. Our process is slightly more complicated, so select the Custom Sort option.

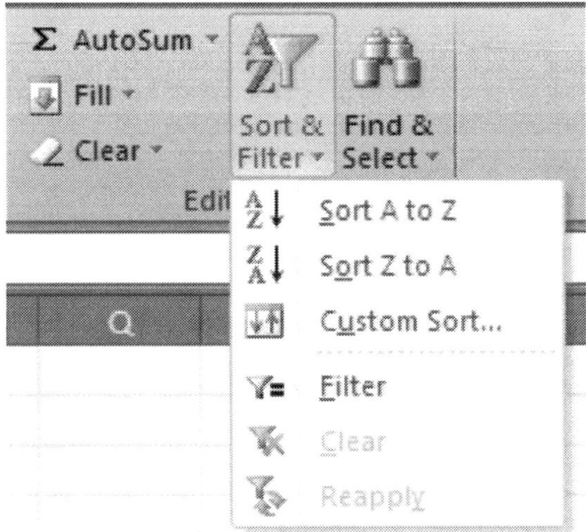

Figure 11.17 - Sort and Filter

Clicking on the "Sort by" field will show us the names of the two columns. Excel pulls these from the cell above the first data entry when selecting a column, which is a nice feature. If you do not have column names, Excel will state "Column A", "Column B", &c., up to however many columns you have selected. Here, select Grade since we want to sort by grade values.

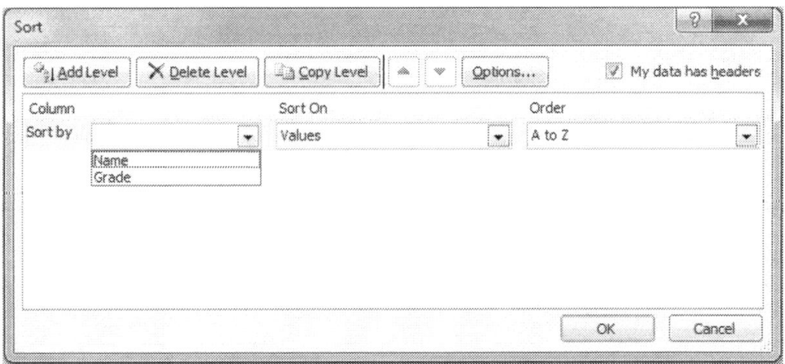

Figure 11.18 - Sorting Menu

When you select Grade, Excel looks in the column and sees that it is formatted as numbers so it changes the order criterion from "A to Z" to "Smallest to Largest". Use the dropdown to select "Largest to Smallest" since we want to start with the best performing students.

Figure 11.19 - Sorting Menu Continued

The sorting options can get more complex. You can add levels to act as tiebreakers. Say that we add a column that says each student's age. We could want to sort for best grades by year. In that case, we could add a level in the sorting menu that essentially tells Excel: "Sort by Age, but when you find students with the same Age, sort those by their Grade." When you finish, you will see each age level sorted by their grade. This multi-level sort can be very helpful.

Name	Grade
David D	100.0
Bobby B	95.9
Greg G	94.8
Aaron A	92.3
Cory C	84.2
Farrah F	82.5
Emily E	78.8
Harry H	64.5

Figure 11.20 - Sorted by Grade

Our sort here was only one level and you see the results above. This example is easy to parse as it only has a few entries, but when you are dealing with hundreds or thousands of entries, it can be essential for understanding to use sorting to present the most important data first.

Conditional Formatting

The other method for highlighting important data is to change the look of the cell compared to its neighbors. You can change the color, font or effects on the text itself to snap the eye to areas you want to see. We will do this with our small data table above.

Select just the grades. Still on the Home tab, look in the Styles section to see the button labeled "Conditional Formatting". Clicking on it opens a dropdown menu. Click on "Manage Rules" so we can see how Conditional Formatting works.

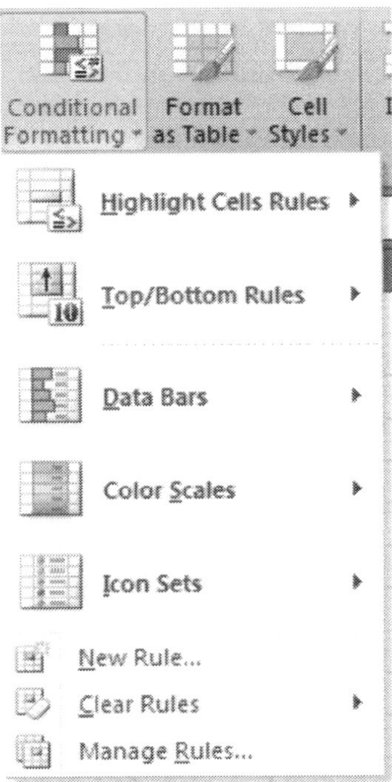

Figure 11.21 - Conditional Formatting Dropdown

We will look at some of the other elements from this dropdown momentarily. Right now you should notice the Conditional Formatting Rules Manager dialog box. Click on "New Rule". This looks drastically different in older versions of Excel.

What you will be doing is telling Excel: "If the data looks like *this*, its formatting should look like *this*."

Click on "Format only cells that contain". This will give you a dialog box similar to the one on older versions of Excel. Now, apply the rule. We want students who have a 90 or higher to be green and bold. Change the condition to "greater than" and then put "90" in the cell next to it. Then click on the "Format" button. Your screen should look like this afterwards:

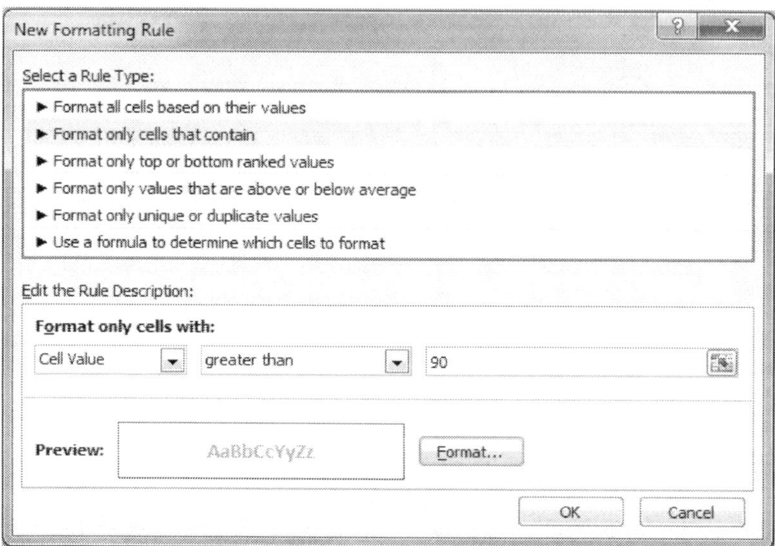

Figure 11.22 - Conditional Formatting Rule

When you click OK, you will see the results:

Name	Grade
David D	100.0
Bobby B	95.9
Greg G	94.8
Aaron A	92.3
Cory C	84.2
Farrah F	82.5
Emily E	78.8
Harry H	64.5

Figure 11.23 - Successful Formatting

More Conditional Formatting

The newest versions of Excel offer some very attractive new ways of drawing attention to particular data. One is Color Scales that automatically puts a heat value based on the minimum and maximum values in your data. This is applied by highlighting your data and clicking the Conditional Formatting dropdown, selecting "Color Scales" and then selecting the color scales or rules you wish to use. In the image below, a 100% is the darkest green, while the lowest score is the darkest red. Of course, in this grayscale image the range is hard to see. Values in the middle go from red to orange to yellow to green.

Newer versions of Excel also let you put icons in cells based on the value contained in the cell. I put the reception bars in the cells in the image below based on the number of reviews. This is not particularly helpful in the below example, but you can see what it would look like. You can also choose "Data Bars" to fill the cell a percentage based on the value in the cell.

Remember to use your formatting responsibly. Too many elements that draw the eye end up making the data just as cluttered and obtrusive as completely plain, unsorted data.

Date	Studio	Game	Platform	Rating	NumReviews
1/1/2011	BioWare	Mass Effect 2	PS3	92.97%	31
1/1/2011	Media Molecule	LittleBigPlanet 2	PS3	92.26%	51
1/1/2011	Visceral Games	Dead Space 2	X360	89.40%	43
1/1/2011	Visceral Games	Dead Space 2	PS3	89.24%	42
1/1/2011	Capcom	Ghost Trick: Phantom Detectiv	DS	84.77%	30
1/1/2011	Southend Interactive	ilomilo	X360	81.52%	26
1/1/2011	Hudson Soft	Lost in Shadow	WII	69.88%	25
1/1/2011	Square Enix	Kingdom Hearts Re:coded	DS	69.64%	29
1/1/2011	Reality Pump	Two Worlds II	X360	69.16%	22
1/1/2011	Atomic Games	Breach	X360	60.38%	24

Figure 11.24 - Other Conditional Formatting

Worksheets

A single Excel file can contain multiple spreadsheets. This can be helpful when you want to only look at certain data at a time (like having each sheet be a year's worth of data) or you want to compare different sets of data that have different parameters (like comparing the features of different lists of automobiles: one worksheet for engine specs, another for interior specs, &c.,)

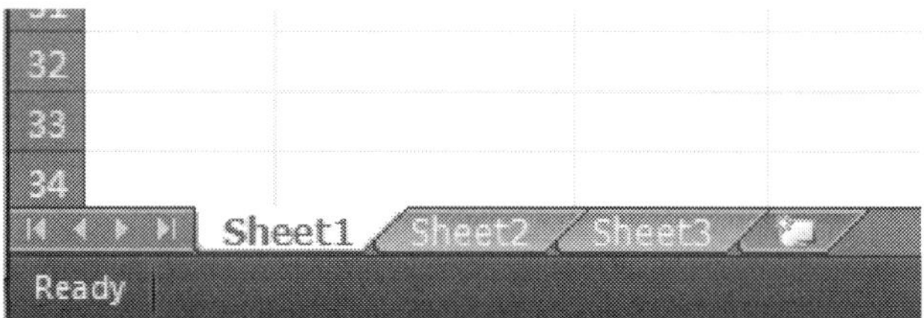

Figure 11.25 - Worksheet Tabs

In the lower left, find the tabs that stick out below the spreadsheet's cells. Each of these tabs is a separate worksheet. Excel defaults to each .XLS or .XLSX file having three worksheets when created in most versions. Of course, you can add or delete worksheets as you see fit.

You can rename a worksheet from its default "SheetN" name by clicking on the name while that tab is selected or by right clicking and selecting "Rename". Proper labeling of your worksheets avoids confusion. The small icon to the right of your worksheets will add a new worksheet to the end of the list. Worksheets can be reordered by dragging them into place.

Formulas can refer to data in other worksheets of the same file. Say you want to refer to cell B3 in a worksheet called 'OldData'. If you were referring to that cell from within OldData, you could simply use =B3 as your formula. But from another worksheet, you can refer to cell B3 by using:

```
=OldData!B3
```

You can also refer to a range in the same way:

```
=OldData!B3:B13
```

By separating your data into logical worksheets, you can make data easier to read and understand and limit the amount of work you have to do when new data must be added to the spreadsheet.

Charts

People love visualizing data. Remember how we emphasized the use of pictures in our chapter on written communication? The same lesson holds true whether you are talking about writing about a feature specification or trying to summarize thousands of rows of data. Charts work.

There is a danger when you first begin to understand the flexibility of charts in Excel. That danger is wasting your time making flashy charts instead of using the power of charts to make simple, effective information out of obtuse data.

Famous information theorist and statistics professor Edward Tufte coined the concept of the **data-ink ratio** in *The Visual Display of Quantitative Information*. Data-ink, to Tufte, is ink that if removed would remove information from the chart or graph. Non-data-ink, likewise, is decoration or ink that can be removed without affecting the information presented in the chart or graph.

Tufte's directive was for chart makers to maximize the data-ink to non-data-ink ratio.

For instance, here is a chart with a low data-ink ratio that you might see in an Excel or Powerpoint file in industry:

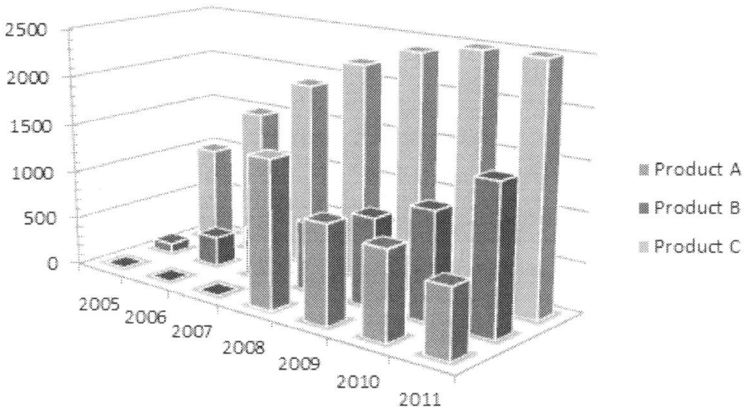

Figure 11.26 - Low Data-Ink

And here is a high data-ink version of the same exact data:

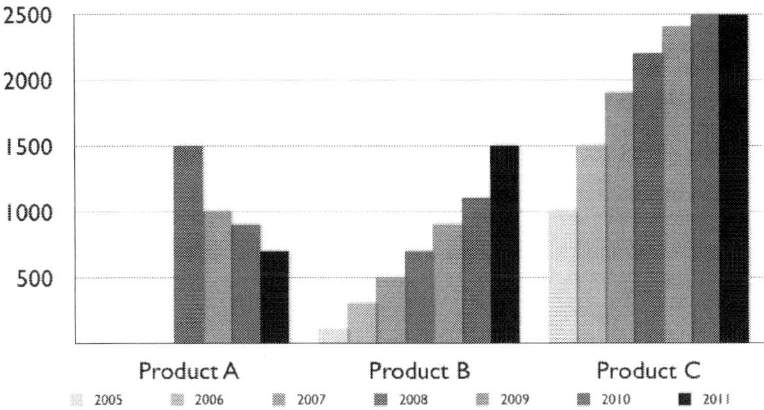

Figure 11.27 - High Data-Ink

The data is the same, but the high data-ink version is easier to read and understand. How can I compare 2007's numbers to 2008 or 2011 in the low data-ink version? The perspective makes it difficult. Charts with non-linear height per data value also violate the principal of maximizing data-ink.

Charts in Excel

It is easy to insert a chart into Excel. Highlight the data and select from the type of chart in the Charts section of the Insert tab.

Class	Strength	Dexterity	Intelligence
Warrior	18	10	6
Rogue	10	18	10
Wizard	8	12	10
Priest	12	8	10
Farmer	14	10	8
Droid	19	3	19
Samurai	10	19	12
Professor	8	8	19
Cheese	2	2	2

Figure 11.28 - Some Data to Chart

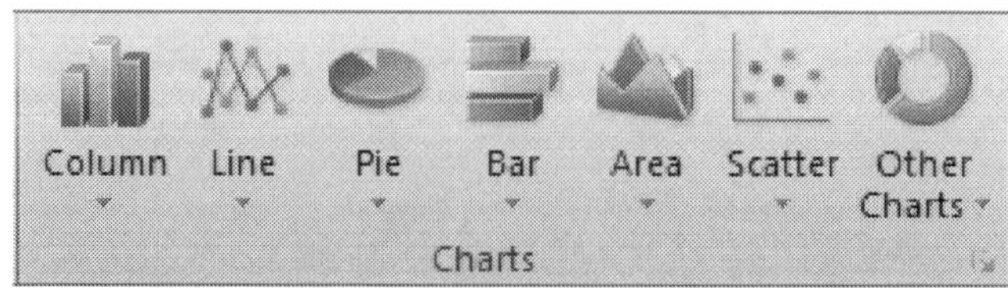

Figure 11.29 - Charts in the Insert Tab

Your choices are:

Column Charts - Good for comparing aggregate data. The histogram add-in for Excel also helps in making column charts. Histograms will be covered a bit more later.

Line Charts - Good for comparing data over time.

Pie Charts - Good for comparing delicious percentages of a whole.

Bar Charts - Similar to column charts.

Area Charts - Rarely used due to the low data-ink ratio.

Scatter Charts - Good for tracking individual data points that are order-independent over two dimensions.

Other Charts - There is nothing in this category that I would recommend using.

For our above data of player classes and their attributes, we would choose to compare the data using a simple column chart. Highlight the Class and Strength columns and click on Column and then the first 2-D column. Excel will generate a standard chart.

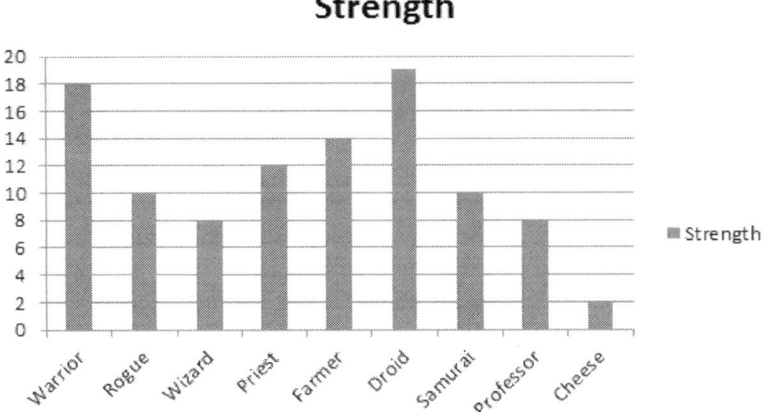

Figure 11.30 - Default Chart

Excel generates the headings based on the labels surrounding the data. Since we had a label "Strength" in the top row, the title and the legend reflect this. Since we don't need a legend for one series of data, click on the legend and press delete. The chart will fill in the remaining space.

Excel also guesses the range you want to see. In this case, it chose 0-20 with 2 between major tick marks. Double click on the Y-axis and you will see the axis options.

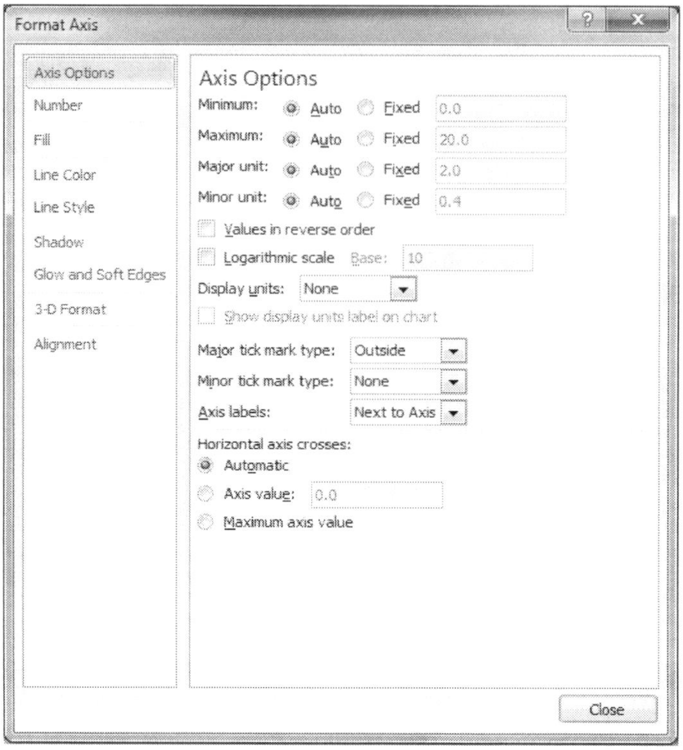

Fig 11.31 - Axis Options

If you click on "Fixed" for minimum or maximum values, you can change the range of the chart. Changing the "major units" will change where the horizontal rules appear. Changing the minor units will change where the tick marks appear if applicable.

Now we will make a time-series chart. We will use the following data:

Level	Experience	Bosses
1	0	0
2	100	1
3	500	2
4	1400	4
5	3000	7
6	5500	11
7	9100	16
8	14000	22
9	20400	29
10	28500	37
11	38500	46
12	50600	56
13	65000	67
14	81900	79
15	101500	92
16	124000	106
17	149600	121
18	178500	137
19	210900	154
20	247000	172

Figure 11.32 - Time-Series Data

Clearly at each level, our player is encountering more and more bosses and gaining more and more experience. But what if we want to chart experience versus bosses using this data. Are we giving more experience per boss in the beginning or the end game? Highlight the experience and bosses columns and select to insert a line chart. You will get this:

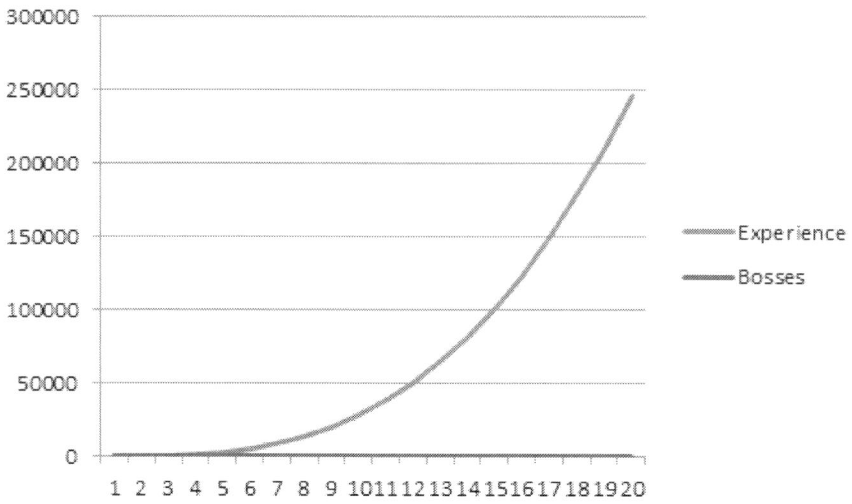

Figure 11.33 - Time-Series

That's not very helpful. First the X-Axis is just the number of each observation, not the number of bosses fought. First things first, delete the legend. Now right click on the chart and go to "Select Data".

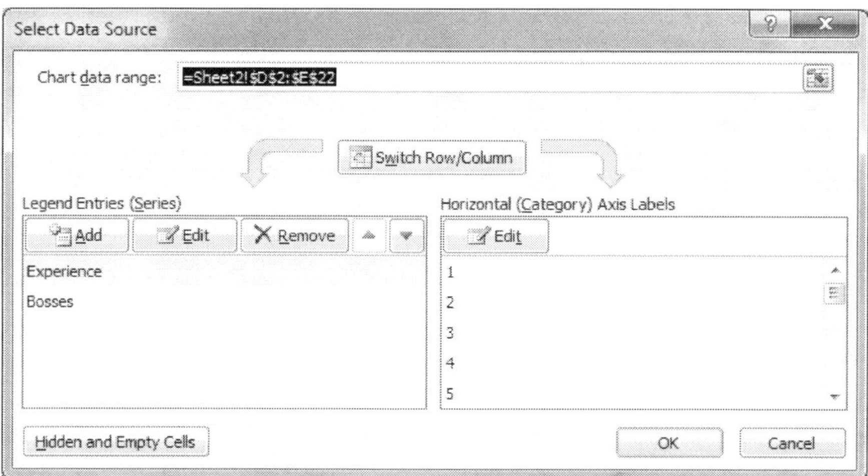

Figure 11.34 - Select Data Dialog Box

The first broken assumption Excel makes is that we want bosses to be graphed. So click on "Bosses" in the Legend Series and remove it. The next incorrect assumption is the 1,2,3 category axis. Click on Edit. Excel will then let you highlight what you want the category axis to be. Highlight the bosses column.

Here is the chart that Excel gives you afterwards:

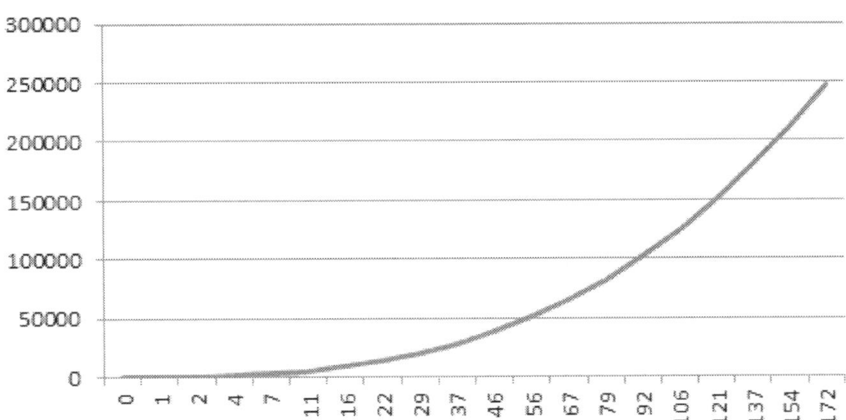

Figure 11.35 - Changed Label Axis

A quick look at this would confirm any suspicion that the player is getting more experience per boss at the end of the game. But look at the x-axis. The first few tick marks have only one or two bosses between them but the end tick marks have ten or twenty.

Right-click on the X-axis and select "Format Axis". Under Axis Type, it is likely that it says "Automatically select based on data." In a text axis, Excel just weights every value equally. But in a date axis, Excel will spread out the values to compensate for different lengths between the values. Think of each boss as a "day". In the later levels, we waited ten or twenty "days" before taking another experience observation.

Go ahead and select "Date axis" and change the major units to 20 days. Click Close. Now we have a chart that better reflects the character's experience points after any number of bosses. It looks mostly linear to me.

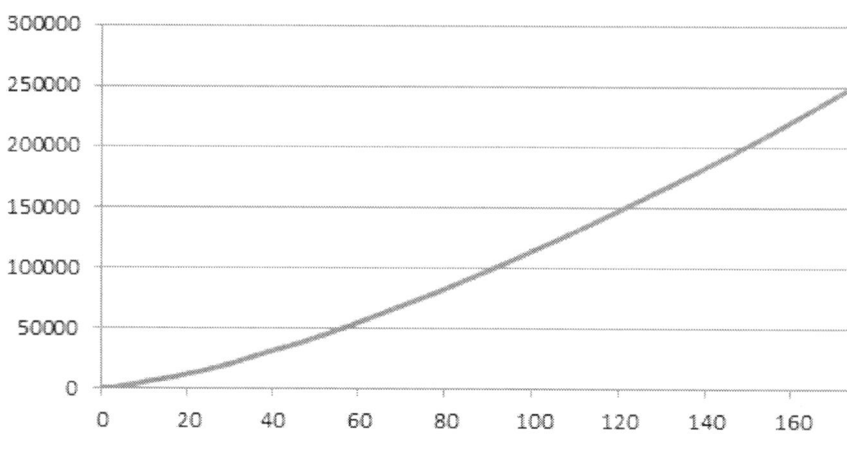

Figure 11.36 – Fixed Time Series

Most charts are not this complicated, but you must be vigilant that your charts are representing your data correctly. You may need to change axis labels or separate data into different graphs for clarity. Changing the minimum and maximum values of the chart can also help tidy up the data to focus on exactly the elements you mind most noteworthy.

Goal Seek

Sometimes you want Excel to solve something for you rather than evaluating a statement. For these times, the built in Goal Seek function is very useful. For more complicated scenarios, the Excel Add-In called Solver is necessary.

Goal Seek is an automated "guess and check" system. You choose one cell to change and one cell with a target value. Excel will then keep guessing and checking until your target cell reaches the target value.

For a simple example, say that you had a set of lap times from some playtesters for a racing game. As the designer for that track, you may have a target time in mind. Say that you want the average lap time for the average player on their first try to be 2:00.

Here are the results of nine playtests: 1:59, 2:11, 1:58, 1:50, 2:20, 2:04, 1:45, 2:05, 2:33. What does the tenth playtest time need to be to average 2:00? If this sounds like a trivial SAT-style problem, that's because it is. But if you can set up the spreadsheet for this, you can always know what result you would need no matter how many times you run the playtest.

Enter the times in column B. Below, I entered the times in seconds because it is easier to read and it is more difficult to make simple math errors this way.

Run #	Time
1	119
2	131
3	118
4	110
5	140
6	124
7	105
8	125
9	153

Figure 11.37 - Times

Now in cell D2, create a formula that averages everything in column B, and the cell below it. Here my formula is =AVERAGE(B2:B1000,D3). The D3 is the hypothetical run that Goal Seek will change to find the correct average.

Now under the Data tab, find the What-If Analysis button and go to Goal Seek.

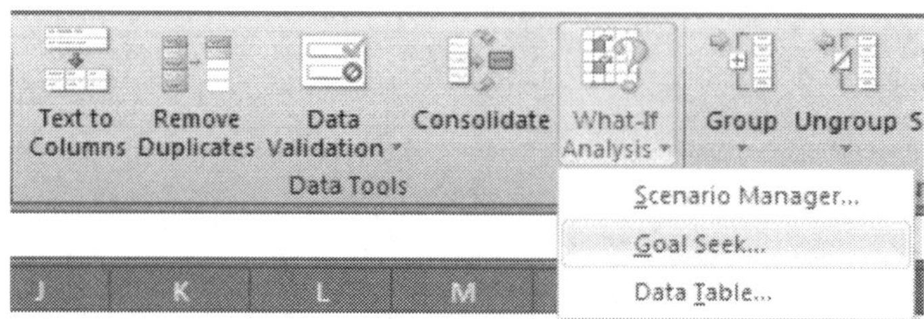

Figure 11.38 - What-If Analysis

Goal Seek

Set cell: D2

To value: 120

By changing cell: D3

OK Cancel

Figure 11.39 - Goal Seek

Goal Seek consists of three values. First, the "Set Value" needs to point to the cell that you want to reach a specific value. "To Value" is the value you want the first cell to be. "By Changing Cell" is pretty obvious; this is the cell we will be changing to try to get the "Set Value" to the "To Value". In our above example, we want the three fields to be D2, 120[11], D3.

Hit OK and watch Excel do its instant magic. 75 seconds is your answer. As long as the next tester does the lap in 75 seconds or less, the average will be two minutes. Now you can run Goal Seek a number of times with either the same observations or new ones. Say you don't want the lap times to go above 2:10. Run a new Goal Seek and you find the new answer is 165 seconds or 2:45.

[11] Remember: we are using seconds as our units.

Solver

This can be really useful rather than doing the guessing and checking on your own, but what if you need to answer a question that is a little more complicated? Solver is an optimization tool used to find maximums or minimums under constraints. If you've taken an introduction to calculus course, you may be familiar with some of the math behind it.

Solver is an add-on. It doesn't come enabled with every distribution of Excel. It needs to be installed. In earlier versions of Excel, the add-ins dialog can be accessed through the Tools menu. In Excel 2010, you access it by going to the File tab and selecting Options (for some reason). Then select "Add-Ins". Here select Solver Add-In and then "Go". Then click the checkmark beside Solver Add-In and hit OK. Got it?

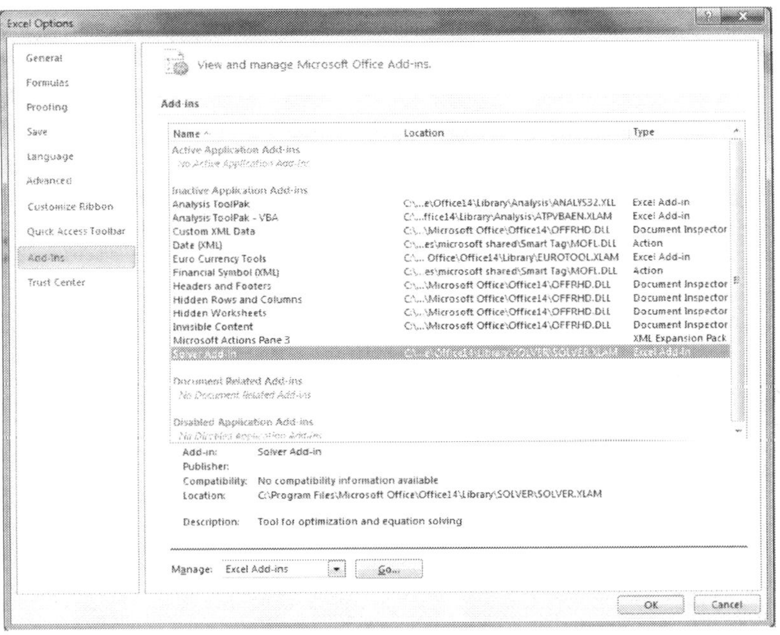

Figure 11.40 - Options/Add-Ins

In Excel 2010, Solver will then be located in the Data tab under the Analysis section. Go ahead and fire it up and you will see this dialog box.

Figure 11.41 - Solver

In Solver, you first select the cell that you are looking to maximize or minimize.[12] Then you select the cells you wish to change and the constraints you wish this to be under. Unless you've done some basic calculus, this can be hard to see in an abstract way, so let us try an example.

Say you have a number of sources of money in your game and each one takes a certain amount of time. That is reflected in the spreadsheet below.

A player can spend time hunting and selling skins, but that gives a weak 15 gold per hour. Or a player can go to the archery game. That starts out being lucrative, but then drops and as the player gets tired of the game, he/she start losing money. He/she makes 20 gold the first hour, 40 the second, 20 the third, breaks even the fourth and loses 20 the fifth. Or the player can do the quest, which results in a treasure chest. He/she gets 50 gold and takes one hour but the player can only do it once. How much can a player make in five hours?

How do we model this in Solver?

First we create a 3x3 table. The first column is labels, the second is hour spent and the third is how much gold that yielded.

	A	B	C
1	**Activity**	**Hours**	**Gold**
2	Hunting & Selling	0	0
3	Archery Game	0	0
4	Treasure Hunting	0	0
5	*Total*	0	0
6			

Figure 11.42 - Solver Table

For the Hunting/Selling gold cell (C2), the formula is simple: 25 * hours. For the Treasure Chest gold cell (C4), this is also simple: 50 * hours. Our archery game gold cell (C3) will be a little trickier. Get out your algebra/statistics skills to model this or just create a long nested if statement along the lines of IF(Hours < 3, Hours*20, 20 – 20*(Hours-3)). Do you see why that is?[13]

At the bottom of the table, add a cell that sums all of the hours (B5). Also add a cell that sums all of the gold (C5).

Now run Solver from the Data menu.

The cell that is our objective is our total gold (C5). Set the objective to that cell. The variable cells we want to change are the number of hours, so select that range (B2:B5).

Now the constraints. Constraints will tell Excel what numbers are valid for this calculation. First, the total number of hours spent must be between 0 and 5. Select our hours summation cell and add that constraint. Also remember that you can only do the Treasure Hunt task once, so limit that to one hour.

---

[12] "Value of" is similar to Goal Seek except that it uses the constraints listed below.

[13] We split up the winnings into two parts: the winnings when they are increasing (hours one and two) and the winnings when they are decreasing.

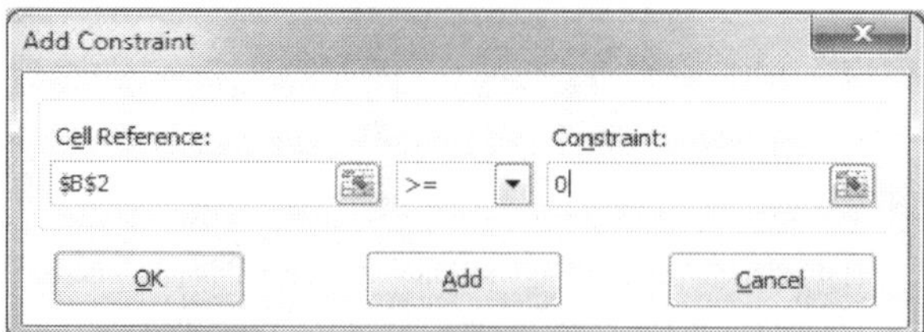

Figure 11.43 - Sample Constraint

Also, none of our tasks can be done for less than zero hours and for the sake of our example, all of them must be integers. Here are all the constraints (phew!):

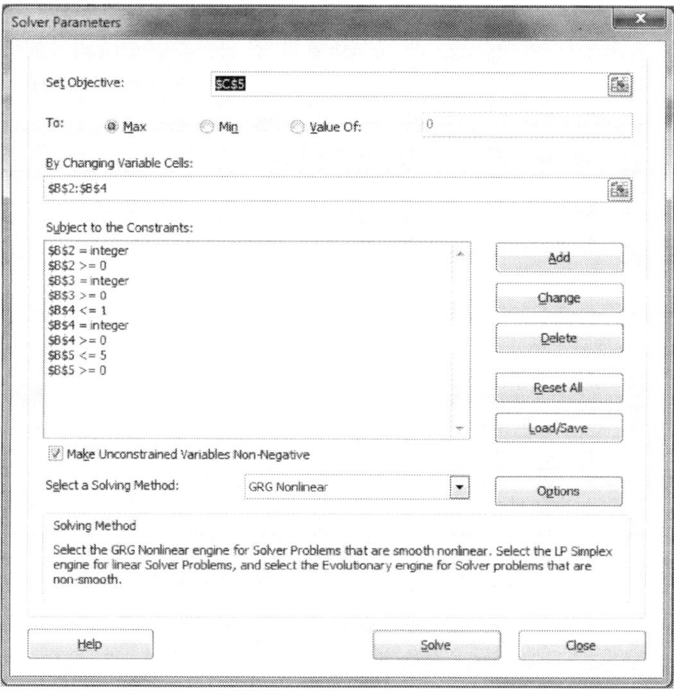

Figure 11.44 - Constraints Finalized

Look at our constraints. Do you understand why they are all there? Now hit the magic Solve button.

	A	B	C
1	**Activity**	**Hours**	**Gold**
2	Hunting & Selling	2	30
3	Archery Game	2	40
4	Treasure Hunting	1	50
5	*Total*	5	120

Figure 11.45 - Results

There are our results: one hour doing the treasure hunt, two hours doing the archery game and two hours hunting and selling. Awesome! Change the variables and try it again. What if you had six hours? What if you double the value of hunting and selling?

Solver can be an extremely valuable tool. Be creative with it.

Floating Headers

When you have a large amount of rows or columns, it can sometimes be helpful to always be looking at the column headers no matter now far down in the chart you scroll. This can be done with a feature called "floating headers" or "frozen panes".

To do so select the row you wish to float (this will usually be the top row or rows) and click over to the View tab. Select "Freeze Panes" from the Window section. You can either freeze your selected rows or freeze the top row. Now when you scroll, the top row will always be shown!

	A	B	C	D	E	
1	Date	Studio	Game	Platform	Rating	Nun
2634	2005	G-Artists	PoPoLoCrois	PSP	67.85%	
2635	2005	EA Canadε	MVP Baseball	PSP	67.81%	
2636	2005	WayForwε	Sigma Star Saga	GBA	67.49%	
2637	2005	Juice Gam	Juiced	PS2	67.48%	

Figure 11.46 - Frozen Top Row

To thaw the panels, click "Freeze Panes" again and select "Unfreeze Panes".

Chapter 12 - Simple Simulation

Now that you are familiar with the functions and uses of Excel, you can wield this mighty weapon and force it to your will. Or you can use it to do some simple simulation. Whatever.

What are some ways you can apply Excel to model a game situation? Here we will go through a long example first and then a simpler one.

The Long One

What if I asked you what the odds were of landing on Boardwalk in the first pass around a Monopoly board assuming no "Advance to.." or "Go back..." cards are drawn, no triple-doubles penalty or you don't hit "Go to Jail"[14]? How would you do it?

Well, there are 40 spaces on a Monopoly board and Boardwalk is 39th. You would assume that the odds of landing on any particular space are 1/40, thus the expected value would be 40 rolls. But you cannot assume that because you cannot reach Boardwalk until your fourth roll (12+12+12+3). You need to know how easy it is after an uncertain number of rolls that you sum up to 39.

The file for this is on the book's website so you can download it and follow along.

First, I created a table that related a space number to a name. This is not necessary, but is helpful for readability. Here is the table:

[14] These assumptions are made for simplicity, but you can adjust your simulation to take these into account. It is a good exercise for the reader.

	A	B
1	0	Go
2	1	Mediterreanean
3	2	Community Chest
4	3	Baltic
5	4	Income Tax
6	5	Reading RR
7	6	Oriental
8	7	Chance
9	8	Vermont
10	9	Connecticut
11	10	Just Visiting
12	11	St. Charles
13	12	Electric Company
14	13	States
15	14	Virginia

Figure 12.1 - Space-Name Table

Next, I created a trial game that has three hundred rolls[15]. I have six columns here: Roll # (which is just the number of the roll), the roll itself (remember that you are rolling two six sided dice so this should be the sum of two RANDBETWEEN(1,6) statements[16]), the sum of all rolls up to now and the *modulus* of the sum of all rolls.

[15] It is quite likely that someone can lap the board 20 times without hitting boardwalk. Always provide more rolls than you think is normal because you want to support the edge cases like the trial where Boardwalk keeps getting missed. 300 rolls is a lot, but it does not guarantee that a user will ever hit Boardwalk.

[16] You cannot put RANDBETWEEN(2,12) here because it is more likely to roll a 7 than it is a 2 or 12. We will cover this later.

D	E	F	G	H	I	J
Trial #	Roll	Sum	Modulus	Lap	Location	Boardwalk Hit?
1	8	8	8	1	Vermont	I
2	4	12	12	1	Electric Compan\	
3	6	18	18	1	Tennessee	
4	5	23	23	1	Indiana	
5	5	28	28	1	Water Works	
6	6	34	34	1	Pennsylvania	
7	5	39	39	1	***Boardwalk***	7
8	10	49	9	2	Connecticut	7
9	4	53	13	2	States	7
10	6	59	19	2	New York	7
11	9	68	28	2	Water Works	7
12	7	75	35	2	Short Line RR	7
13	7	82	2	3	Community Ches	7
14	6	88	8	3	Vermont	7
15	4	92	12	3	Electric Compan\	7
16	5	97	17	3	Community Ches	7

Figure 12.2 - Trial of Rolls

The modulus is just a fancy way to say "remainder". When you lap the board once and reach Mediterranean, you are on space 41. But unless we want our Space-Name table to repeat dozens of times to handle space #500, we can do a bit of math to figure out which space from 0-39 this corresponds to. When you do =MOD(Sum of All Rolls, 40), Excel will keep subtracting 40 from the sum of all rolls until it gets to a number that is between 0-39. In the case of space 41, Excel will subtract 40. The result is 1, which is Mediterranean Avenue on our lookup chart. If the player is on space 222, Excel will keep subtracting 40 until 222 become 22, which is in our lookup table.

In the next column I have the lap (which is not necessary for this analysis, but might be helpful if you want to do additional analysis on this data. Finally, I have the name of the space landed on, which is a VLOOKUP statement on our Space-Name table in Columns A and B.

Now I have a column that specifically tells me if Boardwalk has been hit yet. First, it looks to see if the cell above it says Boardwalk has been hit. If it has, it repeats the number that is in the above cell. If not, it looks to see if Boardwalk was hit this roll. If it was, the cell's value is the roll number. This causes the first roll number where Boardwalk is hit to be repeated down to the bottom.

To the right, I added a **data table**. Data tables are a feature I didn't cover in the Crash Course chapter for a number of reasons. They can be counterintuitive and complicated, so it is best to take your time with them.

If you are interested in them, there are a number of tutorials available online. Search for one that matches your version of Excel specifically. To sum up what the data table function does is that it runs that trial (of three-hundred rolls) one hundred times and lists the result of each trial.

Excel might slow down at this point. Every time you change a cell, Excel will recalculate one hundred trials (of three hundred rolls each). You can change the recalculation rules to only recalculate when you hit a specific key. This is in Options or Preferences under Calculation.

N	O
Data Table	
	7
1	40
2	31
3	6
4	40
5	18
6	74
7	12
8	33
9	17
10	32
11	48
12	74
13	41
14	22
15	11
16	24

Figure 12.3 - Data Table

In the newest versions of Excel for Windows, you can generate histograms automatically. In older versions and versions for the Mac, you must "roll your own" histograms. I will briefly show you how just to be sure.

In the next few columns, I create the "bins" for the histogram. Each bin will hold some range of results like "less than ten", "ten to twenty", "twenty to thirty" and so on. In this example, I use bins of 5 up to 150. In the next column, I run a COUNTIF for each range to count the number of results for each bin. Then I can create a column graph when this is complete.

Q	R
Histogram	
<5	0
6-10	19
11-15	11
16-20	9
21-25	9
26-30	5
31-35	5
36-40	6
41-45	6
46-50	4
51-55	2
56-60	5
61-65	2
66-70	5
71-75	5
76-80	1
81-85	0
86-90	1
91-95	0
96-100	1
101-105	1

Figure 12.4 - Histogram Table

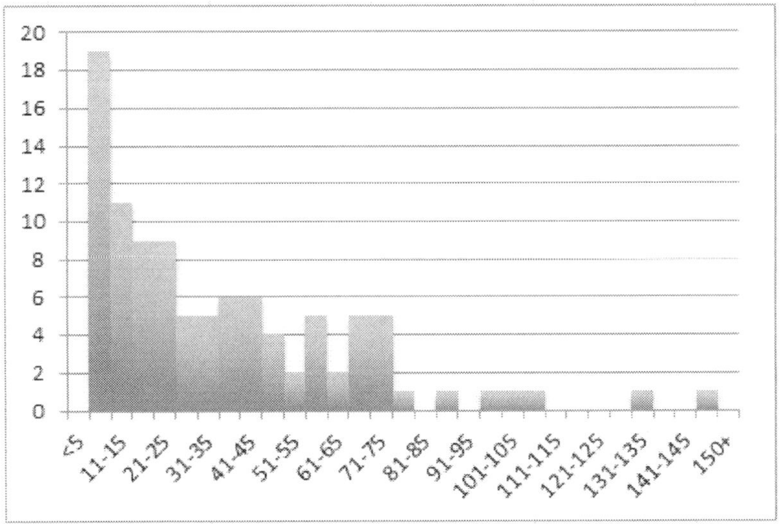

Figure 12.5 - Histogram

Every time you recalculate (when you change a cell or later if you've switched your settings), Excel will do one hundred trials of three hundred rolls and graph the results. You can keep recalculating to see how the results change. If they change drastically every time you change cells, then you may need more trials.

Below the graph, I have marked the mean and median. The mean is indeed near to 40, as expected. With enough rolls, every space is as likely as every other. But the median is much less than forty because the distribution (as seen in the histogram) is skewed. Many of the results are actually below 40, but some outliers are way above 150 rolls. There is a long tail. Why do you think this may be?

What elements can you change for this to answer additional questions? Can you figure out the lap number in which a player will reach Boardwalk? How about Go to Jail? How would you go about adding the triple doubles Go to Jail roll?

A Simpler Example

I chose the long example first because it features most of the functions and techniques we have discussed in the last chapter. Most of your time that you do these things in industry, you will be using Excel to answer a question quickly.

For instance, say you are making a basketball game and you want to implement a hot and cold hand feature[17]. Take a player whose base shot percentage is 50%. Every time the player makes three shots in a row, increase his percentage 10% (maximum 90%). Every time the player misses three in a row, his percentage drops by 10% (minimum 10%).

You could spend the time to code this into your game or you could run a simple Excel simulation.

Here's my version, also available on the book's website in the same file as the previous example:

[17] The concept of a hot hand is that when an athlete is scoring, he or she is "on fire" and more likely to score in the future. Cold hands are just the opposite. If the athlete keeps missing, he or she will be rattled and continue to miss.

	A	B	C	D
1	Shot #	Percentage	Shot Is	Adjust
2	1	50%	Missed	-
3	2	50%	Missed	-
4	3	50%	Missed	40%
5	4	40%	Missed	30%
6	5	30%	Made	30%
7	6	30%	Missed	30%
8	7	30%	Missed	30%
9	8	30%	Missed	20%
10	9	20%	Missed	10%
11	10	10%	Missed	10%
12	11	10%	Missed	10%
13	12	10%	Missed	10%
14	13	10%	Made	10%
15	14	10%	Missed	10%
16	15	10%	Missed	10%
17	16	10%	Missed	10%
18	17	10%	Missed	10%
19	18	10%	Missed	10%
20	19	10%	Missed	10%
21	20	10%	Missed	10%
22	21	10%	Missed	10%

Figure 12.6 - My Simulation of Hot/Cold Hand - The Shots

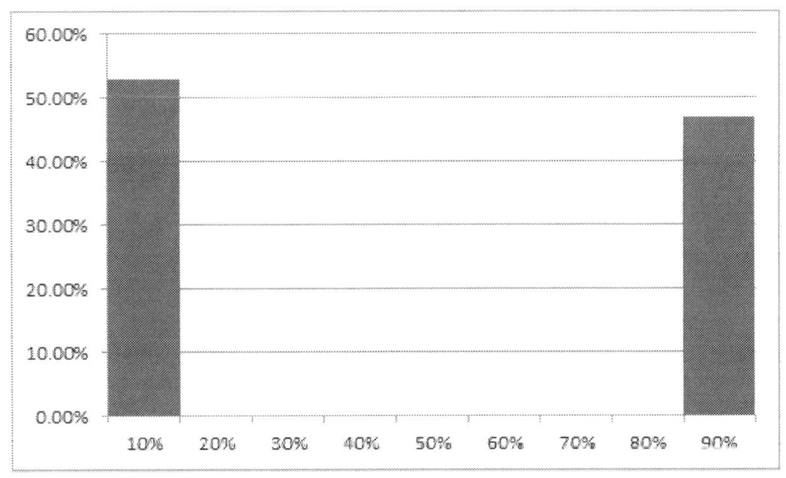

Figure 12.7 - Hot/Cold Hand - The Ending Distribution After 200 Trials of 100 Shots Each

What happens? After a while the players converge to the hottest and coldest values. Once you get up to 90%, it is very unlikely you will ever miss three in a row to get colder. Conversely, once you get to 10%, it is very unlikely you will ever hit three in a row to boost it. With a couple minutes of work, you can see that either you need to change your numbers or drastically rethink the feature.

Chapter 13 - Probability Tools

Designers need to have a fundamental understanding of how probability works. Probability doesn't just enter games in cases of rolling random numbers, but also in aggregate decision making: what's the probability of a baseball player getting a hit? What's the probability that there will be greater than X players in such-and-such area?

Space doesn't allow for a proper examination of probability and statistics for game designers, so here is the incredibly condensed version.

Basic Probability

Many non-technical people are afraid of probability because it is math and math scares them. But probability is not integral calculus, it is *counting*. And you can count, right? Thought so. Most of the time, probability is about counting things that happen and things that do not happen and dividing the two.

You want to know what the odds are that you will draw an ace from a normal deck of cards. This is a simple matter of counting the aces (4) and counting all of the cards (52). Divide the two: 4/52 = 7.7%. We represent the probability of an event by writing P(Event) and this value ranges between 0 and 1 (or 0.00% and 100.00%). So we can write the probability of rolling a six on a six-sided die as P(Rolling a Six) = 1/6.

The above example is trivial. Probability gets interesting when you combine events together. What is the probability of rolling a 7 when rolling two six-sided dice like in a game of Monopoly?

Many people when posed this question would say that 7 is just one value out of 12 so the answer must be 1/12. Some would point out that you couldn't roll a one when you roll two dice, so the answer must be 1/11. But use the tool of counting and you will see that...

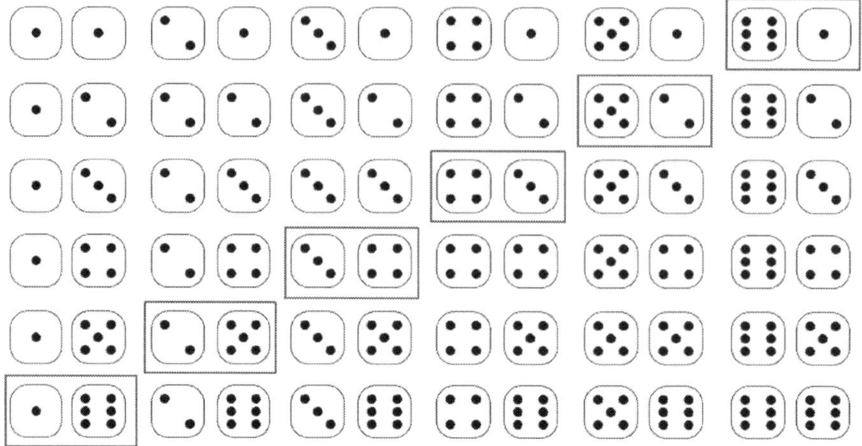

Figure 13.1 - All Possible Two-Die Combinations

...six of the thirty-six possible rolls add up to a seven. 6/36 = 1/6 or 16.7%.

In fact, many do not realize that while the result of a single die roll has a flat distribution, the sum of two of these die rolls is a bell-shaped distribution. This shows the dangers of making assumptions with probabilities when dealing with multiple events.

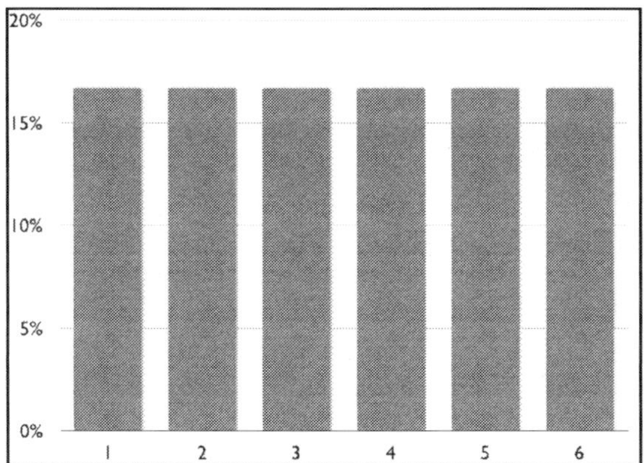

Figure 13.2 – Probability Distribution on One Six-Sided Die Roll

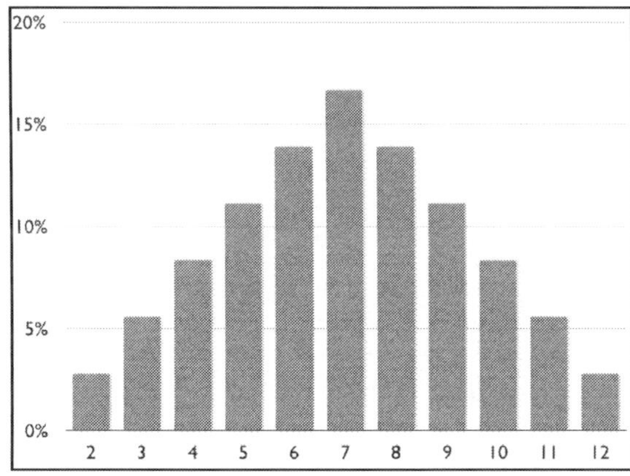

Figure 13.3 – Probability Distribution on Two Six-Sided DIe Rolls

Unions (OR), Intersections (AND) and Independence

When two events are **disjoint**, meaning that they are mutually exclusive or that both cannot simultaneously occur, you can add the probabilities together. Say you are making an RPG and you want to know what the probability is that a player is an offensive class. If you can only have one class at a time you can just add the offensive class probabilities together:

P(Warrior or Thief or Barbarian) =

P(Warriors) + P(Thieves) + P(Barbarians)

Figure 13.4 - Disjoint Sets

But when you are examining areas where groups may overlap or areas where one group affects another, you cannot simply add together. If there is any overlap, then you must subtract out that overlap.

Say you run an online game service like Steam or Xbox Live and you are interested in the proportion of users who were banned. Say also that you only ban for two offenses: hacking and being offensive jerks. These are not mutually exclusive: being a jerk doesn't mean you are or are not a hacker. Some are both, some are one, and some are neither:

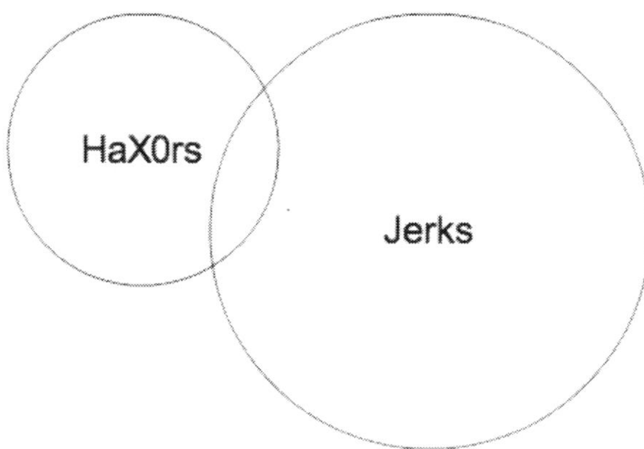

Figure 13.5 - Non-disjoint Sets

If 1% of your users are hackers and 5% are jerks, that doesn't mean that 6% of your users have been banned. If you count people who were banned for multiple offenses for each category, you will end up double-counting users. So here is a more formal probability statement:

P(A or B) = P(A) + P(B) - P(A and B)

In cases where A and B are mutually exclusive (or disjoint), that last term is zero. In our above case, say that 0.5% were hackers AND jerks. Then the probability of being a hacker OR a jerk would be 5.5%. Do you see why?[18]

Have you ever played *Roulette*? In the game you can bet on red or black numbers to come up on a spun wheel. In many places, the last few spin results are placed on a board. A gambler comes in and sees that red has been spun four times in a row and says, "Looks like black is due!". This is called the **gambler's fallacy**. It is the mistake of treating independent events as if they had some sort of memory or effect on other events. The wheel does not know what it spun before. A coin does not know what is flipped before. A patient's height and weight are not affected by the person who saw the doctor last.

We call events **independent** when one event does not make another more or less likely. Rolling a die is considered the prototypical independent behavior.

When we have independent events we can find the probability of all of the events happening by multiplying their probabilities together. For instance, if there is a 50% chance of rain tomorrow and a 10% chance the first number drawn tomorrow in the state lottery will be a 1, then the probability of it raining AND a one being drawn is .5 * .1 or 0.05 or 5%. The weather does not affect the lottery picks.

Probability Trees

Much like the addition rule's dependence on mutual exclusivity, the multiplication rule is dependent on independence. But like the more general rule given for OR probabilities that always works, there is a more general rule for deriving AND probabilities that is rock solid.

P(A and B) = P(A) * P(B *given* A)

---

[18] P(Hacker or Jerk) = 5% + 1% - 0.5% = 5.5%

What does this new term mean? The probability of B given A means: "what is the probability of B if A is already decided?"

Think about drawing balls from a bag. There are two red balls, four green balls and four purple balls in the bag. What is the probability of removing two red balls in two choices? If draws were independent events, you would say the answer is simple: 2/10 + 2/10 = 4/10. But this is not a situation where you can add probabilities because the first draw changes the number of red balls in the bag.

We can model this with what is called a **probability tree**. We split the exercise into two discrete events. On the first draw, there are two red balls in the bag and eight non-red balls. So we draw boxes for each of our outcomes and arrows pointing to them with the probabilities of that event listed with them. All probabilities leaving a box must add up to 1. This is how you know you are covering all events.

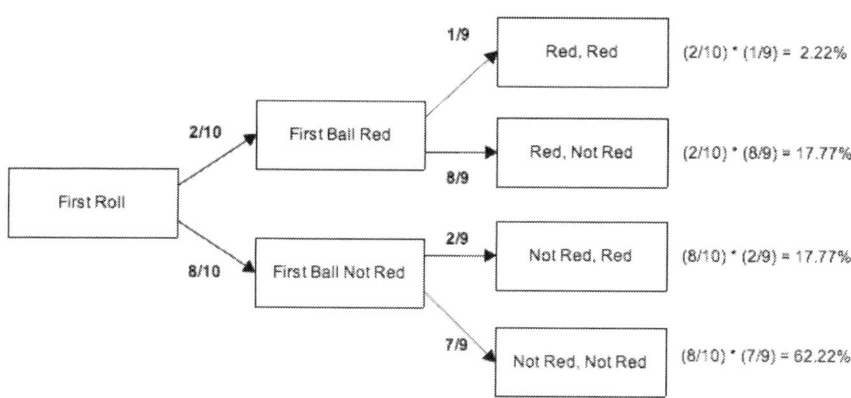

Figure 13.6 - A Decision Tree

After the first draw, there are nine balls left in the bag, but there may be one or two red balls left in the bag depending on whether or not the first pick was a red ball. We draw two more boxes for each of the boxes we drew for the first pick, determining the red/not red event of the second pick. The tough part is defining the probabilities, but again this is only counting. If you got a red ball on the first pick, then there is only one left in the bag of nine. If not, then there are two red balls in the bag of nine.

We can multiply all the probabilities from left to right with our rule (because the first probability is P(A) and the second is P(B given A) to get the final probability of any particular node. That is shown on the image above. From that we can see that the answer to our original question of the probability of drawing both red balls on two pulls is 2.22%. Using diagrams like the above can help visualize these complex chains of events.

One Minus P

There's a trick you can use if you are stuck on a probability problem. If you know the probability of something you know the probability of that something *not* happening:

P(A) + P(Not A) = 1

It is one of the things we checked to make sure our probability tree was solid above.

Say you are playing an MMORPG like *World of Warcraft* and you want some Super Uber Loot Drop that the Ugly Monster drops. This item drops 20% of the time. If you kill the Ugly Monster five times, what are the odds that you still won't have the Super Uber Loot Drop?

There is little we can do with the 20% as is. If we multiply 20% together five times, we would be getting the probability of dropping *all five times*. The naive user would say 0.2 * 5 = 1 so we are guaranteed to drop the loot! But since we know the trick, we can change this formula around:

P(Not Dropping on Kill 1 *and* Not Dropping on Kill 2 *and* Not Dropping on Kill 3 *and* Not Dropping on Kill 4 *and* Not Dropping on Kill 5).

These are all independent. Whether or not the loot drops does not factor in whether the user got the loot in a previous kill. We know what the probability of loot not dropping thanks to our trick: 1 – 0.2 = 0.8.

P(Not Dropping All Five Times) = 0.8 * 0.8 * 0.8 * 0.8 * 0.8 = 0.3276 or 32.76%.

A designer who wants it to be likely to have dropped the loot after five battles will need to raise the drop percentage!

More on Statistics

There are a number of topics in probability and statistics that are valuable for designers to know. Variance, normal distributions, power law distributions, and statistical inference are just four topics that the aware designer should understand. Here's the super high-level overview of each to whet your appetite to go off and learn more:

Variance can be used to describe the spread of a variable. Say you are rolling five six sided dice versus rolling one thirty sided die (yes, they have those!) Much like in the bar charts above, the one 30-sided will have a flat distribution. There will be just as many 3s as there will be 15s (the average result). With the handful of six-sided dice, the 15 result will be much more likely than a 3 (try it!). Thus, we say that the one die result has higher variance or spread. If a designer wants to group a value around some range, he or she needs to use a method that has a low variance.

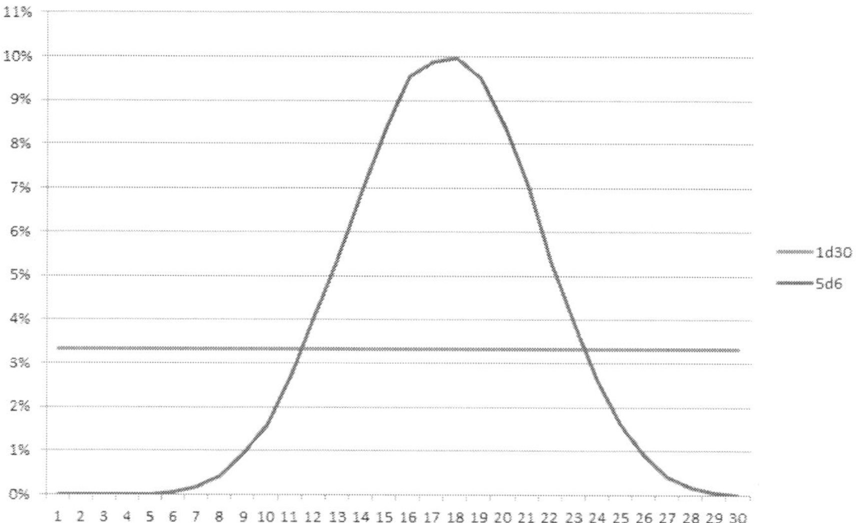

Figure 13.7 - One 30-sided Die Versus Five 6-sided Dice

The **normal distribution** is the granddaddy of statistical distributions. A variable that is normally distributed fits in a type of bell curve like this:

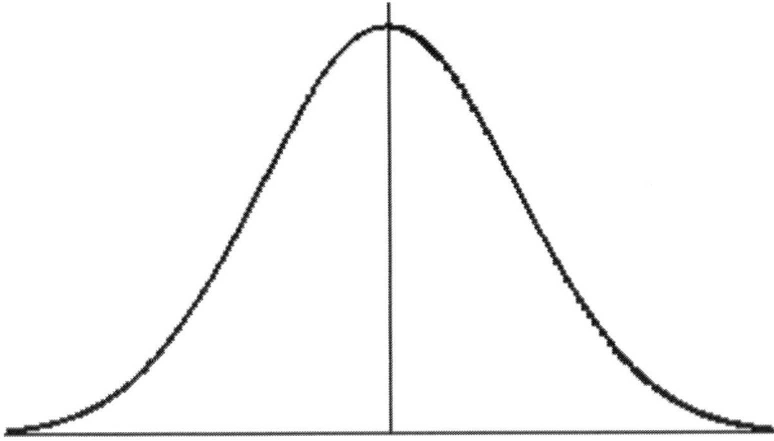

Figure 13.8 - The Normal Distribution

The normal distribution is important because it happens so often in nature. Additionally, it is important because of what statisticians call the *central limit theorem* which underlays a lot of the assumptions in statistics and is just all-around handy. The normal is often applicable to games. For instance, the location of a bullet shot in an FPS is generally normally distributed around the crosshairs. The bullet is most likely to hit where the crosshairs aim, but can diverge to the left or the right, periodically being way off mark.

A **power law distribution** is less often seen but no less important. Power law distributions explain many economic systems such as how much wealth is generated per individual or how much users will spend in an unconstrained transaction like buying virtual goods in a Facebook game or spending in a casino. A common stating of a power law distribution is "the 80-20 rule" or the "Pareto principle". This was developed by the Italian economist Vilfredo Pareto in 1906 who observed that 80% of the land in Italy was owned by 20% of the people. Businesses notice that 80% of their revenues come from 20% of customers. Games see 80% of their traffic from 20% of users. There is nothing special about the numbers 80 and 20, any proportions can work. Another interesting facet of a power law distribution is that it even works when you zoom in. Say your Facebook game gains 80% of its sales from 20% of its users. If you look at those 20% "whales" that give most of the revenue, you will find that the top 20% of *them* contribute 80% of what all "whales" contribute! Handy!

Statistical inference is a deep topic. It concerns taking a sample of statistical data and using it to make some judgment at some level of confidence about the world as a whole. Say you want to know about the playing habits of your players: how often they play, what areas they stay in, et cetera. If you don't have the ability to generate this information for all of your players, you can generate these numbers from a sample subset of your users[19] and then use techniques of statistical inference to make guesses about the population of players as a whole. This topic is significantly complicated but so enlightening that it is worth the study.

[19] Sampling only a hundred users can provide great detail about the whole population.

Chapter 14 - Game Theory

Game Theory is unfortunately named for our purposes. It is the area of mathematics that deals with the examination of the decisions of players where one's decisions affect another. This field was pioneered by John von Neumann, the mathematician behind dozens of fields and theories that are helpful to modern game designers. (In addition to game theory, von Neumann had significant contributions to behavioral economics and computer science.) You may also have heard of game theory if you watched the 2001 film *A Beautiful Mind* that profiled one of the most prominent minds in game theory—John Nash.

The Prisoner's Dilemma

The standard example of game theory is the Prisoner's Dilemma. Here's the setup:

You and a co-conspirator are accused of committing a crime. You are kept separate and cannot communicate with each other. If you snitch on your friend and he remains silent, you will go free and he will get ten years in prison. Likewise if he snitches on you and you remain silent, he will go free and you will get the ten years. If you both snitch on each other, you will each receive five years for cooperating. If both are silent, you can each only get nabbed for a misdemeanor charge and have to pay a fine. What should you do?

	He Snitches	He is Silent
You Snitch	(5, 5)	(0, 10)
You are Silent	(10, 0)	(0.1, 0.1)

Figure 14.1 - The Prisoner's Dilemma

The standard way of looking at this is with a table. The first number is the punishment for you and the second number is the punishment for him. What we try to look for in these situations is **dominance** or one choice that is clearly better than another no matter what your opponent does.

For instance, assume that your partner snitches. The only choice you have control over is your own. If your partner snitches, your best option is to snitch as well, cutting your hard time in half from ten years to five. Now assume he is trustworthy and silent. Looking at your options, your best option is to snitch since you will get no time at all. Thus, *it doesn't matter what your partner does,* you should snitch. He is, if rational, facing the same reasoning and thus he will snitch as well. Both you and your co-conspirator will rationally choose a result that is the worst for you both.

Look at another example. Say you have a big slice of pie or cake and you and a friend want to share it equally. Now you could let your friend cut it and then choose which piece is his, but what is to stop him from making a cut that gives him 55% and you 45%? You each want as much of the cake as possible. So you go with the rule that one person cuts and one person chooses which slice to take. Why? Look at it from a game theory perspective:

	He Chooses Left Piece	He Chooses Right Piece
You Cut 50/50	You: 50 Him: 50	You: 50 Him: 50
You Cut 51/49	You: 49 Him: 51	You: 51 Him: 49
⋮	⋮	⋮
You Cut 99/1	You: 1 Him: 99	You: 99 Him: 1
You Cut 100/0	You: 0 Him: 100	You: 100 Him: 0

Figure 14.2 - Game Theory of Cake Cutting

This is a game with a solvable equilibrium. Given your cut (a row), your friend will always take the bigger piece. This means he will always choose the left column. So since you know he will always take the left column, you can make a cut that maximizes your piece size, which would be the 50/50 cut. The 50/50 cell is the dominant result.

Many games are not so straightforward. In fact, this is an area of mathematics that has been rigorously studied in the past few decades.

As game designers, it is important to look for situations of dominance like in the prisoner's dilemma or the cake-cutting game. Look at a table for rock, paper, scissors where a 1 is a win, a 0 is a tie and a –1 is a loss:

	He: Rock	He: Paper	He: Scissors
You: Rock	(0, 0)	(-1, 1)	(1, -1)
You: Paper	(1, -1)	(0, 0)	(-1, 1)
You: Scissors	(-1, 1)	(1, -1)	(0, 0)

Figure 14.3 - Game Theory of Paper-Scissors-Rock

This game is different and doesn't have a pure strategy equilibrium like the prisoner's dilemma. If you expect the opponent to pick Rock, your best bet is to pick Paper. If he picks Paper, you pick Scissors. If you expect Scissors, pick Rock. There is no dominance.

These "mixed strategy" situations make for the best games that are played as entertainment because the decisions are more interesting than in solvable games.

The Zero-Sum Game and Virtual Economies

One special type of game is worth mentioning: the zero-sum game. The zero-sum game is one in which the resources are transferred among players but resources are not created or destroyed. A good example of a zero-sum game is *poker*[20]. For every chip a player wins, another player has lost one. An example of a non-zero-sum game is *Monopoly*. As players round the board, they get more and more money from the bank[21]. The total money in the game increases until it is all in the hands of one player.

It is important to take heed of which interactions in your games are zero-sum and which are not. An imbalance of non-zero-sum mechanics that drains money from the system will impoverish a game's economy. An

[20] That is, when the house doesn't take a share of the money called a *rake*.

[21] You may not simultaneously complain the *Monopoly* is boring and also play with bonus money for landing on Free Parking. The free money unbalances the game and helps to draw it out. This is a house rule along with skipping auctions for unbought properties that helps destroy the game dynamic. It is a personal crusade of mine to stop people from playing this way.

imbalance towards creating wealth can flood a game economy with resources and cause inflation[22].

You need forces on both the wealth creation side and the wealth destruction side to avoid runaway economies. Take a sample MMO for example:

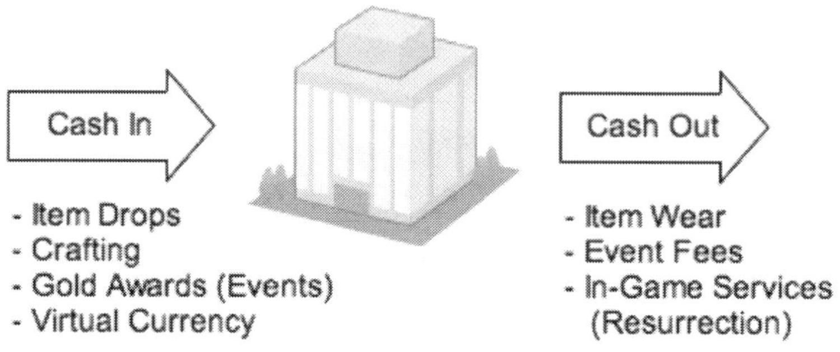

Figure 14.4 - Inflationary and Deflationary Features

If you have a number of techniques both adding and removing wealth from your game, you can turn any number of dials to adjust in-game inflation or deflation. For instance, if it is becoming too easy to buy fixed-price goods or if auctions are slowly creeping up in average price, a designer can increase the impact of some of the "Cash Out" features. Perhaps raise the gold cost to resurrect a character? Increase the rake of the in-game auction house? Increase the rate at which equipment wears so players have to spend more money on equipment?

The popular MMO Eve Online has an economist on staff just to deal with the complex dynamics of virtual economies. You don't need to be as advanced, but you should understand some of the sources of potential problems with both single player and multiplayer economies.

---

[22] More on this: Money Supply Impacts on an online economy (2003): http://www.flyingscythemonkey.com/Money_Supply_White_Paper.htm
Also: http://www.mine-control.com/zack/uoecon/uoecon.html

Exercises

1. In Excel, generate 1000 random numbers between 1 and 100. Take the average and standard deviation of this list. Does the answer make sense? How can you create a list of random numbers with the same average but a larger standard deviation?

2. Say you have a Facebook farming game. Your player gets one farm square per level. Every hour, the player can click it and get a random number of experience points from 10-20. The player "levels up" at 100, 200, 400, 800 and 1600 points. If the player plays optimally, how long will it take the player to reach 2000 points? What is the distribution? Simulate this in Excel.

3. How many flips will it take to have a fair coin come up heads four times in a row? What is the distribution?

4. A player has a 1% chance of his or her sword breaking during a battle. What is the probability that the sword lasts 100 battles?

5. You are on a game show with another contestant. Each of you has a choice. You can take $1,000 or you can take what is in the box. If you both choose the box, neither of you get it. But if only one player chooses it, he or she can keep it. You cannot communicate with each other and you only get to play once. If $2,000 is in the box, what should you do? If $1,001 is in the box, what should you do? If $1 million is in the box what should you do?

Summary

- Excel is a powerful calculation tool, not just a way to format tables or make graphs.
- Using the RAND, IF and COUNTIF functions, you can simulate complex interactions.
- A mastery of the basics of probability can take you a long way in being able to analyze game situations.
- Game theory can help us to understand the decisions of our players when they are put in the competitive space.

Part Four - Generating, Testing & Presenting Ideas

Open up fandango.com and look at the movies there. Garbage, right? Hollywood must be out of ideas, we say. It is a common excuse. It is as if some people think that Hollywood can't come up with an original idea. There wouldn't be so many struggling gifted screenwriters out there if that were true.

Hollywood is not out of ideas - they have an idea surplus. What Hollywood lacks are decision makers who can turn ideas into quality final products.

The same is true in the game industry. Ask any burnt-out designer and they will tell you their One Great Idea for a game. Ask a producer, they will tell you their epic RPG idea. Ask an artist, they will tell you about their anime-inspired beat-em-up surefire-million-seller. Here they are, in the industry, but still powerless to turn their ideas into products.

People often think designers just sit around, come up with ideas, and kick their feet up while the worker bees make it. Not true at all! That initial idea has to be communicated and sold to a chain of decision makers. And here is where rigid or poorly thought-out ideas die and mediocre vague ideas flourish until they become the next Sci-Fi Space Marine Shooter or Michael Bay movie.

This is a section about ideas: how ideas are generated in the industry, how they are tested and how they are sent up (or down) the chain to be sold to decision makers and teams. Those that think this process is simple, that the best ideas bubble up and objective viewers will find the quality, will be the ones grumbling in a few years that none of their ideas have sold and that no one appreciates their genius.

You must respect that while ideas do indeed have internal quality, it is the presentation, evaluation and execution of those ideas that put them over the top.

Chapter 15 - Generating Ideas

Brainstorming

The "where do ideas come from" question that opens most texts about brainstorming is naive. We have no problem tracking down where ideas come from; they happen all around us. When we sit in traffic, at the computer, in the shower, right before falling asleep[23] - if you are anything like me and many other designers, then you do not worry about coming up with ideas. Ideas are easy! If you are interested in being a designer, you are likely more concerned with how ideas are organized and shepherded in the industry. That is what we will cover.

The most popular cudgel for generating ideas in the corporate setting is the "brainstorm". In your classic brainstorm, members from one or many disciplines that are stakeholders in the project get together in a conference room. It may include just designers or it may include QA, programmers, artists, producers and executives. The brainstorm tends to have a theme or purpose; there is some kind of problem the brainstorm session is trying to solve. Someone moderates the meeting and all the members just spout out possible solutions while someone else records the proceedings.

Alex Osborn presented this technique in the 1950s in his book "Applied Imagination". In this book, he coined the term "brainstorming" and its cardinal rules. The rules he created mostly carry over to properly-run brainstorming meetings today:

- Quantity, Not Quality - Worry about "good" ideas later. In brainstorms, just try to come up with as many ideas as possible.
- Build on Ideas - The reason the brainstorm is a communal activity is that you are to use other people's ideas to spur the creation of new ideas from different perspectives.
- Encourage "Crazy" Ideas - Anyone can come up with the obvious ideas. If the obvious ideas worked, you wouldn't be having the problem causing the brainstorm session in the first place! Even if

[23] "The eye sees a thing more clearly in dreams than the imagination awake." - Leonardo da Vinci

the ideas you come up with are ridiculous, maybe a kernel of that idea will inspire some other, better and more feasible idea.

- No Criticism - Here is the one that is most often violated. Not only do we self-censor, but also when we hear ideas, our critical evaluation centers go active and we try to evaluate why the idea won't work. In corporate environments, there is also often a political motive to stamp out other's ideas to develop one's own standing. This is counter to the brainstorm's goals.

Osborn found that when these rules were followed, that idea generation was more productive than in a normal meeting situation.

Unfortunately, research on brainstorming versus other techniques in the corporate environment since has not been so kind. In fact, research has shown that using the brainstorming rules in an *individual* setting provides more (and higher quality) ideas per person than the traditional group brainstorming setting.

What this means is that if you take five individuals and have them brainstorm on a topic, they may average six ideas each. A group of five with the same makeup who brainstorms in the group setting may come up with twenty or less ideas - less than the individuals combined even when adjusting for duplicates. The group brainstorms do create more ideas than *any one* brainstormer can create on his/her own which is why brainstorming is so popular: it looks like it is effective in isolation. But when the group brainstorm is compared with the collected whole of individual brainstorms, the numbers do not add up.

Problems with Group Brainstorming

So the rules themselves were good, but something else was holding them back in the group setting. Researchers took a look at this problem and came up with some reasons for the discrepancy:

Evaluation Apprehension - Anyone with any sort of social anxiety understands this at heart. One of the rules of brainstorming is that quality does not matter. Yet in the corporate environment, we are constantly being judged on the quality of our work. If you are a designer, your very livelihood is the quality of the presentation of your ideas! As a result many, even subconsciously, will hold back and "test the waters" to see what kind of ideas are being received appropriately. They then will use that as a guide for the risk-level of further ideas, essentially turning off the "wild idea" center for fear of being judged if the idea is not of high quality. Simple body language cues such as frowns or raised eyebrows can turn us off and make us feel uncomfortable about delivering ideas. The research has shown that this affects even folks without a conscious level of social anxiety.

Social Loafing - When I lived in New York City, my fiancée (at the time) and I loved enjoying nice days in Central Park. One day, we rented a tandem bike and took a couple laps around the park:

If you've ever ridden a tandem bike, the person in front can pedal, steer and brake. The person in back can only pedal and pray. When you go up hills, you share the work. You can split the work and each pedal equally hard or you can enjoy the breeze and let your partner do all the work. If your feet are moving around the pedals but not pushing, to any outside observer, it looks like you are working just as hard.

This is the concept of social loafing. In a brainstorm, you will usually find that a couple people will provide the lion's share of ideas. Sometimes these are Type-A personalities that by compulsion have to dominate every meeting. Sometimes these are just naturally prolific idea-people. In practice, everyone else in the meeting sits back and lets these people take the helm. Maybe they do not want to break the "flow" of ideas. Maybe folks just want to be polite. In any case, they reduce the output ideas by not pedaling as hard as other members.

Interestingly, in studies of social loafing, when the researchers would conduct exit interviews, the "loafers" always compared themselves to the *least* producing member of the group, in effect saying: "Well, I didn't do *the least*" or "I did almost as much as *that* guy" rather than comparing themselves to the highest producers of the group.

Production Blocking - This is an unfortunate side effect of the human attention span. When we sit in a room together and generate ideas, we have to wait for everyone else in the room to be silent before we can chime in and have our ideas heard. This pause is, in essence, limiting individuals from contributing as much as they could. In an individual brainstorm, ideas are recorded as fast as they are generated; there is no pause.

We can take these three problems and turn them on their heads to formulate rules for a better brainstorm.

Electronic Brainstorming

Many studios now use wikis or other shared software for recording their brainstorms because it fixes the aforementioned problems.

The *anonymity* of digital systems fixes the evaluation apprehension problem. In a digital environment, your contributions can be made anonymously depending on the software. Who cares if you throw something dumb into the mix if it cannot be traced back to you? If it is impossible to be punished for bad ideas, then apprehension should diminish.

Additionally, digital systems allow for *parallelization*. This fixes the production-blocking problem since multiple participants can contribute simultaneously.

The downside of electronic brainstorming is that it does nothing to promote team camaraderie and can actually exacerbate the social loafing problem since there is no accountability for nonparticipants. These negatives have to be weighed according to the composition and methods of your team.

Mind Maps

A mind map is a freeform diagram used to record ideas. Mind maps start from a center **node** that then **branches** out to further related topics. While this is mathematically equivalent to a hierarchical list, the radial presentation affords a more non-linear approach to its creation and is thus why it is a favored method for recording brainstorms.

Mind mapping software is diverse. The most popular specialist mind mapping software on Windows is probably MindManager by MindJet. It is fully featured and easy to use but is unfortunately not free. FreeMind is an open-source alternative for Windows. On Mac, I like to use the free software called MindNode. MindNode has a pro version that adds useful functionality, but the free version should be enough for experimentation.

Now it is time to make a mind map. My examples here will be in MindNode but MindManager and other software acts similarly.

Say we are writing an article about the best games of all time and wanted to do a brainstorm to shout out and collect ideas and then use the mind map to cull the original output down into a more ordered list.

Figure 15.1 - The Blank Page

We start with a simple center node from which all of our ideas will be connected. From here, we come up with some categories so we can order our ideas. We never have to lift our hands off the keyboard. Type what you want and hit enter. A new branch will appear. Type and hit enter. A new branch will appear. We can keep adding branches to the highlighted node by typing.

Figure 15.2 - Some Category Ideas

When we want to add a new branch off of the branch, we just click on the name of the branch, hit tab (it is tab in MindNode; in MindManager it is the Insert key. In whatever software you are using, look for the command to enter a new child node) and type away. Many mind map programs will automatically move nodes so they do not overlap, but you can click and drag nodes to position them you. In less than a minute, here's what I was able to create brainstorming by myself:

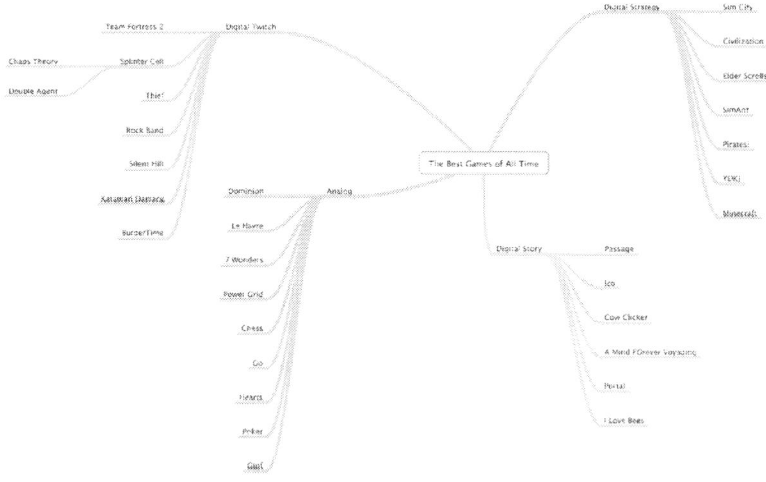

Figure 15.3 - A Mind Map

Now this was just one cheeky designer in a minute (okay, I lied, closer to two), so imagine the output when you have a room full of people shouting out ideas. Mind maps make recording easy and since the point of the game is speed, every keystroke counts.

When the brainstorm is done, the mindmap can be exported as an image or (in some packages) a hierarchical text list (good for combining brainstorms). From this list, you can start whittling the list down to good and/or feasible ideas to be more thoroughly investigated.

Beyond Brainstorming

While brainstorming is one of the most popular idea generation techniques, it still doesn't beat good old-fashioned inspiration for quality and innovation. Unfortunately, inspiration cannot be scheduled, managed, coerced or predicted and is thus unpopular for a business to rely upon for revenue. It is also highly personal and thus not reducible to a task.

You must build a mind that is ready to produce inspiration. This requires a wide experience and immersion in books, movies, music, culture, science, and human affairs. It is a prerequisite to idea generation that is rarely touched because, simply put, it takes a long time. Some stick to their comfort areas and never branch out to the unfamiliar or challenging. It is like expecting to run a three-hour marathon based on expert tips and ignoring the fact that you need to be in excellent shape.

Like much of design, idea generation is exercised by practice. Make games or write all of the time and you will find the process less mysterious.

Chapter 16 - Analog Prototyping

So you have a great idea, the Next Big Thing. Of course you do! Everyone has their own ideas (which are to them overwhelmingly great) and there is no why to tell *a priori* which ones are the greatest.

In fact, this gluttony of ideas can make a preproduction stage of development into a real hell as designers and other stakeholders battle for who has the best ideas. But these are futile arguments. We can only guess as to what will be a good idea.

Prototyping is the solution to this roadblock. Prototyping is the act of **quickly** creating something that has the same feel as what you are aiming for to gain a more intuitive understanding of the pros and cons of building it for real.

There are many ways to prototype but I will split them into two divisions:

Digital Prototyping is the most common. We will talk about it more thoroughly in a further section. In digital prototyping for video games, we literally build the feature in the quickest and cheapest way possible. It is chosen because it yields a result that it is closest to the final product. More on this later.

Relatively ignored is its brother **Analog Prototyping**. In analog prototyping, we use what are essentially board game bits: dice, pawns, coins, and other physical objects to attempt to create the dynamics of the system that we are interested in testing.

Analog Prototyping is extremely cheap compared to the digital alternative. Programmer time needs to be spent so that a digital prototype is robust enough to not crash and handle all reasonable inputs without assistance. But a board game only needs designers to tend to the game to anticipate and handle edge cases. Most can be thrown together in a day or less and iterated on instantly.

There's a bit of a stigma to it though. In a multibillion-dollar company like the biggest developers, who would stoop to using some chits and dice?

Figure 16.1 - A Professional

Well, EA did. That handsome gentleman up there is me in 2005 working on a Nintendo DS game. The game contained a multiplayer mode that was rigorously playtested in that very room by analog methods. When our game shipped, the part we spent hours and hours mocking up with post-it notes, playing cards, dice and little candies ended up being the strongest and most coherent part of the game.

So How Do You Do It?

There is no easy way to teach someone how to do analog prototyping as there is no step-by-step formula on how to make a game. There is a bit of mystery as to how creativity works. I will try my best to abstract out the bits to focus on.

Worry First About the Dynamics of the System - I am going to explain dynamics more thoroughly in a moment. What this means at a glance is that foremost in your mind should be how the players will act in the prototype and what decisions they will make. For instance, if you were prototyping a cover system, your focus would be: where the cover is, how much it protects, how long it takes to get there and how it affects offensive power. You wouldn't particularly care about aiming or grenade tossing distance or other bits that well may be important to your final game.

Approximate the Mechanics with Rules - Now you know what decisions you need your players to make, craft the rules with those decisions in mind. In the above example, we talk about cover. So create a map with varying types of cover at varying distances. Then write some rules governing how pieces that represent the players move and deal damage.

Get the First Version Running as Quickly as Possible - The benefits of analog prototyping are that it is very quick to get a first version up and running comparing to coding something from scratch and that it is nearly effortless to make changes as you go. Use this benefit to get your first versions running as soon as possible.

Evaluate It As You Go, Making Changes as Necessary - When you are playing it (and remember that you can make yourself all of the players, including the AI) always be evaluating whether the prototype has the same feel as you desire in the final version.

Do Not Make Design Decisions Based on What Is Easy To Make - What is easy to make in board game form may simplify things for you now, but will it be the best decision for when it is coded and made final? Sometimes a particular mechanic will need to be rough in board game form just due to the lack of AI crunching numbers at light speed. This is okay. Remember your final product won't (likely) be a board game, so don't design with the goal of making a fun board game. Instead design to inform how your mechanics interact with each other.

When It Is Fun, Move On - It is tempting when a paper design is working to continue to refine it until it is perfect, but this can backfire. The digital version that you will eventually make will by nature have significant differences to your analog prototype. The key is to make sure that the important parts are the same. If you spend all of your time making your whole game in analog form, when it comes time to make the final digital version there will have to be time spent on converting mechanics that don't make sense in the final digital version and all of that balance time you spent on the analog version will be lost.

Be Creative - Too many analog prototypes are of the roll-and-move variety. This means there is a pawn and players roll a die to see what he does or where he moves. But in your digital game, is this how the player will make decisions? Randomly? Instead encourage the same decision making processes that the players and AI will make behind the scenes in your final version. This means you may have to use odd materials or methods. I once saw an analog version of *Tetris* where a player threw tetromino cards at a player who had to chase them, pick them up and then place them. This seems silly at first, but if it captured the frantic decision making of *Tetris* then it is effective. If it gets you closer to your goal, then it is worth it.

Chapter 17a - Aside: MDA Framework

This book is centered around the tools that designers use in the field and thus tries to stay away from theory to focus more on practice. I am going to go against that general trend in order to discuss a theoretical tool that can assist you when designing and is particularly helpful when dealing with designing prototypes.

In 1994, veteran designer Greg Costikyan penned an article in a British role-playing journal titled (in an homage to sci-fi writer Harlan Ellison) "I Have No Words and I Must Design" which lamented the lack of formal definitions in the field of game design and attempted to start an examination of possible definitions.

Years later, in 1999, Doug Church (of *System Shock* and *Thief* fame) penned an article for Gamasutra called "Formal Abstract Design Tools" which also attempted to answer the question of how we explain this magical experience one gets while gaming. Inspired by the work in that article, a "framework" called MDA was developed with the work of designers Marc LeBlanc, Robin Hunicke and Rob Zubek.

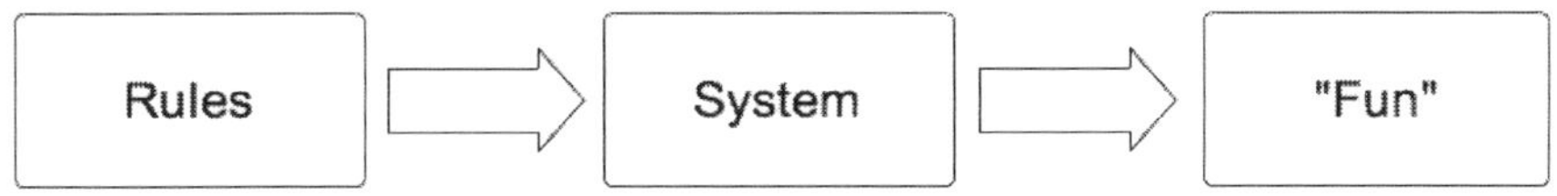

Figure 17a.1 - The Less-Formal Version

Let us look at a board game as an example. All that you are presented with when you buy a board game are the pieces and the rules. A consumer reads the rules and plays the game by exercising those rules. When he or she does, those rules become a system. We see holes not in rules solely by examining them, but by how they play out to become a system. And then that system elicits some sort of response from the player. In many cases, we just aim for "fun". But that is too vague. Sometimes we aim for tension or horror or drama or to make a societal or political point.

This three-tiered system is the MDA framework. Except instead of the above words we have these three more expensive words:

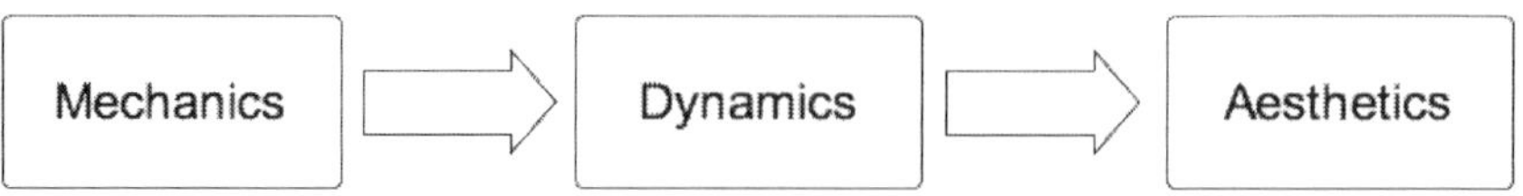

Figure 17a.2 - MDA

Mechanics refers to the rules and building blocks of the game.[24] **Dynamics** refers to how that game plays out as a system and **aesthetics** (while a loaded term philosophically) refers to the subjective qualities that players experience.

When designing a game, the only "knob" that you can turn in this machine is the mechanics knob. You can affect the rules of the system[25] and see how that affects the dynamics. You do this primarily by playtesting, which we will discuss later. Farther down the line, you are aiming for some sort of aesthetic response.

If you are making a survival horror game, you cannot add more "scary", but you can build monster closets (rules as to where monsters will spawn, mechanics) to create situations where the player is trapped having a monster between him/her and safety (dynamics), which can in affect be "scary" (aesthetics).

Realizing this is the only knob you are able to turn is a great discovery when prototyping. It allows you to examine strictly *the effect of mechanics changes on the systemic results* instead of sort of firing blind in a guess-and-check manner.

When you are crafting your analog prototypes, you can focus on the dynamic events that you want to replicate in your final target. Since the mechanics will be different by necessity[26], you must focus on recreating the chosen dynamics.

If you don't grasp this right away, that is okay. It can be heady stuff and generally has to be learned through experience. Let me take you through a few more examples that may help you understand. Notice that the mechanics are the only things the designers can directly touch.

---

[24] In my interpretation of MDA, I like to include the 'Milieu' the game is in addition to the formal mechanics. This is both the art and sound of the game as well as the cultural setting and assumptions of the game. These all can lead to wildly different dynamic and aesthetic results.
[25] Or parts of the milieu, from above.
[26] In a paper prototype you may move spaces on a piece of paper, in the computerized version you may count space by pixels or world-feet.

Electronic Arts' *Army of Two*:

- Mechanic: Players enter a "back-to-back" level where time is slowed and the two players are situated back-to-back. Enemies spawn from all directions.

- Dynamics: Since players are back-to-back, they have full coverage and must rely on each other to "cover them" by eliminating any enemy forces in their view.

- Aesthetics: Tension and Cohesion/Adversity with teammate.

Hasbro's *Monopoly*[27]:

- Mechanic: Any property not purchased after a player lands on it goes into auction. All players can bid on this property. The highest bid takes the property. Bids can be as low as $1.

- Dynamics: Instead of buying everything a player lands on, players may hold back money to bid up an unpurchased property that an opponent lands on. This can be to further the player's own interests or to spend money to avoid another player from consolidating power. Money becomes tighter.

- Aesthetics: The game gets highly tactical (puzzle-solving), teamwork strategies burgeon (social).

area/code's *Parking Wars*:

- Mechanics: Place a car on the street of a friend. While you cars are parked, they make you money. There generally are not enough open parking spots to park all of your cars legally, so you must resort to parking illegally. If your friend finds you parked illegally on his/her street, your friend can ticket you and take the money you have earned. Parking rules change from day to day so what is legal today may not be legal tomorrow.

- Dynamics: If you know a friend is on vacation or somewhere he or she will not check Facebook, use his or her street to park illegally

---

[27] Generally, people who hate the game the most tend to be the ones who play by "house rules" that ruin the game. Two easy examples are this rule about auctions and the house rule that gives people free money for landing on Free Parking. By examining the dynamic situations these cause, designers can see why adding a few simple house rules can turn a tactical game into a random game.

and reap the rewards. Or enter into a mutual parking agreement with a friend where you can park illegally on each other's streets. Or at least wait until your cars are off his or her street before breaking the agreement and ticketing all five of your friend's cars.

- Aesthetics: Social Engineering - a combination of fellowship, competition and puzzle solving.

Chapter 17b - Aside: The d20 System

Here I will take an aside to tell you about a system of game mechanics that may help you in making prototypes.

Many of the mechanics in the games you play derive from the grandfather of "game designer" games *Dungeons and Dragons*. In 2000, Wizards of the Coast, the owners of the Dungeons & Dragons franchise, released what is called the "d20" system under a license that allows other games to use elements of their system. Of course, video games have been using concepts from *Dungeons & Dragons* informally since the 1980s.

The basic concept of d20 is used to compare two game components that may or may not be equal in a random manner. In Dungeons and Dragons, this covers so many events that it is called the "Core Mechanic". Examples of this could be: a player attempting to pick a lock, an enemy attempting to strike a player's armor, or a player finding out whether he survived ingesting poison.

Here is how it works. A player has some sort of **modifier** (or modifiers). We will use the example of a player fighting a goblin. Say he is using a "+1" sword and has a "+2 strength" modifier, meaning his modifier for this is +3. He/she then rolls a 20-sided dice (hence the name d20) and gets a 19. He/she compares this result with the object's **difficulty**. Perhaps that Goblin is wearing armor that has a difficulty of 15. Since 22 >15, the attack is a success!

In short: If (Roll + Modifiers) > Difficulty, then the action is a success.

How does this apply to you? Take a game as popular as *Madden* for instance. How does the game decide if a player catches a pass when they are covered? The answer is a strikingly similar manner to the d20 system. The receiver's "catch" rating is modified and compared with a random roll and a defender's "pass defense" rating.

In your prototypes, you can use this system too. Use it when you have to compare any two (possibly unequal) forces with uncertainty. It is not applicable to every situation but it can be used for prototypes where the CPU will do the math behind the scenes and where the encounter needs to be randomly determined.

The math savvy will notice that the probability of winning is zero if the difference between the difficulty and the modifiers is greater than twenty. Likewise, the probability of winning is 1 (assured) if the modifiers are greater than the difficulty. In every other case:

(Difficulty - Modifiers) / 20 = Probability of Losing[28]

And, of course, the probability of winning is 1 - the probability of losing.

You can use the math to help you choose the difficulties and modifiers. Do you want a particular encounter to be difficult or easy? How much so? The "tweakability" and simplicity of this system has made it valuable for numerous prototyping designers.

---

[28] This is constrained between 0 and 1. Obviously, you cannot have a probability of 360%. Values above one become one. Values below zero become zero.

Chapter 18 - Digital Prototyping

Digital Prototyping is the method more commonly used in industry when any prototyping method is used at all. In digital prototyping, the goal is to make a playable version of your idea in digital form as quickly as possible. Unlike a normal production, a digital prototype may use placeholder art, may break down outside the area being tested and may ignore other aesthetic concerns that would need to be addressed in a full public version.

Often prototypes are considered "throw-away" meaning that the code used in the prototype will be scrapped after the prototype is done. The reason you would want to throw out work is that the speed-driven nature of the exercise can lead to shoddy code and art that would never be used in production. Sometimes prototypes are converted into production versions, but this intent should be clear from the start.

Most professional studios will prototype in whatever tools they use for their production games. If they make games in UDK, their prototypes will be in UDK. If they use a proprietary engine, their prototypes will be in the proprietary engine. It just makes sense. Since the goal is speed, why relearn a new tool? And if it turns out that the code and art is robust enough by sheer luck to be included in the production model, so be it.

Since digital prototyping methods are so dependent on the tools and engine used to create the prototype, little can be said about commonalities. Actually, many of the tips from the analog prototyping section carry over nicely here with one addition that I will mention at the end:

Worry First About the Dynamics of the System - When faced with an empty Visual Studio window, anyone with coding experience starts thinking about code and what methods it will take to get something quickly up and running. While it is good to focus on "quick", you must also focus on how you want your prototyped system to function *to the players* not how it will function under the hood. This slows down most prototyping projects when the how becomes more important than the what.

Get the First Version Running as Quickly as Possible - Digital prototyping is generally slower to a get a first version playable than its analog cousin unless the functionality is extremely similar to something you already have made[29]. That said, the focus is on getting something playable as quickly as possible. Only playtesting can gauge whether the idea is fun or not which is the whole reason you are prototyping in the first place.

Evaluate It As You Go, Making Changes as Necessary - Prototyping is an iterative exercise. You create. You evaluate. You change. You repeat. Sometimes this evaluation step happens during the creation step. This can be an "ah ha" moment as the idea burns in your subconscious while your conscious mind is trying to understand why the code doesn't compile. Embrace the change!

Do Not Make Design Decisions Based on What Is Easy To Make - Be mindful that you are not changing just because an alternative may be easier to implement. The point of the prototype is to find fun (hopefully created quickly) not to create quickly (hopefully finding fun). If prototyping in a team environment, try not to make major changes that are not easily revertible without buy-in from the other team members.

When It Is Fun, Move On - It is tempting when a design is working to continue to refine it until it is perfect, but this can backfire. The refinements can happen in the production stage. Once it is fun either move onto another idea that needs to be prototyped and let your brain relax on the particular idea or move into production mode and make the idea in earnest.

Be Creative - Prototyping is designed to minimize the effect of failures. So go wild! Test the boundaries of your creativity. You may fail, but at least you didn't fail in an expensive production environment. That is, make *calculated* risks that have large potential upside. You are likely in this field to be creative. Prototyping is the most acceptable arena for creativity!

---

[29] For instance, when we were working on sports games at EA Tiburon, we had last year's stable game to build from and could prototype quickly from a real code base if given the opportunity.

Scope

One final issue is much more of a concern in digital prototyping than in analog and plagues student and professional projects of all kinds. That is the issue of **scope**.

A popular software development mantra is "Good, Fast, Cheap: Pick two." The implication is that you can have something of high quality and on schedule, but it will be very expensive. Or that you can have something on budget and on schedule, but it will be of poor quality. Or that you can have something on budget and high quality, but it will take forever.

In games this is particularly true: shovelware games are fast and plentiful. High quality titles are either pushed back constantly or tied to studios that go bankrupt.

In student projects, one of these variables is fixed: schedule. You likely have a due date that is immutable. This is often true in business as well. This leaves two inversely changing variables: quality and scope. You can choose to make a very small feature set at high quality or a very large feature set at middling quality. Framed like this, most independent observers would choose to make something of high quality. Yet when this truth is not identified, teams try to have all three: a high quality game, on schedule with a sprawling scope. This leads to massive failure as one or more of these variables spiral out of control.

The best thing a student can do in one of their projects is to manage scope effectively so that he or she will have time to make it of the highest quality possible. This is hard to do. "Wouldn't it be neat if..." is a common stray thought that gets everyone in trouble. Yes, it would be neat, but you will have to sacrifice other features or quality to implement it. When it is phrased as a trade-off the decision is often put it the proper perspective. Prototyping helps define vague or out of scope features quickly.

Chapter 19 - Playtesting

It is extremely difficult to look at any of your game creations objectively. After all, you were there when they were just sketches. You've sat through the bug fixing. You've followed a plan to the T. Many observers throw out the term "polished". But how do you know what to polish? How do you know when something is objectively good, not just good in comparison to where it was?

This is the goal of playtesting. Playtesting answers questions that you are incapable of answering yourself. You are too neck-deep in the process to be objective anymore.

Playtesting is the simple act of setting down an *external* user or player and letting them experience your work and give feedback. Sometimes this will be helpful. Sometimes it will save your neck. Other times it will be frustrating, painful, obvious, oblivious and dull. Playtesting can be excruciating. But it is good for you. It is a lot like exercise: everyone knows they have to do it, but everyone makes up excuses as to why they cannot. Then when our games are fat and bloated we pass the blame around.

Playtesting is different than quality assurance, which will be covered later.

First, you and your team will want to cover the scope of the playtest. Generally, playtests are not used to spot bugs per se, but focus on a specific feature or features for fun, understandability, length or other metrics. Deciding what questions you want to answer allows you to not waste time with levels that are not ready or on problems that are already identified. You will want to a) independently validate design concerns and b) become aware of unknown design problems. *It is not the role of playtesting to come up with solutions to these problems, only identify them.*

There are two methods you can choose: guided or ad hoc. Guided playtests take users through specific features to get their feedback. Ad hoc playtests just put the user in the game to see what happens with little or no prompting. Generally, guided playtests are more useful because they can be done while the game is still in progress without playtesters being distracted by bugs and unfinished sections.

It can difficult to find useful playtesters. You want to find people who are the target market for the game, who understand what they like and do not like, who can articulate those preferences, who can fairly evaluate a work in progress, and who can come to the game with as blank of an impression as possible. While getting your mom to playtest may be convenient, she may not have the gaming knowledge or interests to be of much use gauging the difficulty of your first person shooter.

Think Aloud and Removing Prejudices

The reason you use external playtesters and not people familiar with your game is that these people are prejudiced. They have a pre-judgment on the state of your game. You are the most prejudiced of them all! Your playtesters must come to the game as purely as possible to get the best results.

A simple comment can unravel this purity. Imagine a game where the interface was poor and players would not know where to go. In a playtest, the playtester struggles and the observer leans over and says, "Go up where that statue is." The tester then gets it and finishes the level. He rates it well! Unless you are planning on shipping yourself free with every copy, you cannot give any help or opinions. The only times you should intervene is when a playtest has completely stalled. In that case, something is catastrophically wrong and should be identified.

It can be very difficult to shut up when people are struggling with what is patently obvious to you. Researchers have come up with various user-testing protocols to handle what an observer and tester should do. My personal favorite when it comes to games is called the **Think Aloud Protocol** first published by an IBM researcher in the early 1980s.

In "Think Alouds" as they are sometimes called, the observer sits with the tester and prompts them like such:

"In this test you will be playing a level from suchandsuch. I want you to go ahead and play the level as you would if you were playing at home. While you are playing, I want you to say aloud everything you are thinking about what you are doing. For instance, if you are jumping say, 'I'm jumping so I can get onto that platform because it looks like there might be something interesting up there'. Or if you are fighting with a bad guy say 'I'm hiding behind this rock because I think he'll walk by and I can ambush him'. Never stop talking. Always be talking."

There are two jobs for the observer: One: internalize and record what happens in the playtest. Where does the tester stumble? What decisions does he make? Two: constantly prod the tester to keep talking. Generally, test subjects will remember to keep talking for about ten or fifteen seconds and then they will get sucked into the task at hand and will quiet up. It is the observer's job to remind them to keep talking.

An observer can record by taking notes, but often a playtest session contains so much usable data that one cannot write fast enough to catch everything accurately. A more useful technique is to both take notes and record the session.

Advanced playtesting suites are being developed at many major publishers that record video of the tester's facial expressions, hands, and screen outputs in addition to play metrics. It is a wealth of data of which you would be lucky to gain access. Often these publishers and large studios do playtesting without the designers present or involved. I find this to be a huge mistake. The design and playtest teams need to be in constant communication to understand what needs testing and what questions need to be answered.

What Now?

When you think you are done playtesting, playtest more. I have yet to have heard from a team that has ever complained that they did too much playtesting. I have heard many examples where teams did a little playtesting and then either ignored it or simply quit and released to confused masses.

When you stop getting useful feedback, it doesn't necessarily mean you are done playtesting. It does mean that you should try harder to get different viewpoints. Ask different questions or find new sources of playtesters.

Take problems (not solutions) presented in playtests and prioritize them by their frequency and/or severity. Then decide which you want to tackle and how. This should be integrated with your bug tracking and fixing procedures.

It is important to return to problematic issues in playtests after they have been resolved. An unfortunately common occurrence is to have a problem come up in a playtest, ("Players are unsure which door is the exit") implement a fix, ("Okay, we added an arrow") and assume the problem is fixed. Often on secondary playtests it is found that the "fix" is ignored or misplaced.

The Pepsi Challenge and Metrics

All this playtesting comes with a major caveat. It is a huge assumption that almost every game player makes—that he or she knows what makes a good game. You are the designer and they are a player for a reason. Don't take playtest suggestions as gospel. You will always find someone that "gets" a feature and someone who does not. Any single data point is not sufficient to change course. But a collection of data can be a useful suggestion that something is unnecessarily difficult or confusing.

There is no rule that says, "If X people say Y, then Y is a good idea." People who believe in design by committee and the worship of metrics and end up making truly soulless and awful games. Playtests are a way to see from another person's eyes[30] and should be used as a guide, not a rule.

A famous example of this from the corporate world comes from the soft drink wars between Pepsi and Coca-Cola. Pepsi's marketing aim was to put their crosshairs on the Coke giant by showing public taste tests where Pepsi was put up blind against Coke. This was called the "Pepsi Challenge". And indeed, even when Coke recreated the experiment, Pepsi won by a wide margin. This caused Coke executives to scramble and led to the genesis of "New Coke".

If you've never seen New Coke in a store, it is because it was a short-lived experiment. It was a drastic market failure despite Coca-Cola spending millions on marketing and designing to the same kinds of taste tests to go head-to-head with Pepsi. But if all the metrics said that Coca-Cola Classic is inferior to Pepsi, why did New Coke fail? And why is Coke still a market leader despite the same test tests in 2011 yielding the same results?

Malcolm Gladwell in his popular book, *Blink*, studies this case and comes to the conclusion that the test itself is measuring the wrong thing. Since "Pepsi Challenge" subjects only take a sip, they are judging on sweetness alone. Pepsi is clearly a sweeter-tasting product. But consumers do not only

---

[30] "The hardest thing to see is what is in front of your eyes." - Johann Wolfgang von Goethe

sip, they drink whole bottles. And when this is compared, Coke ends up ahead.

The moral of this for game designers is that metrics and consumer studies can be incredibly misleading. Coke spent millions of dollars thinking they were following simple preferences. How easy would it be for you to mistake a few playtest feedback data points for scientific truth[31]?

Once you decide the area in which you are going to playtest, you must find *appropriate* playtesters, conduct the playtest, evaluate your notes and decide whether to create a new playtest or fix the issues that arose in your first playtest. In either case you are not done. Notice this flow has no natural endpoint. Playtest until you can playtest no more.

---

[31] Or a few hundred or reams of collected user metrics?

Chapter 20 - Quality Assurance

Quality Assurance positions are popular entry points to those who would get into the industry at way they can. QA, as it is commonly abbreviated, is a job role that is absolutely critical to the development of a successful title but is often characterized by a high turnover workforce with little training and long hours.

Popularly, QA positions are seen as playtesting positions, yet those two could hardly be further apart. A QA tester generally does not have carte blanche to explore the game, pausing only to find bugs. Testers are tasked to replaying the same systems over and over again in attempts to break the game and generate bug reports.

A **bug**[32] is generally a defect with the game. Either a feature doesn't work in the way that the feature is described in the GDD and test cases or an unlisted feature breaks down in a noticeable way. For instance, there is generally no GDD that says "The game should not crash" but a crash is so obvious and overreaching that it must be a bug.

Bugs have to be compared to some design-based document to evaluate whether the behavior the game is producing is a bug or a feature. Perhaps the AI's pathfinding is not optimal: it always uses the same route to track down the player. If the player knows this, they can break the system. Is this a bug? Only the design team knows for sure. Maybe it was designed to be breakable!

[32] Use of "bug" as an engineering term dates back to the 19th century, but is popularly misattributed to Grace Hopper and the Harvard Computation Library who found an actual moth in a relay causing system errors in the 1940s.

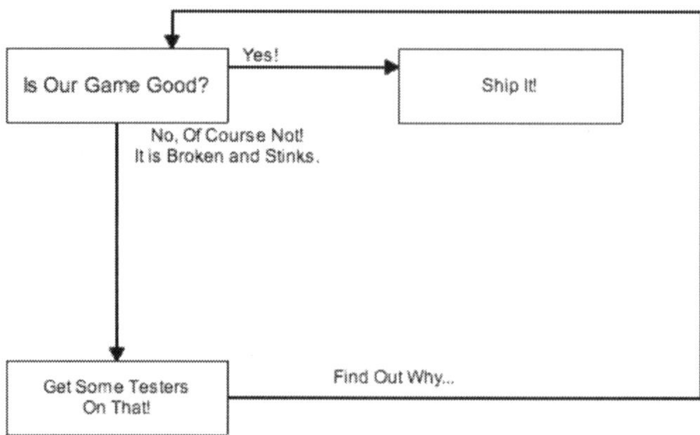

Figure 20.1 - The QA Cycle

The fantasy that QA is a dream job where one plays fun games all day is just that - a fantasy. I always tell students that QA testers play broken games over and over again for ten plus hours a day and once the game is finally playable and good, it ships and testers have to play an unfinished broken game again.

Testers generally live in a sort of contentious battle with developers. Developers submit their code and data and assume it is bug free. When testers come back with bug reports, there is often a shoot-the-messenger mentality. It is often an Us vs. Them mindset. In the end, if managed well, this back-and-forth will lead to a relatively stable game.

This functional friction is why one of the most important assets a QA tester can have is the ability to clearly communicate. Does that sound like a designer at all? If you read earlier in the book, you will pick up the similarity. Testers must tactfully and clearly communicate game issues back up the chain to the game team and convince them to act on it.

Have you ever played a game that you would consider obviously buggy? We all have. How does a game release that way? Is it not obvious?

Imagine a game with the level of complexity of a modern sports console game. Even though it starts year after year from a stable feature set and engine, a one-year cycle can add upwards of twenty thousand bugs to a bug-tracking database. If there are ten engineers working on the game, they need to fix *two thousand bugs each* in addition to their normal workload!

Bug Tracking

Any project of nontrivial size will track their bugs using some sort of database. Numerous third-party companies supply bug tracking software. Mozilla's BugZilla database tools are very popular as is the closed-source DevTrack bug management tool. QA testers or QA leads will often enter bugs directly into a database after checking to make sure the bug is not already entered. A producer then looks at bugs as they come in and will recategorize them, reject them or assign them to a team member's "bin". Team members then check their bins regularly to see if any bugs have been assigned to them and on what they should work.

Bug Classifications

Bugs can be classified in many different ways, but generally they are all given two attributes: a severity and a status.

The **severity** of a bug is how critical it is to the project's health. Severities are often classified by letter grades. A-level bugs are "showstoppers". They are bugs that are so severe that the game cannot ship or, in some cases, even be tested without the bug being eliminated. A-level bugs are crashes, impossible levels or legal issues such as displaying a licensor's logo incorrectly.

Bugs then decrease in severity by letter grades. A B-level bug is serious and will usually be fixed, but is not blocking anyone's progress. These are usually features not working as intended or features that just look bad. A C-level bug is your average bug. It may not appear in every playthrough and it may not cause a huge effect on the game experience. A C-level bug may be a line of dialogue cutting off early or a texture being misapplied. D-level bugs are tough to reproduce and of little consequence. An object having poor clipping that is in a difficult-to-reach portion of the map is still a bug, but affords the lowest severity.

Producers then prioritize bugs by their severity and attempt to direct the team to fix the worst offending bugs first so that when the team runs out of time only minor issues remain.

The **status** of a bug indicates where it is in the project's workflow.

An **open** or **pending** bug has just been entered but has not been examined by a team member to be fixed. Once a producer assigns the bug to a team member, it becomes **in progress**. If the bug is a **duplicate**, it is marked as such and **closed out** or removed from the open list. Other ways to close out a bug are to mark them as **designed** (meaning the behavior that the tester thought was a bug was intentional) or **cannot reproduce** (when the team cannot get the behavior that caused the bug to happen again). Bugs that are too minor to be added are marked as **known shippable**. This often happens to minor open bugs at the end of the project when the team knows they will not have the time to address the problem.

When an engineer, artist or designer thinks he or she has fixed the bug, he or she marks it as **claimed fixed** and sends it back to QA. The bug is not closed out here as QA has to verify that the fix actually worked. This is called running a **regression**. While the bug is in this process the bug is marked **pending regression**. The testers try to reproduce the bug on the new post-fix build. If they cannot reproduce it, the bug is closed out. If they can, the bug is marked **fix failed** and returned to the team.

Using these severities and statuses the QA team can produce reports that show the status of the quality of the project. Using the database software, QA or production can ask questions like: "How many severe bugs (A or B) do we have open and unassigned?" Or: "Which engineers are producing the most failed fixes?"

Anatomy of a Good Bug Report

Of course the severity and the status is just the tip of the bug report iceberg. QA testers that communicate well and write well-formed bug reports are almost always the ones who see promotions and get put on the most valuable tasks.

A good bug report clearly and concisely (remember: engineers hate reading lots of text!) describes the steps leading to the bug so that the bug can be tracked down and the behavior analyzed.

Here's an example of a bad bug report:

"Level 3 has some graphical glitches around the midpoint."

I have seen literally hundreds of bug reports like these in my career. They are not helpful and usually get sent back to the QA team. What are the glitches? Where exactly do they happen? What choices did you make before the glitches? What mode are you in? Was this from an earlier build? What system is this on? None of these questions are answered.

Here's a better example:

"There is an odd-looking model near the castle section of the third level. I have attached an image of the model and a map of the area where this model was found.

I was able to reproduce the bug in every class I tried (Paladin, Rogue, Fighter). The bug was first found in Wednesday's build (#3211).

Steps to reproduce are also attached.

Attachments: model.jpg, map.jpg, steps.txt"

In this one, the producers and artists know exactly where to go to see this because the tester has attached a map. They know what they are looking for because the user took a screen shot. The team knows when this was uncovered and knows the steps taken to get there. They even know that this is a reproducible bug meaning it likely won't be a waste of time trying to fix.

Besides being complete, the best bug reports have a respect for spelling and grammar. If the report is tough to read because the writer forms sentences poorly, the wrong impressions can be made and time could be wasted trying to figure out what the tester was saying. On numerous occasions, bug reports were passed around teams I have been on where the language was so massacred that no one on the team had the Rosetta Stone that would decipher the tester's unique tongue. Those testers rarely lasted.

QA For Student Projects

Even if you are not particularly interested in becoming a professional tester, your design projects will still need QA. The smaller the project becomes, the closer the QA process resembles ad-hoc playtesting. Even on small single-person projects, it helps to set up a database for defects even if it is as simple as an Excel spreadsheet list. Find anyone who will test and give feedback and listen to his or her bug reports. By using a list, you will ensure that you never forget about a bug that someone else thought was crucial.

For student projects, I have found that a quid pro quo arrangement can be very beneficial. As a student, your cohort will likely be working on similar projects. Offer to put in X hours of QA testing for them in return for X hours of QA testing for your project. Set a specific date or dates for this exchange to avoid having only one end of the bargain fulfilled. Even one set of outside eyes can break your game in ways you've never imagined! A student game without any proper QA will be obvious. Us professionals are experts at breaking projects.

Exercises

1. Set a timer for ten minutes. Brainstorm on ideas for features of one of your favorite complicated games. Sports games work the best for this. Try *Madden* or *Fifa*. If you don't play sports games, pick something with a lot of interconnected systems like an MMO. Record these features in a mind map. Go for quantity.

2. Take a feature area of a game you know very well and make an analog prototype of it. Using what you learned in the MDA chapter, how is your prototype dynamically similar to the actual game?

3. Take a feature of a game you know very well that you think is quite effective. Analyze it from an MDA perspective. What are the mechanics? What are the dynamics those mechanics create? What aesthetic values follow?

4. Using the d20 system's "Core Mechanic", try to do the following ten times and record how many successes you have:

    a. A thief attempts to use his good lockpicks (+5) to pick a locked door (Difficulty:20).

    b. A student searches (Awareness: +2) his messy room (Difficulty: 12) to find his Textbook of Learning.

    c. A politician attempts to deceive (Silvertongue: +10) a veteran reporter (Difficulty:27).

5. Use Excel to run each of the three above rolls a thousand times.

6. Think about the quality, scope, and budget triad from the digital prototyping section. Think of three games you know of that succeeded in two of the areas but failed in a third. Which sacrificed quality? Which sacrificed scope? Which sacrificed profit?

Chapter 21 - Pitching Ideas

Pitching is about telling a story. Before the tablet, the Kindle, the bookstore, the library, before even movable type, our ancestors have been telling stories. Since the dawn of language, generation after generation based their values and histories through the use of stories. We are wired to hear stories. And whether you are pitching a feature idea to coworkers or a title idea to publishers, you too are telling a story.

What is the story about? The story is about the idea you want to sell. That is where most presenters stop. Excellent storytellers know that the story is just as much about the audience as it is about the idea.

Mind The Gap

Nancy Duarte give a wonderful presentation at TEDxEast that is available online[33]. In it she analyzes and maps some powerful speeches to get a sort of DNA of what makes them compelling. In her presentation, she puts forward the idea of the "What Is - What Could Be" gap.

Figure 21.1 – Nancy Duarte. Image care of Flickr user designbyfront.

The idea is simple. Most successful presentations about new ideas make a stark contrast between the terrible world of today and the euphoric world of tomorrow. Think about one of the greatest presentations of all time (done without slides, mind you): Martin Luther King Jr's "I Have a Dream" speech. It starts with the what-is:

"But one hundred years later, the Negro still is not free. One hundred years later, the life of the Negro is still sadly crippled by the manacles of segregation and the chains of discrimination."

And it soon moves into the meat, the what-could-be:

"I have a dream that one day this nation will rise up and live out the true meaning of its creed: "We hold these truths to be self-evident, that all men are created equal."

You can rewatch[34] the speech yourself and watch Dr. King oscillate between the what-is and the what-can-be. There are a number of techniques that Duarte identifies in her analysis that amplify the impact of his speech, but the what-is/what-can-be gap is something that can be used to form the structure of your pitches. The larger the gap, the more powerful the comparison.

The form itself requires only a change in thinking, but probably what holds back its widespread adoption is that identifying the what-is can often require research and work. If the presentation is important enough to give, it is important enough to spend the time gathering the data you need.

Say you are pitching a user interface re-haul. The team is justifiably worried about it: deadlines loom, a working version is in the game and it seems like more work than its worth.

You can do the standard approach that most take: state that the transition from in-game to quitting the game takes too long and then propose a solution.

But why simply state the what-is? Take a video of the twelve steps it takes to get from in game to where they want to go. Superimpose a timer using a standard video program. Then contrast it to a mockup of a three-step version. I guarantee you this latter version will be better received. Without directly stating it, you've shown the what-is and the what-could-be. The audience's mind fills in the gaps. They get excited about the possibilities.

---

[33] http://blog.duarte.com/2011/03/nancy's-talk-from-tedxeast-you-can-change-the-world/
[34] http://www.americanrhetoric.com/speeches/mlkihaveadream.htm

Plan Ahead

Preparing a presentation is not about throwing some junk into a slide-making program and reading it off. To be successful you must prepare.

1. Design Your Flow

Most presenters put words and images into slides in the order they think of them and then present that way. Maybe they follow someone else's template. Both these methods are insufficient. Later, we will look at the Slide Sorter in Powerpoint as a tool to help you visualize the flow of your talk. It should have a beginning, middle and end. It should reiterate your point and illustrate the gap between what-is and what-could-be.

2. Anticipate Objections and Deflate Them

Maybe you will be lucky and you will present to a smiling, attentive audience who loves your ideas at face value. Maybe. It has never happened to me. Imagine your harshest critic sitting in the corner, interrupting you on every point. That man or woman might be there. Prepare yourself.

Thriller author Barry Eisler says: "All effective personal protection, all effective security, all true self-defense, is based on the ability and willingness to think like the opposition."

Know the weak points of your argument and address them *before* the objections come up. Most people do not do this because they are either so tied up into their argument that they cannot see the other side or are too afraid of pointing out problems that they think they will be helping to damn their cause. As long as your responses to these objections are sound, you will look highly prepared (because you will be) and the rest of your presentation will take on additional gravitas.

This is a hard thing to do on your own, so share your presentation with coworkers who will be creative and honest players of Devil's Advocate. Tell them to be brutal. It can only make your arguments stronger.

Few things feel better in presenting than having someone object and bring up a point and then you say: "Funny you should say that", advance the slide and there is the data supporting your rebuttal large as life.

3. Control the Environment

You spend hours and hours agonizing over your slides, but do not forget the importance of the venue itself. Arrive early and test the equipment if you can. Are the screens bright enough? Does the Internet connection work? Can the farthest row back read your text? These are all things to try out.

First impressions are everything. Research shows we make value judgments of arguments *before the argument is made* based on the likability of the presenter. Shine your shoes, shave, do what you have to do to make yourself presentable. That goes without saying. But we have all been to a presentation where the speaker spent forever just trying to get the projector to warm up, the slides to download or the sound to work (God forbid). Don't be that person. Do not be late. If you are late, you have already lost. You will have objectors; don't give them extra ammunition.

Objectors are not necessarily curmudgeonly people out to destroy you and your ideas. Sometimes these objectors are passive. Their mind wanders. Their Blackberries buzz. Heaven help you if you are scheduled to present in the post-lunch food coma period.

One of the things you can do to help this passive objection is to create an environment that helps your argument. Arrange the seating to where you can walk by and engage with your audience. Don't ever present from behind a podium if you do not have to. If you control the lights, don't dim them. This puts people to sleep and makes it very difficult for you to judge how you are doing by making eye contact.

4. Have Fun

While this is not necessarily a planning point, it speaks to something broader. Many people are deathly afraid of public speaking. I have my irrational fears, but this was never one of them.

In college, I helped run our on-campus movie theater. It was completely student-run and we showed films that were coming off of their original theatrical run. Often the reels of film themselves were in bad condition, having been mailed from theater to theater for months before ending up in our student center. These films had the tendency to, on occasionally, jump from the projector's sprockets, get stuck next to the ultra-high intensity projector lamp and burn to a crisp. This gave off a terrible noise both from the burning soundtrack and from the burning mad students who paid a whole dollar to see a second run of Monsters Inc.

Someone had to go advise the surly and mostly drunk patrons of the problem and advise them to come back in 10, 15, 20 minutes, depending on how bad the problem was. I was the guinea pig. I stood at the bottom of the McConomy Auditorium and watched as 400 sets of eyes burned holes in my forehead and 400 mouths booed at me. Anyone could get frightened in that situation, but I used comedy to have fun with it.

When one of the *American Pie* movies went down, I told an off-color joke about having time to handle any business they suddenly felt the needed to handle somewhere outside the theater and to come back 12 minutes after they finish, or 15 minutes total. A lucky break happened with *Men in Black* as we dressed up in black suits like the characters and we had one of the electrical engineers make a "mind wipe" device out of a disposable camera flash beforehand. I dragged him out to the front, had him "flash" the audience and told them that they weren't angry about the movie breaking after all and that they needed to go stretch their legs and come back in 15.

The point is not to be a bit of a jester like I was but to realize that, like Judo practitioners that use their enemy's energy for their own offensive maneuvers, with the right frame of mind you too can turn bad luck into opportunities to impress.

I didn't think about being in front of four hundred angry university students. You should not think about being in front of impatient people that make ten times what you make. Think about your message, your purpose and your delivery. You practiced, right? You spent a lot of time on this presentation, right? Why? What's your purpose?

In my student days, my purpose in the theater was to entertain the student body, so that's what I tried to do. In my pitching design days, my purpose was to create marketable ideas for the companies I worked for. Everything else is and was inconsequential. In *Dune*, Frank Herbert has his protagonist repeat the mantra: "Fear is the mind-killer."

You have a choice to embrace pitches as experiences or to hide behind fear. Given the choice, why not have fun with it?

Chapter 22 - The Many "Don'ts" Of Powerpoint

In 2007, I had the opportunity to pitch a game idea my group was working on to senior staff at EA Tiburon. I had given many presentations since I started working there. I enjoy presenting ideas - most designers do. I had studied the art of giving presentations long before it was part of my career. The things I have learned make up this section of the book. I stayed late the previous nights before the pitch polishing the flow of the presentation and practicing it in my head so I wouldn't have to refer to notes too often. I knew the senior staff (it was not like these were some legendary icons shrouded in mystique), but still I had butterflies.

The day of the presentation came and I went to the conference room early. I had a backup of the slides ("the deck") on a thumb drive in my pocket in case the network was down. I made sure my videos were working as intended. I tested my wireless remote. All was well.

The staff made it to the meeting late, as usual, talking still about whatever was the topic of their previous meeting. When they were settled, my boss introduced me and I started. I was about thirty seconds into the presentation when the executive producer's Blackberry came out. He started checking his mail. Was I boring him? Okay, I'll get to the meat of the presentation. I won't screw around.

Five minutes in, I'm really rolling. I'm telling a story about the heart of my game and the executive producer looks up and stops me.

"Zack, hold up."

I stop.

"This slide is just an image."

I look back at the screen for the first time.

"Yes, it is."

"Where's the content?"

I pause. "I'm telling you about the content. The slide is just a mockup of the idea I'm talking about."

He grimaces.

"Where are the bullet points? How am I supposed to know what I'm looking at?"

I'm pretty sure I start sweating at this point. "I... just spent the last minute and a half describing it..."

The executive smiles and puts his Blackberry down on the polished maple conference room desk.

"Your job is to present the slides. I'm not going to listen to you. I'm going to read the slides."

I have always had a problem with keeping my mouth shut. The following I do not recommend to future underlings in the corporate world, but one of my main strengths is that I will always tell you what I believe unadulterated.

"Oh," I said, "Well, I can just make a short document describing this and email it to everyone. Then we don't have to waste everyone's time finding a meeting time and place where we are all free and it will be a lot quicker to just read the document than have the document read to you."

The executive looked impatient. "Just finish the presentation." He picked up his Blackberry and didn't listen to another word. I was told by the other senior staff that attended that the presentation was great and one of the most interesting they had seen.

But the executive producer didn't come to listen to a presentation; he was used to a workflow that suited him: look up, read the wall of text on the slide, then spend the next two minutes while the presenter read the slide aloud to check his email or play *Tetris* on his phone. Emailing a pitch document or summary would have saved him and everyone else there a load of time and delivered the information just as well, but he was so used to bad presenters wasting his time that he set up defenses against it.

This was a disheartening encounter.

I had a choice after that meeting: I could continue to present in ways that research has suggested to be more effective (and honestly, this way is way more fun), or I could do what everyone else does: make slide documents, read them aloud and put my audience to sleep in the hopes that it gets through to some people who are used to the status quo.

I chose the former.

The next time I presented to that particular executive, we had a joke about my style ("Oh, if you didn't like me having two words on a slide, I'm sorry. I use 50% less this time.") But he was way more attentive. He knew what he was getting into.

If you haven't had a lot of exposure to Powerpoint presentations, consider yourself lucky and blessed. Most of them are awful because they are not planned well and don't suit the format. Most presentations don't need slides, but we are expected now to have them, so we take the path of least resistance. We use the default Powerpoint template: title, bullets, clip art. And we don't think about it.

But there is a better way. Some simple tweaks can amplify your message. In this chapter, I'll highlight many of the don'ts of Powerpoint and other slide-making software (coined "slideware" by Edward Tufte) and will conversely highlight the ways to fix the problem and make your presentations beautiful and effective.

1. Don't Read Your Slides Aloud

It is only natural. There's a bunch of text on the screen and you don't know what to say next. Just read your point aloud to reinforce it, right? No! Research has shown that it is more difficult to process information when it is being both spoken to an audience and presented as text. The reason is simple: we read much faster than we talk. We can finish reading the slide in a few seconds while the presenter lags behind with his monologue. The two don't sync up and it causes interference.

If you have a quote in a slide, it is far better to pause to let the audience read it than to read it for them.

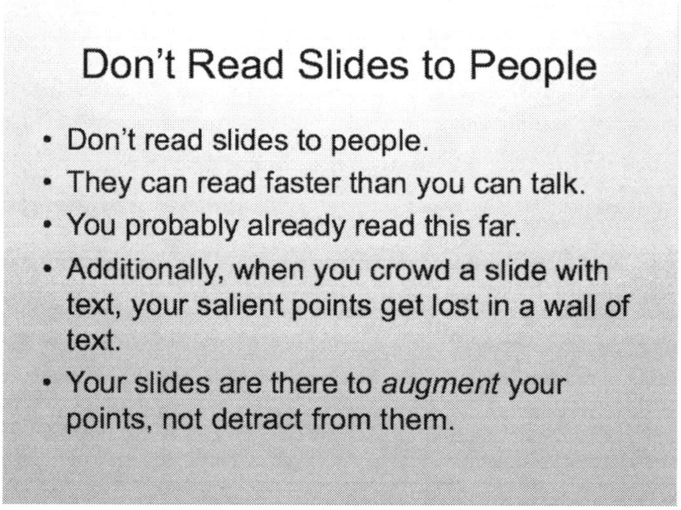

Don't Read Slides to People

- Don't read slides to people.
- They can read faster than you can talk.
- You probably already read this far.
- Additionally, when you crowd a slide with text, your salient points get lost in a wall of text.
- Your slides are there to *augment* your points, not detract from them.

Figure 22.1 - Yeah. Don't

Your slides cannot exist without your narration to guide them.

2. Don't Make Your Points Through Slides, Have Slides Reinforce Your Points

If this seems like a reiteration of point one, it is because it is. DON'T READ YOUR SLIDES ALOUD. If you must use slideware, use it to show supporting facts or figures or, in lieu of that, short text phrases or images that support your ideas.

The point of giving an oral presentation is not to serve as narrator for your slides. It is to convey information in a group environment. Your slides are there to support your argument. You are not there to support your slides.

3. Don't Use Text

The average Powerpoint slide has forty words[35]. This is FAR too many. Seth Godin puts a cap at six words[36]. Guy Kawasaki at ten[37]. I am not in favor of an artificial cap because it limits creativity. My rule is to use as little text as possible while still feeling natural.

Figure 22.2 – Compare and Contrast Image vs. Text

Most of my slides have no text or only a phrase. An exception is made when you are showing a quote.

4. Don't Meander - Have a Theme

The human brain is remarkable, but very limited. We can only hold about seven pieces of information in working memory for less than thirty seconds[38]. Longer-term storage than working memory gains additional retention when repeated. By repeating the most salient elements of your presentation, you increase the chances that your audience will remember your points.

For instance, if I was to tell you right here to **never ever read your slides aloud**, then it might be sinking in for you since I mentioned it in the points above.

---

[35] John Medina, "Brain Rules".
[36] http://sethgodin.typepad.com/seths_blog/2007/01/really_bad_powe.html
[37] He also states that a business model should be explainable in ten words.
[38] http://www.brainrules.net/short-term-memory

While brevity is important, it is not wholly effective for message retention. By returning to the same points but presenting them in different configurations, you help to reinforce your message.

5. Don't Use Clip Art

Want to make a terrible impression? Use the clip art provided in Powerpoint. Everyone has seen the lo-res guy-in-front-of-a-chart or stick-figure-scratching-his-head clip art a thousand times. Subconsciously (or maybe consciously!) your audience is thinking that you spent no time on your presentation if you resort to the packed-in clip art.

All images are not created equal. Use images that resonate with your point. For every hands-shaking-in-front-of-a-globe image you use, I die a little inside. Don't be lazy and pretend the images do not exist. They do. In the "Finding Images" section below, I'll detail some great services that provide hi-res images you can use.

Figure 22.3 - Where are their faces?! AHHHH!

6. Don't Make Your Text and Images Hard to Read

Contrast and readability are incredibly important. How does your text blend with the background? How do your images blend with your background? Can you read the text from the very back row of your presentation room?

We tend to underestimate the text size needed when sitting a foot away from our computer monitors. Always overestimate.

Figure 22.4 - Which is more readable?

As a bonus, things that stand out from a list are easier to remember as well. It is called the von Restorff effect. Be careful when using this, however. If everything stands out, then nothing does. Use contrast for emphasis.

7. Don't Use Transitions

Transitions are really slick looking. You can make it look like your slides are all on a cube and then the cube rotates when you advance! Unfortunately, this is all style and no substance. Not only does it artificially stretch the length of your presentation while you wait for the spinning text to settle into place, it provides no information. Using the transitions that come with slideware is a surefire way to get eyes to roll in your audience. I feel confident saying that no one in this millennium has ever said: "Did you see those rotating text bits in his presentation? That presenter knows what he/she's talking about!"

There is one exception where I find transitions wonderfully useful. The appear/disappear transition used on text and images can save time and space when used properly. I talk more about that in the section about transitions later.

8. Don't Use Sound Effects

Unless your presentation is literally **about sound**, there is no reason to use sound effects in your presentation. Some see it as witty and cute, but most will see it as attempting to focus on shine instead of substance.

Other than that, focus on the message not on multimedia tricks. We will discuss sound and video later.

9. Don't Create Slide Handouts

Sitting down for a presentation, the supposedly prepared presenter hands you a freshly printed set of handouts, six slides to a page, which shows all of the slides the presentation will cover. You look at the front page and you patiently follow along in their presentation, right?

No, of course not. You read ahead, flipping through the pages looking for interesting bits. Remember, we process images and text way faster than we can deliver information orally. And in business, we are incredibly impatient. If you want folks to pay attention, don't give them slide handouts beforehand.

What about afterwards? Because you are designing slides to *augment* your talk, not to give your talk, your slides by themselves won't be useful. Why print it at all? Instead create a summary handout that you can give to your audience afterwards that contains a one or two page version of your points and supporting data. This can be designed in a normal word processor, giving you better information density and control over your presentation.

Do not give this beforehand either or it will be read ahead just the same. If the handout is a better way to present the information, why give the presentation at all? Just give folks the handout and save everyone's time!

10. Don't Act Neutral

Most presenters try to deliver in a detached way as if they were supposed to be neutral and feel nothing about the content. You worked so hard to create this presentation/story/argument, own it! Present enthusiastically. Content is important, but so is delivery. How do you expect someone to be excited about your idea if you don't appear to be?

The worst possible presentation style is to appear falsely or unevenly enthusiastic. Once I gave a presentation for an idea I thought was not very good (it was not my idea, but I was the "presentation guy" on the team). I tried to sell it, but when objections came up of which I agreed, I was clearly not at the level of convincing enthusiasm established in my other presentations. It was obvious. The best thing I could have done was to refuse to do the presentation because even my subtle lack of enthusiasm was enough to sink the idea.

11. Don't Waste Ink

Edward Tufte, probably the leading expert on data presentations coined the concept of the data-ink ratio in his legendary book *The Visual Display of Quantitative Information*. In a presentation, data-ink is ink that cannot be erased from the image without erasing information; ink that if removed would change at least some of the meaning of the chart or graph being shown. A good chart or graph, Tufte argues, is that which maximizes data-ink and minimizes non-data-ink. No aspect of the image should be superfluous. Take these two versions of the same data:

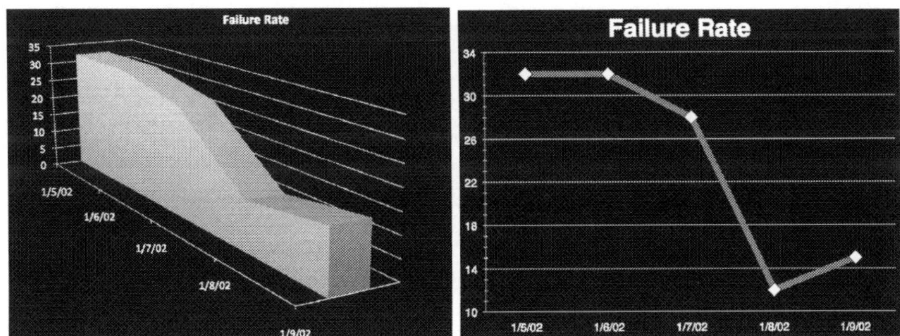

Figure 22.5 – Data-Ink Comparison

The first graph wastes space and makes the decrease in failure rate harder to understand. The second graph uses less "ink" and gets the point across in a much clearer manner. It could be clearer still!

Research has shown[39] that completely eliminating non-data-ink is often preferred less when compared to a minimal data-ink alternative. Focus not on eliminating non-data-ink, but instead on making the point of the slide as clear as possible.

Remember: you do not speak to the slide's point, the slides speak to yours.

[39] Inbar, Tractinsky and Meyer, Minimalism in information visualization: attitudes towards maximizing the data-ink ratio., http://portal.acm.org/citation.cfm?id=1362587

12. Don't Repeat Boring Information

I have lost count of the number of team-based presentations I have seen in my life where the team of four splits twenty slides into four equal parts. At the end of every fifth slide, the presenter goes "And now I will hand it off to Steve, who will talk about the demographics." She hands the clicker to Steve and he begins: "Hi, I'm Steve and I'm the market research analyst for Soandso Games and I will be talking about the demographics." He then clicks to a slide that says "Demographics".

What a waste of time!

If I see you handing off the slide advancer, I won't go "Whoa, what's happening?! Did she quit!?" All audience members understand that different people can present. You don't have to have an introduction and conclusion to every few slides. If you introduce everyone at the beginning, that is more than sufficient. How many times above did "Demographics" need to be said? The answer is zero. Once on the slide is enough. The first speaker should conclude her section, hand off and Steve should start going into his spiel. It should be like a NASCAR pit crew: change the tires and speed off.

Okay!

You have heard about what not to do, now it is time to go into Powerpoint and look at the features you can use to create a presentation. Naturally, before you even got to this point you would have brainstormed ideas, created a flow of how you want to present your theme and prepared the best way to present for your audience. In the following examples we will be working through an imaginary presentation, so we will focus more on the features of the program and less on creating a cogently flowing presentation. Naturally in your presentations you will have to worry about these things, but for the examples in this book it is necessary to gloss over that part in order to show the features in isolation.

Forward!

Chapter 23 - Powerpoint

Powerpoint has the ability to be your best friend or your worst enemy. We have already had a whole section on how not to use Powerpoint. It is dangerous to put that section before the section that teaches you how to use the software, but I will trust that you will go back and read "The Many Don'ts" section before preparing your next presentation.

Powerpoint is ubiquitous. You will see it in nearly every studio or publisher you visit. Powerpoint has some fully featured alternatives like Prezi and Apple's Keynote, but it is rare to find an office not dominated by Microsoft's presentation behemoth.

Now we dive into the software itself and see what features can be used to create a simple pitch presentation.

Setting Up The Presentation

Before you start adding images and text to the presentation, you will want to set up the environment to make creating a great presentation easier.

Aspect Ratio

The first thing to notice is that if you fire up the default presentation, it will look like this:

Figure 23.1 - 4:3 Aspect Ratio

Notice the black bars on the side? You will if you are viewing the presentation on anything but a 4:3 monitor. This number is the aspect ratio or the ratio of width to height. Most modern monitors and projectors are 16:9 or 16:10. For instance, your widescreen television at home is likely 16:9. Unless you plan on presenting on an older projector that has a 4:3 resolution, you will want to change the slide size so that you can avoid having those bars.

On the ribbon, click the "Design" tab and then select "Page Setup" from the left. We are unfortunately still stuck with these physical metaphors like "Pages" even though we will never be printing these slides out.

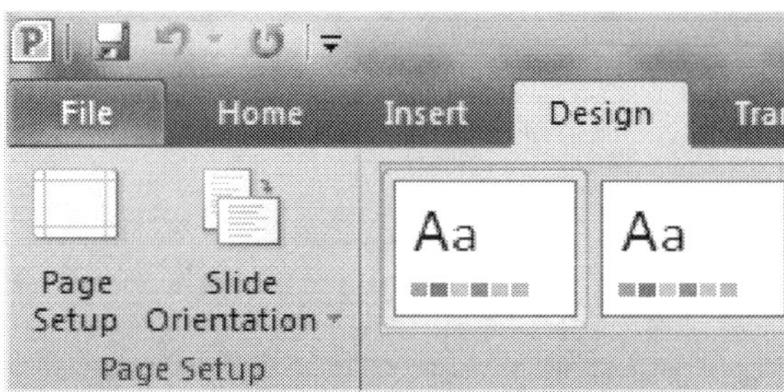

Figure 23.2 - Page Setup

From here, that first drop-down which is currently set to "On-screen show (4:3)" we can change to "On-screen show (16:10)" or whatever the ratio of your presentation screen is. 16:10 is common. Click okay and watch as the sample slide grows wider. It's alive!

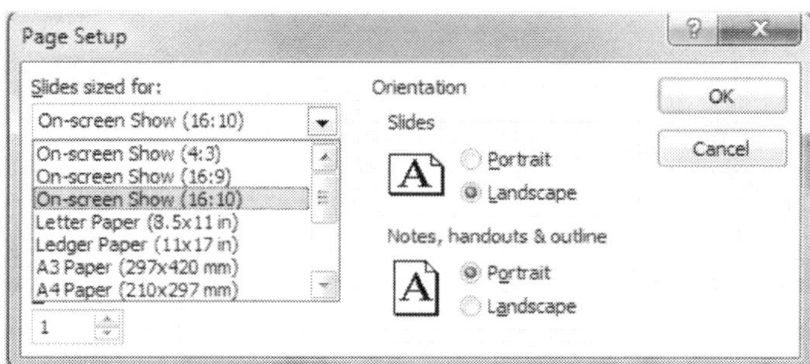

Figure 23.3 - Choose the Aspect Ratio

Guides & The Rule of Thirds

Photographers have a heuristic called "The Rule of Thirds". The idea is that if you split an image into a 3x3 grid, placing your focal images along one of these grid lines results in a more aesthetically pleasing image than the standard "centered image" composition.

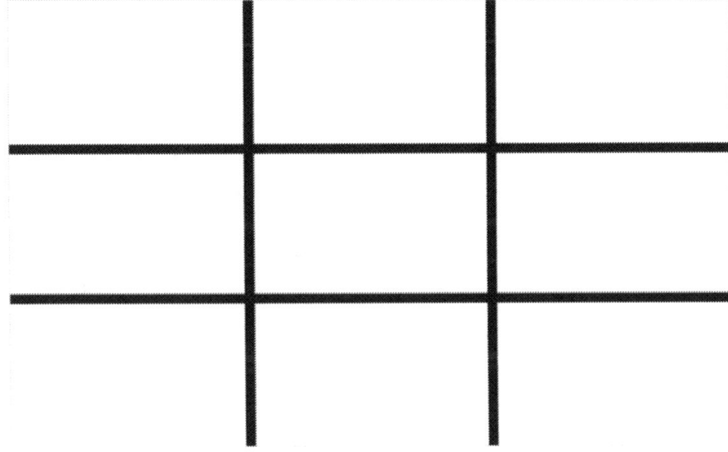

Figure 23.4 - A Three by Three Grid

Figures 23.5 & 23.6 - A Traditional, Centered Image vs. An Image Following the Rule of Thirds

This ends up working even better in slide preparation for an additional reason: often we are pairing this image with a small amount of text. By moving the focal point over from the center, we have more room to play with text placement. Look at two slides using the same images but different placement:

Figures 23.7 & 23.8 - Compare and Contrast the Placements

You can see that on the first image, I had no room to place the slide text but near an already-crowded part of the image. I had to make the background of the text box darker to compensate for the visual clutter. The second image is more palatable. It follows the rule of thirds.

A great feature of Powerpoint is the ability to place "guides" on each slide that only appear during editing that help you compose your slides according to the rule of thirds. Set up your three by three grid:

Go back to our default slide. Go to the "View" tab and make sure that the "Guides" checkbox is ticked. If it is, you will see a dotted horizontal and dotted vertical line on screen.

Figure 23.9 - Guides

Click on the vertical line and hold. You will see your cursor replaced with a number. By default, this is inches from the center that the guide will be placed. This can be changed to be distance from the left edge, so make sure you know what the number means before you go on to the next step, because it requires a little math.

We want our guides to split the slide into three equal parts. In "Page Setup" you can easily see the slide width and height. If it is set to the default 16:10 on screen show, the slide is probably 10 inches wide by 6.25 inches tall. If this is the case, then we want our guides to be at 3.33 (10 * 1/3) inches and 6.67 (10 * 2/3) inches from left vertically and 2.08 inches (6.25 * 1/3) and 4.16 (6.25 * 2/3) inches vertically from the top.

If your cursor changes into inches from the left when you drag your guides, you can skip to the next paragraph. If your number is inches from center, then you need to do a little more math. The 0 on your cursor is actually at the 5-inch mark (10 / 2). So we need to change the above numbers to compensate. 3.33 – 5 = –1.67 or 1.67 inches left of the 0. 6.67 – 5 = 1.67 inches right of center. The horizontal guide is also counting from the middle, so it sits at 3.125 inches (6.25 / 2). Thus our guides need to be 2.08 – 3.125 or –1.04 or 1.04 inches above center. The other guide will be at 1.04 inches below center.

	General 16:10	On 10" x 6.25"
Left Guide	-Width/6	-1.67"
Right Guide	+Width/6	+1.67"
Top Guide	-Width/6	-1.04"
Bottom Guide	+Width/6	+1.04"

Now all we have to do is drag the guide over until it is at the number we desire. If you have the slide size 10 inches by 6.25 inches, drag the vertical guide to 1.67 inches left of center. It may snap to 0.02-inch increments. If that's the case, landing at 1.66 or 1.68 is fine as these are just guides. Place your horizontal one as well.

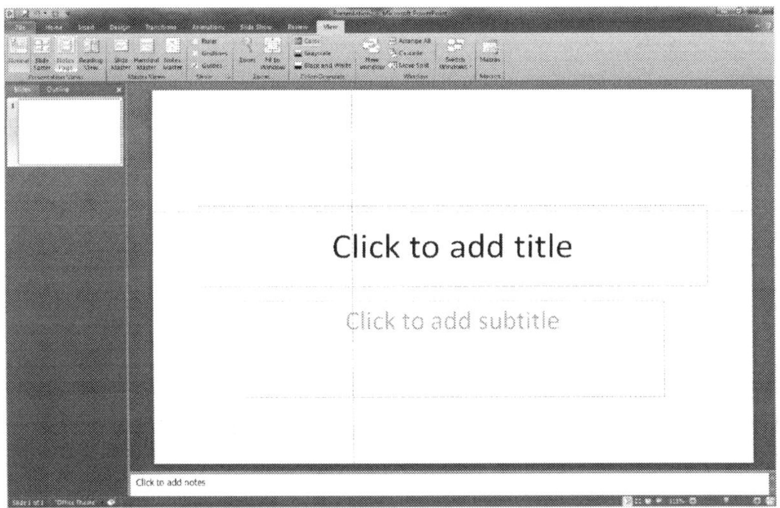

Figure 23.10 - Needs More Guides

Now you need an additional horizontal and vertical guide. To add guides, hold down the Control key while clicking and dragging. This will create a new guide instead of moving the old guide. Add your final two guides and you have a nice 3x3 grid. Some folks like to put additional guides on the slide edges just to have somewhere to align images when you cannot see the background of the slide. You can do that now if you wish.

If you create too many guides, you can remove a guide by dragging it off the edge of the slide.

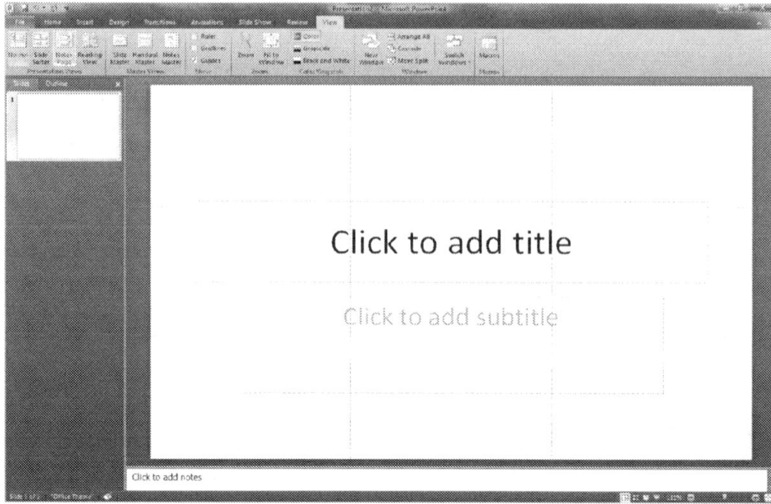

Figure 23.11 - A 3x3 Set of Guides

The Tyranny of the Slide Master

Now that we have our grids, we can deal with this ugly title slide staring us in the face. One of the problems with Powerpoint is that its default layout forces you to make changes to present something in a non-ugly way. You can fix that now.

Go to the "View" tab and select "Slide Master". You will see off to the left all the different ways Powerpoint wants to force you into smashing text into a slide. Time to get rid of them.

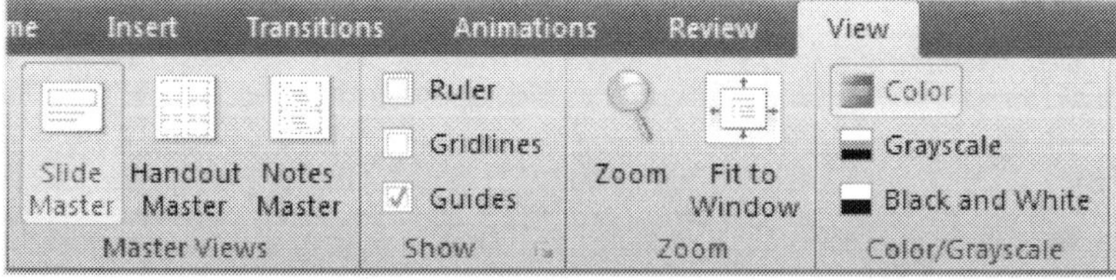

Figure 23.12 - Slide Master

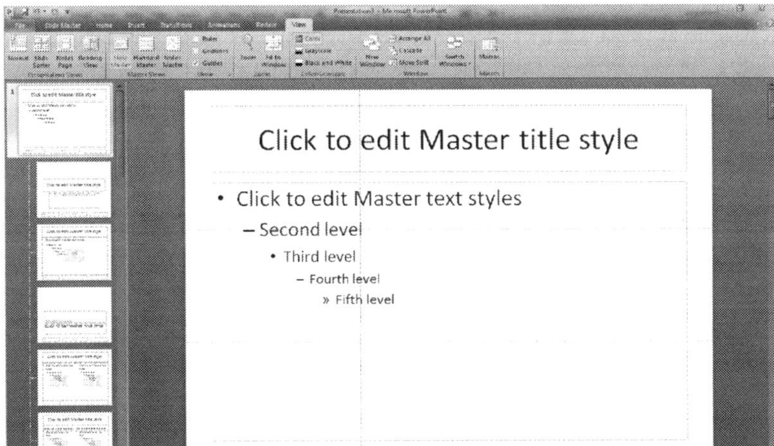

Figure 23.13 - Slide Master View

Go into each slide template and press Control+A and then Delete. This will remove all elements from these templates, meaning every slide you make will have to have thoughtfully placed text and images. There is another way to do this (of course) that preserves your Office theme, but I much prefer nuking from orbit.

Figure 23.14 - Clean as a Whistle

Saving The Empty Template

Now that we are satisfied that we blew up the masters, go to File and then to Save As. It is important that you save this presentation as a template. In the "Save as type" dropdown, be sure to select "Powerpoint Template". Name it whatever you wish. It will have an extension of .potx

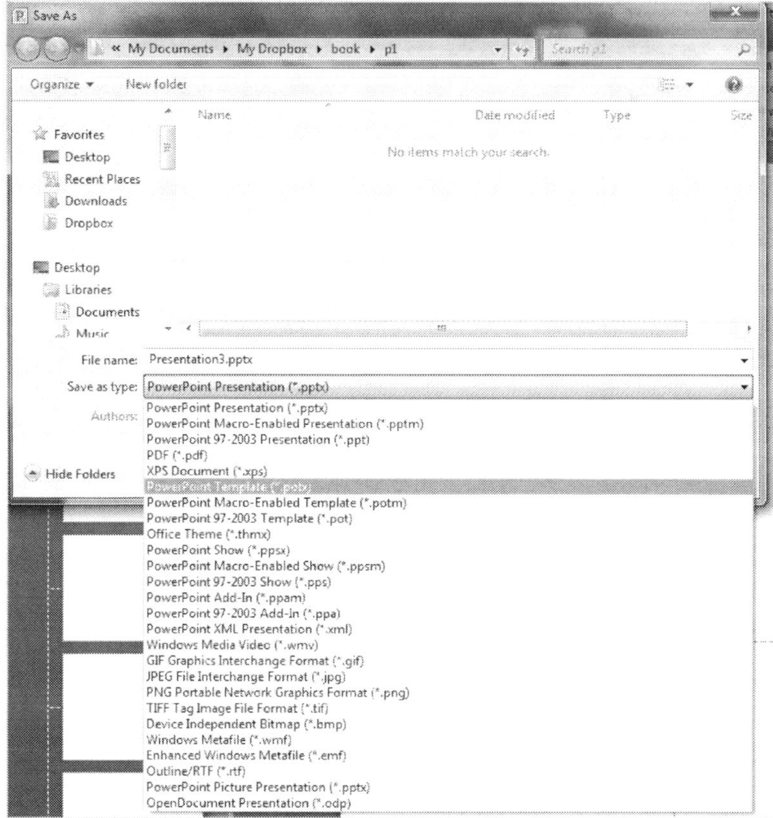

Figure 23.15 - Save the Template

When you go to create a new presentation, be sure to create it from your saved template and your slides will be spic-and-span. You do this by selecting "My Templates" instead of "Blank Presentation" when starting a new presentation. Oddly enough, our template is even blanker than the blank presentation!

Figure 23.16 - "My Templates"

Planning, Flow and Slide Sorter

Before you start typing away in Powerpoint you should have some semblance of a plan as to the content of your presentation and the relative order of that content. This requires planning beforehand and can be done either inside or outside of Powerpoint.

Planning inside of Powerpoint is easily done. Add a bunch of blank slides and then either drop in notes as to what your content will be in a temporary text box (see Text Boxes, later) or in the speaker notes (see Speaker Notes, later).

Many presenters like to plan outside of Powerpoint. They do this either digitally by typing notes in Notepad or physically by sketching out ideas on paper or note cards. There is no one right way to do this. Organize your thoughts in a way that it is easy to move them around and visually understand the flow of your presentation.

Flow is an ephemeral quality that is nearly impossible to measure directly. Its absence is always noticeable. You want your presentation to have logical transitions[40] so that one topic becomes another without glaring shifting moments. The more brusque the transition, the more it jars the audience. Sometimes that is the point - to shock the audience into noticing, but it also gives the audience a chance to be distracted.

Once the rough draft of your presentation is created, use the slide sorter feature to get a grasp of how your presentation flows by topic. What is the cadence? Do you have one Big Idea per slide or three? Do some slides contain a lot more information than others? Will this be jarring to your audience?

Slide Sorter is found under the View tab in Presentation Views.

---

[40] Not slide transitions! More on these evil things later!

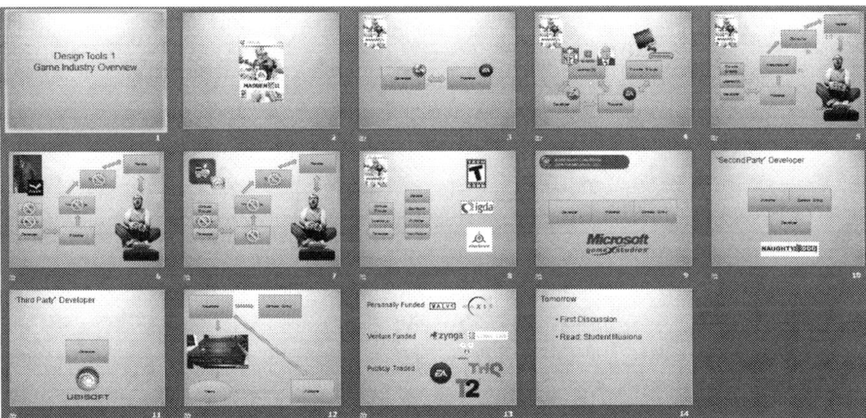

Figure 23.17 - Slide Sorter

In Keynote, another popular slide presentation package for the Mac OS, the slide sorter goes by the name "Light Table[41]". You can reach Light Table from the View menu.

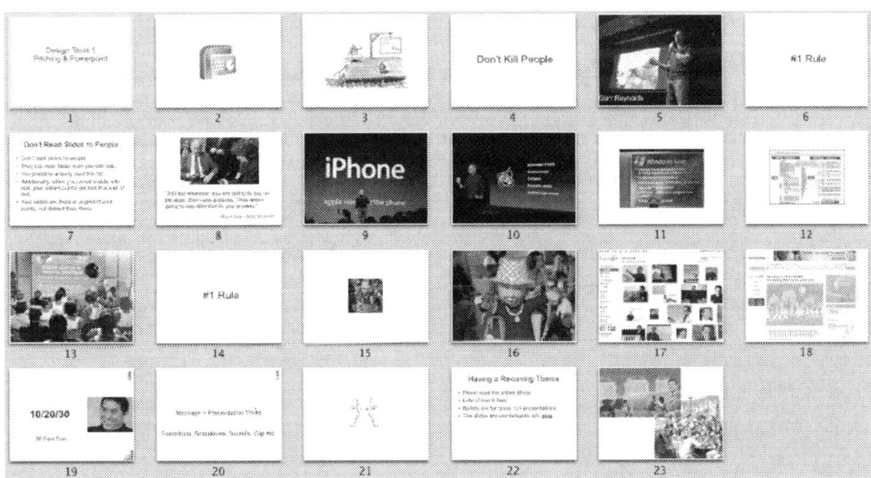

Figure 23.18 - Light Table in Keynote

In Slide Sorter or Light Table, the thumbnails will be able to tell you a lot about the composition of your slides. At the 66% zoom level, can you read all of the text? If not, it may be too small. Can an outside person understand what the images are at that zoom level? People in the back of your presentation may struggle with its legibility.

---

[41] The name comes from the time when people putting together presentations with 35mm film slides had to use a physical table lit from behind to sort the exposures into the right order.

Planning and flow are important because they represent how the message is best transferred to your audience. If you have no message, no amount of fussing with Slide Sorter will help you.

Speaker Notes

Most Powerpoint presenters use their slides as their speaker notes, looking up and reading off a line to know what to say next. This is absolutely the wrong way to present for reasons we have already covered. But in lieu of memorizing your presentation (most people, myself included, do not have the skill for that), how do you guide yourself through the presentation without broadcasting your info to the audience before you say it?

The speaker notes field in Powerpoint provides a popular way of leaving yourself presenting notes. This field attaches a text box that the audience will not see to each slide.

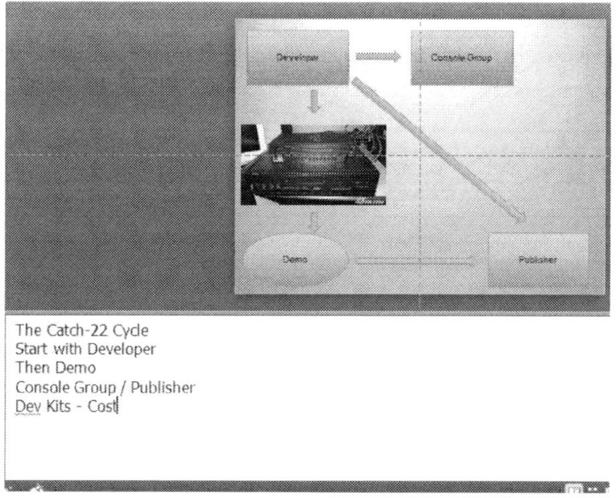

Figure 23.19 - Speaker Notes on an Ugly Slide

When you present, you will likely be presenting from a laptop hooked up to a projector. When Powerpoint notices you have two displays, it makes one display the slides and the other display things that are useful to the presenter. This display can look different on various versions of Powerpoint or Keynote.

Here's the look on Office 2008 Mac:

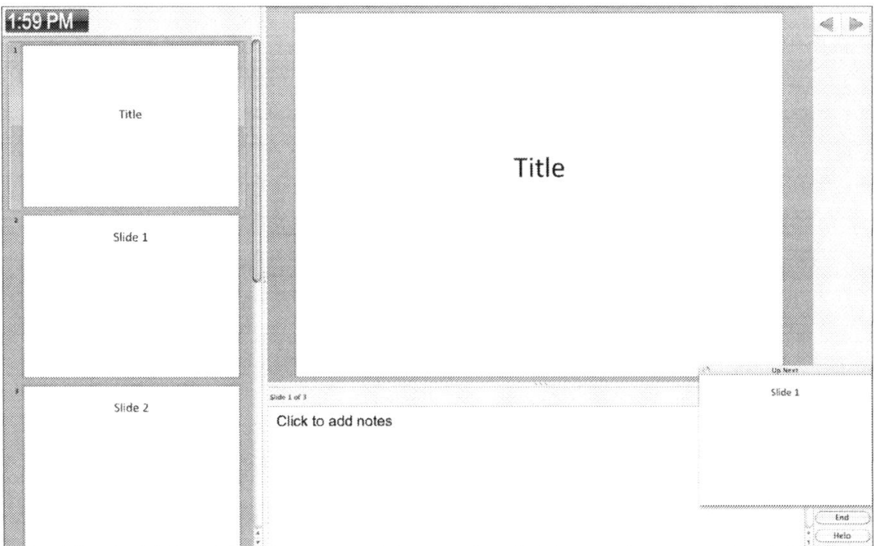

Figure 23.20 - Office 2008 Mac Presenter View

It shows the current slide (so you never have to look behind you and talk to the wall), the upcoming slide and large-print speaker notes. Other versions[42] have additional features like a Pen button to draw on your slides in real-time, timers to note your progress (See Pecha Kucha later) or a slide navigator[43].

Some presenters eschew speaker notes entirely. On-screen notes require you to be behind the podium or screen and to stay put, sometimes squinting at notes. One alternative is to use old-fashioned index cards. Each card represents a slide and is wholly portable so you can walk around and make dynamic contact with your audience. You can even use these cards as a proto-slide sorter to best organize your presentation by laying your note cards out on a table.

Physical cards also show a level (perhaps subconsciously) that you have prepared for this presentation. Another benefit I have found is that if you fidget like I do, cards allow you to shuffle something without being wholly annoying on stage.

[42] For some reason, this feature seems to change drastically with every major revision and from Powerpoint to Keynote. Practice with a particular version to be familiar.

[43] For emergencies: If the projector is showing the audience your notes and the slides are being shown on your laptop screen, press X to switch them.

Figure 23.21 - Best Friends

In any case, notes are essential to ease the human tendency to forget. Your notes should contain key phrases or facts that help you connect points together. Your note cards should not be full sentences or so jam-packed that it is tough to pick up information at a short glance. Reading directly from your note cards is only slightly less nefarious as reading your slides aloud. Your note cards are a safety net, not a crutch.

An additional help is to put facts on your cards that support your arguments but are not necessarily going to be presented in the presentation proper. I remember doing this once for a game pitch. I referenced an obscure game being used as inspiration during the pitch. During the questions and answers at the end, someone tried to trip me up saying that the game I cited was a critical success but a commercial failure. Luckily, I had the worldwide sales for that title in my notes and was able to correct him. Everyone looked at me like I was some kind of powerful wizard for having information that was not listed on the slides. That kind of information is extremely persuasive and makes you look supremely read-up on your subject matter.

Finding Images

It is fine to say that you should fill your slides with appropriate and evocative images. But how do you do that? There are many sources of high-quality images across the Internet that you can use in your presentations.

Resolution

One of the most important things to consider is the original resolution of your image. This is a pair of numbers that describes the width and height of the image in pixels. If you stretch the image, you can increase the resolution but any program you use to stretch the image will have to guess on how to fill in the new pixels. Often this causes an image to look pixilated and low quality.

If you want your image to cover the whole slide, you need the original resolution of the images you find to be larger than the size of your slide. Remember in the preparation of your presentation how you selected a 16:10 resolution? What is the resolution of your projector?

Figures 23.22 - Low-Res Image Stretched To Fit A Slide. Ick.

Figure 23.23. - High Res-Image Slide. Better.

Whatever that resolution is, your full screen images should not be much smaller than that. You may stretch a little, but I recommend not stretching by more than ten percent. For instance, if your screen is 1280 x 800 then your minimum image size for full-screen should be 1152 x 720.

If you have the perfect image for your slideshow but can only find it in a smaller resolution, consider surrounding it with white space if you believe it will still be visible at that size at the back of the room. Never ever crowd a slide with smaller images just to "fit everything in".

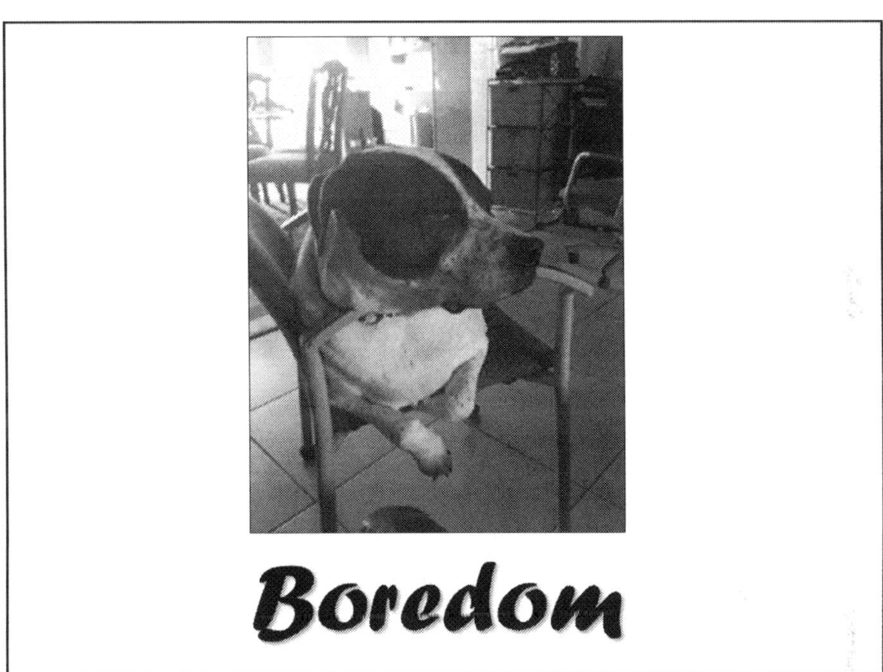

Figure 23.24 - Unstretched Smaller-Res Image

Locations

There are a few go-to locations for images online. My first stop is always stock.xchang at http://www.sxc.hu. This is a repository of high-quality free, royalty-free stock images owned by Getty Images. They provide this service in hopes that you will upgrade to their iStockPhoto site that has paid stock photography. Stock.xchang doesn't have great images on all topics, but for generic searches like note cards (used above!) and game pawns, it is a wonderful resource. Morguefile.com and Dreamstime.com are also reasonably stocked sites.

The next location to search is Google Images. Google offers the largest database of available image files, but there are many caveats. First, since these images are pulled directly from the websites Google crawls, they are in the resolutions native to that site. Most sites do not publish their images at a resolution high enough to be full-slide images. To search only large resolution images, use Google's advanced search options located below the search bar.

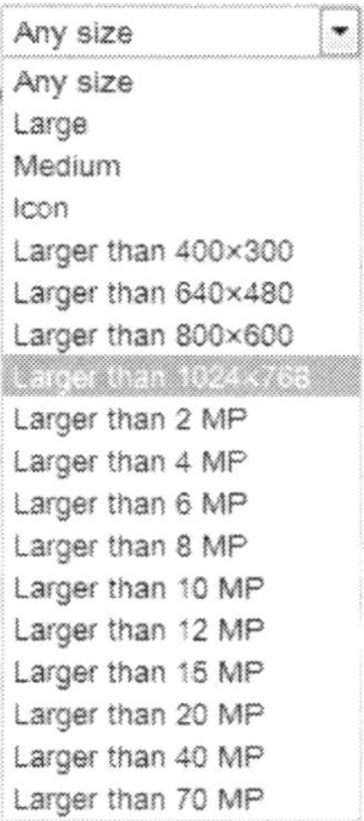

Figure 23.25 - Google Image Size Adjustment

Second, since these are not public-domain images (most likely), you don't have license to use them publicly. I can make what I think it a pretty strong fair-use argument for using them internally, but still you are using someone else's work for financial gain which can be a legal gray area. If doing this publicly, I would read up a bit on what is fair use and who would be most likely to sue you before spitting other's images all over the public.

Third is Wikipedia. Images on Wikipedia come in all sizes but generally have their licensing use restrictions right on the image file's page.

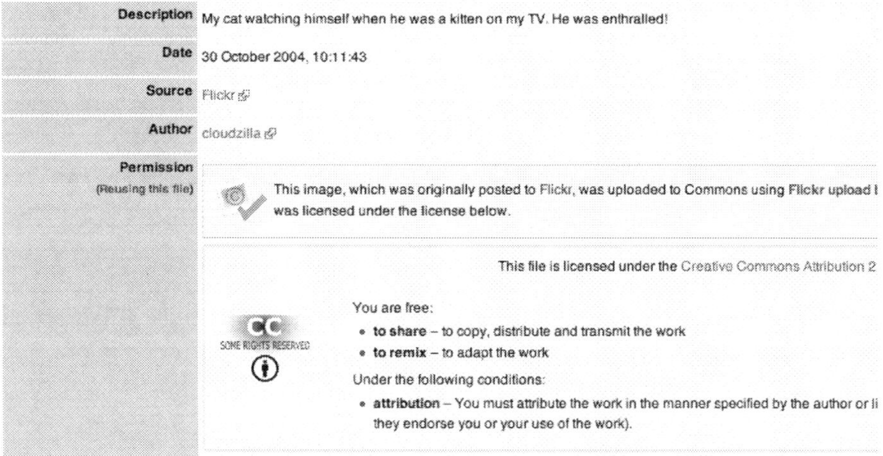

Figure 23.26 - Wikipedia Image Licenses

Lastly are game sites. As game designers, often what you want to present are images from other games. Sites like IGN and Gamespot often keep large databases of promotional images for games before their release that publishers send to them for public distribution. This doesn't mean you have license to use them, but often they are the only source. Again, I wouldn't use these without proper attribution and would never use them publicly without attempting to gauge the legality of doing so. Images are not often large enough to be full screen, but for the purposes of providing reference, they are large enough to be the focal point of the slide surrounded by white space.

Text Boxes

Since I remove the default boxes from my default theme, whenever I need to put text, I need to add a text box. A text box is simply a position to place text.

To place a text box, click on the Text Box button and drag to place the size. From there, type away and make adjustments in the formatting palette. This is easy and hardly worth mentioning, but there are two important notes to discuss regarding text boxes.

Text Box Backgrounds

If you are producing image-heavy slides as I recommend in the previous sections, it can be difficult to produce legible text on a multi-colored image.

Figure 23.27 - Text on an Image with Contrast Issues

Figure 23.28 - Text on an Image with a Colored Fill

To do what I have done in the above image, right-click on your text box and select Format Shape. Under Fill, choose Solid Fill and choose a color with a strong contrast to the underlying colors of the image. If the solid fill is too jarring, try adding some transparency to your fill color so that the background of the slide seeps through a tiny bit.

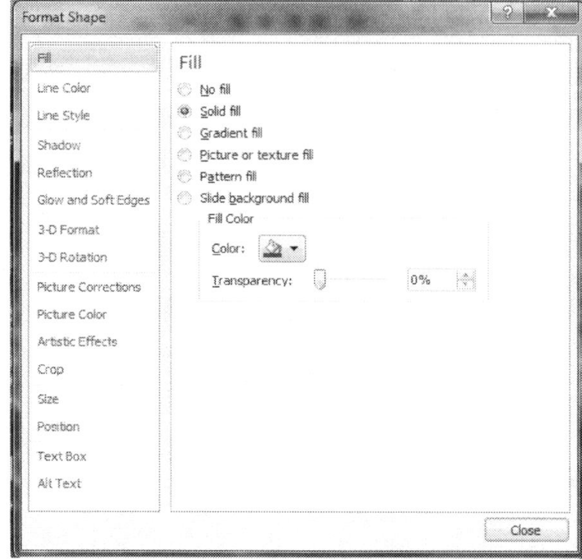

Figure 23.29 - Fill Options

Pacifism

One of the things that Powerpoint and Keynote make it so easy to do is to create a text box and litter it with bullet points. The default template on both assumes this is what you will do. But the problem with bullet points is that if you summarize your argument on screen your audience won't listen to the full explanation. They will just file away the bullets as the argument. Try to avoid using bullet points. Instead use evocative images to accompany your points with relative facts in your speaker notes. In the above slide about power usage, I show a particularly egregious electricity user. This frames the discussion when I start talking about how much the average user uses in a neighborhood versus the energy "hogs". The average presenter would just put the argument on the screen, leaving little reason to have the presentation at all.

Lists are perfectly fine without bullets. Just create text boxes without the telltale circles. Separate text boxes also allow you to use appear transitions to show one at a time (which will we cover later) in a method similar to the bulleted list.

Links

To add a hyperlink, select text in a text box or an image and either press Control+K or select Hyperlink from the Insert menu. This is fairly straightforward. Use of links is really only recommended if you are presenting about the features of a website and want to interrupt the presentation to jump to that website to show functionality. Links as a bibliography are useless as the slides won't be distributed.

Additionally, you can use links to direct to a file on your hard drive. This is useful if you are directing to a file for an external program that cannot be directly embedded in the presentation. For instance, I have done this for Flash SWF files.

Usually it looks better to create an image and attach the hyperlink to that versus doing the same to text.

Video

It is quite popular in the video games industry to provide embedded video in presentations. This is helpful if you are talking about a feature or competitor and want a moving image of the topic going on behind you.

First, be well aware that this will not embed the file itself into the Powerpoint presentation as it does with fonts (see Fonts below), you should keep the video files in the same folder as the presentation or some versions Powerpoint may have trouble seeing it.

You insert video by (oddly enough!) going to the Insert tab and selecting "Video".

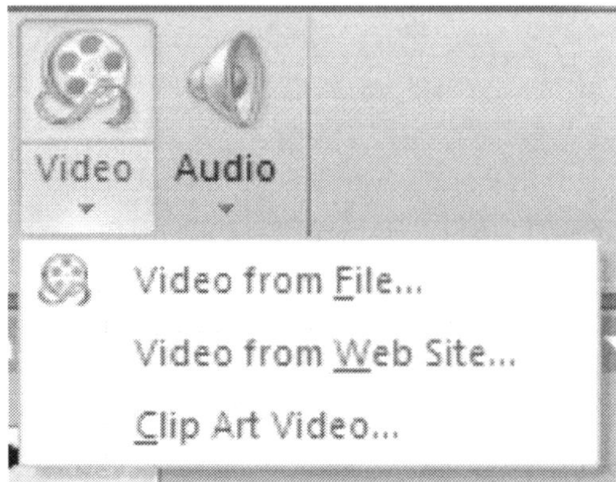

Figure 23.30 - Insert Video

Video from File picks a file from your hard drive. Video files must be in the AVI or WMV formats on Windows. QuickTime MOV files are available on Macs. Movies saved from YouTube are in the Flash Video (FLV) format and will need to be converted before they can be embedded.

Video From Web Site is supposed to allow you to embed clips from sites like YouTube and Vimeo straight into the presentation. The trouble with this is that these sites change so frequently that I have pretty much never been able to get this feature to work without a hitch.

Clip Art Video is awful and should never be used.

Once inserted, you can change it so that the video is started on a user click or started automatically by selecting the video and accessing the Video Tools Playback tab.

How to Convert

One of the best ways to ensure that a video will actually play is to strip it from YouTube, Vimeo or wherever and keep it on your hard drive. Generally, sites discourage this practice, but these safeguards are easily circumvented.

There are plugins for your browser of choice that will allow you to download from YouTube and other sites: "Easy YouTube Video Downloader" for Firefox, "YouTube Downloader" for Chrome. In Safari, you can press Command+Option+A and double-click on the largest file in the list. KeepVid.com is a site that allows you to save videos from any modern browser.

Once you have the FLV video file, you still have some work to do. Powerpoint doesn't recognize FLV files natively. You must convert these files to something Powerpoint will read like an AVI. There are many proprietary pieces of software that will do this like Handbrake or AVS Video Converter. Free implementations like FLVtoAVI vary in usefulness. Some websites even try to convert video on the fly, but your mileage may vary. Since there is no standard here, I will leave this as an exercise to the reader to find the best converter for your uses.

Copyright Warning for YouTube Files

Video is no different than pictures or music you find on the web. It is likely that unless specified you do not have the license to exploit the work for commercial uses. Creative Commons license for video are few and far between at the time of this writing, so unless you hold full copyright over the video, don't use video in public for commercial purposes.

The Hideous Realm of Transitions and Sound Effects

"Talking out of turn? That's a paddlin'. Lookin' out the window? That's a paddlin'. Staring at my sandals? That's a paddlin'. Paddlin' the school canoe? Oh, you better believe that's a paddlin'." - Jasper

If a lot of this chapter seems like it just your humble author telling you about features of Powerpoint that are Forbidden Knowledge never-to-be-used, then you are absolutely right. But don't take my word for it:

"Despite the lush graphics effects so easily produced through modern presentation applications, most contemporary presentations should return to formats nearly as spare as the old overhead transparencies. It is not necessary to copy their specific limitations (there's no need to go back to, say, a single-size typewriter-style font or total lack of color in charts and graphs), but the equivalent level of disregard for extraneous decoration would be helpful, for the sake of both presenter focus and audience comprehension."

Who do you think made that quote? Some surly marketing wonk or curmudgeonly professor-type? No, that's actually Robert Gaskins, the man who (jointly) invented Powerpoint. If you are looking for an expert, it is hard to find someone with more gravitas.

For some reason, the feature that tempts the most is the use of transitions. A slide transition is a special kind of transition animation that ties two slides together.

Figure 23.31 - Unnecessary 3D Slide Transition

But transitions are not limited to just slides, oh no! Text boxes and figures can have animations tied to them. They can spin into place, dissolve or explode onto screen. You can even define motion paths to animate your text or still image over an invisible path. Why this would help cement your audience's knowledge is anyone's guess.

Why are transitions so bad? The question should not be that, but instead the burden of proof should be shifted: why are transitions *good*? They create unnecessary pauses in your presentation, they do not add content and often they can be seen as pedestrian and juvenile. Few see transitions and stare mouths agape in wonder and awe. Why add something with no upside?

The One Transition You Can (and Should) Use

There is, however, one transition (really two if you are technical) that has great utility and this I will show you how to use. It is called "Appear" in Powerpoint. (Its cousin is "Disappear" for those who want to separate the two.) Appear/Disappear cause an element to appear or disappear on a slide when you hit the "Next Slide" button. This allows you to hide information until you want to use it.

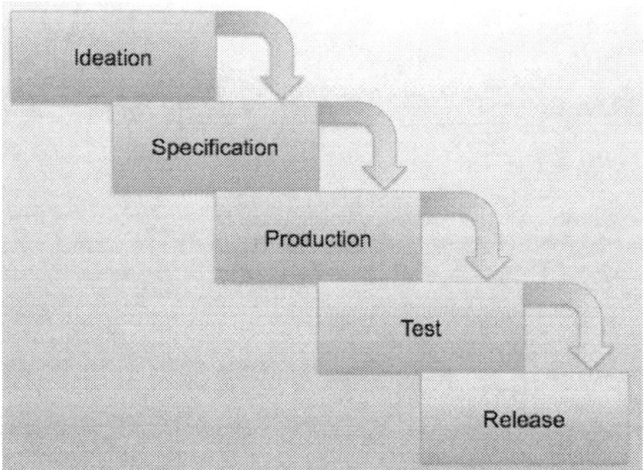

Figure 23.32 - Slide With Appearing Elements

The slide above begins only with the "Ideation" box on screen. Each time I click, an arrow appears followed by the next box in the waterfall. Eventually, I have all five on screen. This is much better than having all five on the screen at the start, which would be a very crowded and confusing slide out of context.

Counterintuitively, object transitions are not found in the Transitions tab, but in the Animations tab. In the Advanced Animation section, turn on the Animation Pane. The Animation Pane shows the order of all animations on the slide.

Figure 23.33 - The Animation Pane

An animation has one of three trigger states: On Click, With Previous or After Previous. Each time the mouse is clicked, Powerpoint will trigger the next animation on the Animation Pane list labeled as "On Click". Any animation listed as "With Previous" will also play. After that animation is done, any animation listed as "After Previous" plays. The animations stop when the next "On Click" is hit on the list. Powerpoint then waits for the next click to trigger.

The figures after the names in the animation pane are a timeline of sorts. If the animation takes a long time, this effect is much more noticeable, but since we are using instant appears and disappears, you will not be able to easily notice this.

Now we will create a slide with a number of animation transitions to show this effect. It will look like this:

Figure 23.34 - Powerpoint Animation Example

Create these boxes and then assign the events stated in the text box to each. You assign the events by selecting the object and then clicking "Add Animation" in the Advanced Animation section of the Animations tab.

You will be presented with a large number of animation types: Entrance Animations deal with how the element comes on screen, Emphasis Animations move or change the element on screen and Exit Animations remove the element from the screen.

Even though I have lectured on only using Appear and Disappear, highlight all of your objects, select Add Animation and give them a slow, annoying entrance animation like "Grow & Turn". This is for demonstration purposes only.

Figure 23.35 - A Gluttony of Options

Now that all eight of your boxes have animation, it is time to change when these animations trigger. For each box from one to eight, select it and then go to where it says "Start" in the Timing section of the Animations pane. Duration allows you to extend the length of these animations (in seconds) if you really hate your audience.

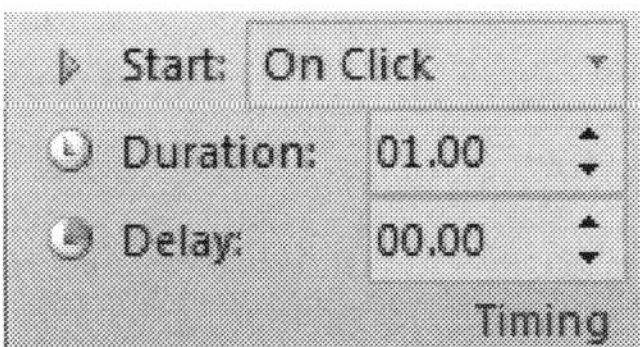

Figure 23.36 - Timing

Change each one to what I have listed in the diagram above. When you are done, the squares in your animation pane that form a rudimentary timeline should look like the order I positioned them in the above diagram.

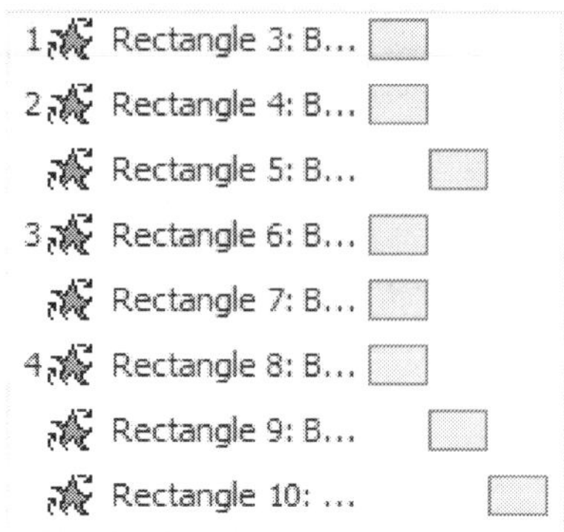

Figure 23.37 - Final Animation Pane

Run the slide show. Each time you click, the animations will trigger until they hit the next number listed in the animations pane. Watch how "With Previous" animations occur simultaneously and "After Previous" animations wait.

You are now a slide transition and animation master. Carry your knowledge with great responsibility.

Why Sound Is (Almost) Never a Good Idea

Sound offers a lot of opportunities to sink your presentation.

What happens often is that the presenter did not test the speakers beforehand and so the sound blares at 130dB. The audience flinches, the presenter scrambles to figure out how to mute, eventually forwarding the slide and everyone takes a sigh of relief like they just missed a car crash. It will take a few minutes for the audience to recover and start paying attention again.

Or the speakers don't work at all and the presenter fumbles and goes back and forth trying to get the sound to play, wasting the audience's time.

Or the presenter succeeds and stands there with a cheesy grin on his or her face.

None are really helpful.

In presentations about music, or where sounds must be heard to convey the instructional or emotional content, then by all means use sounds that are not part of the standard sounds shipped with Powerpoint. But make sure that you test the room in which you are presenting beforehand to ensure that the equipment works and the volume levels are appropriate. Test early enough that you can find help if things are broken or have the time to move your presentation as a last resort.

Here is how you attach sounds in Powerpoint 2010[44].

At the far right of the Insert tab is the Audio option. You are given three options: Audio from File, Clip Art Audio and Record Audio.

Figure 23.38 - Audio Options

"Audio from File" is the one you generally want to use. "Clip Art Audio" should never be used. "Record Audio" is useful in specific situations where you do not already have a recording to use. If you are presenting live, whatever audio you can record at home could probably be better done live at the presentation if possible.

Select the file you wish to add and a speaker icon will appear on your presentation. Once the speaker is selected, you can click over to the Audio Tools Playback tab to find a number of useful options including whether to start the audio with the slide (Automatically), or on clicking the speaker icon (On Click). Additionally, you can loop the sound to play continuously. Your audio clip will appear in the Animation Pane if you want to fine-tune when the sound starts.

If you only want to use part of your audio file, you can right-click on the speaker icon and select "Trim Audio" or select "Trim Audio" from the Audio Tools Playback tab. This is recommended to cut down on the file size of the presentation.

---

[44] As always, these instructions are for the latest and greatest version of Powerpoint. In older versions, sound was easier to find. In older versions, the Sound menu is found under Insert, then "Movies and Sounds", then "From File".

Embedding Fonts

A Princeton study published in the journal *Cognition* recently found that retention is enhanced when text is presented using non-standard typefaces. This suggests that using simple easily-legible fonts (like the one used for this book) actually act *against* cognition because they allow the eyes to read too quickly whereas more non-standard fonts make the brain slow down and process what it is reading.

I am not wholly convinced, but there is much to be said about using interesting typefaces in your slide presentations. An attractive and unusual font can draw plenty of attention:

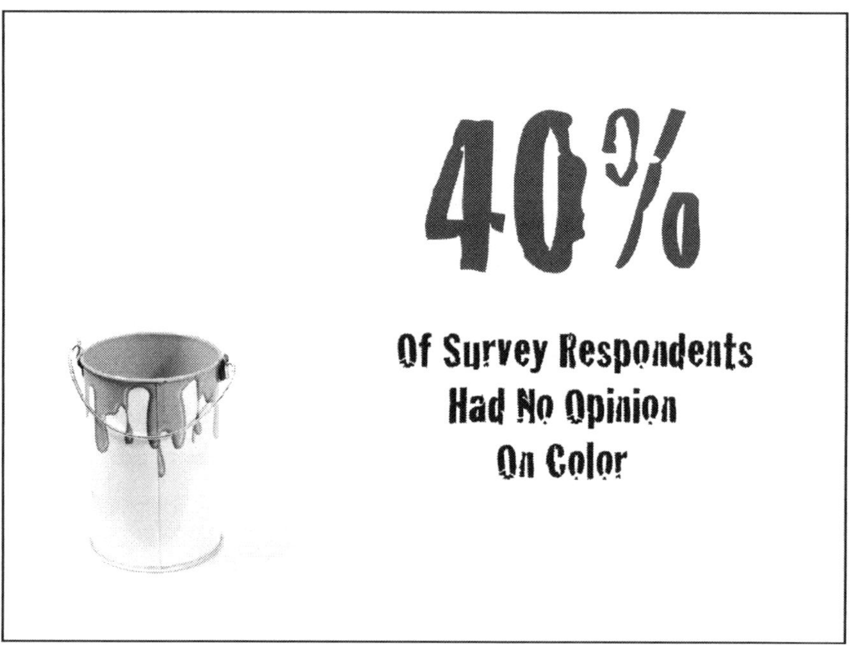

Figure 23.39 - A Slide with a Non-Standard Font

However, when you move your Powerpoint file around to a presentation room computer, you cannot be certain that the presentation computer has the same fonts. You may be surprised to find your text transformed from your perfect typeface to plain and boring Arial!

You can avoid this in Powerpoint by **embedding** your fonts into the Powerpoint file. What this does is save the font file with the presentation. Only certain types of fonts (TrueType fonts with proper licensing) can be saved, so it is best to test your embedding attempt on another computer (or best: the presentation computer) before entrusting that your fonts will look correct.

Note that each font you embed will increase the size of the presentation and can do so drastically if done carelessly. If you plan on emailing your slides, this is a concern you will have to consider.

To embed your fonts, go into Options from the File tab and select the Save Options dialog. Here you can choose to embed the whole font or only the characters you use. If you don't plan on changing anything in the presentation on other computers, you can embed only the characters. Otherwise, you need to embed the whole font. When embedding the whole font, this can add megabytes per font, so use wisely.

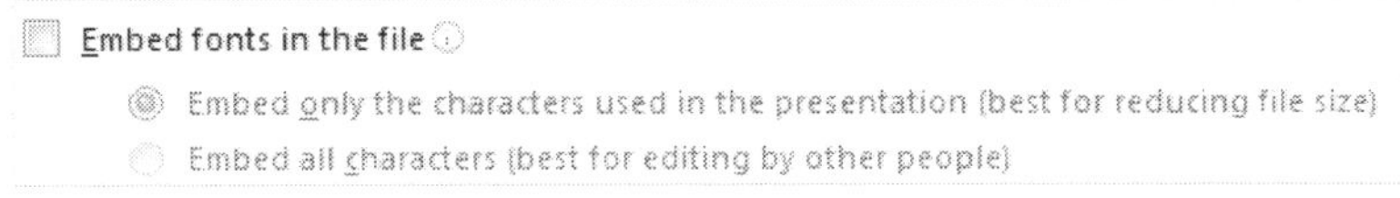

Figure 23.40 - Save Options

The Black Slide Button

At least once in your presenting career you will reach a point where you are on a roll, riffing on ideas and generally producing very valuable content. But you look out on your audience and everyone has their eyes fixed on a slide as if it was a jack-in-the-box ready to pop.

"Hi? Eyes up here? I'm saying cool stuff!" You may want to scream out loud. But that would make you look egotistical. You don't really want them to focus on you, but on your message. If they are not paying attention, there is a built-in tool in Powerpoint that can get your audience to snap back to you with limited jarring. I use it often.

This is the Black/White Slide Button. Press B or W (respectively) and the current slide switches to all black or all white. Your audience then goes all-eyes-on-you because their visual obsession has been removed. It works wonders! Then, when you are ready to move on, press B or W again to toggle back to the slide you were on or space or right arrow to advance the slide as normal.

Pecha Kucha and Practicing

Pecha Kucha (pronounced peh-CHAK-cha) is an interesting method of presentation developed in Japan in 2003. In what is called a Pecha Kucha night, twelve presenters present on twelve topics. They are accompanied by a slide presentation of twenty slides set to automatically advance every twenty seconds[45]. Every presentation is designed to last exactly six minutes and forty seconds (although some go over slightly).

The format is specifically designed to keep presenters brief and on point without the crutch of Powerpoint safety. It is certainly not for presentations on deep topics. But the constraint is actually quite liberating. Presenters will focus more on their unique point and selling it versus the libraries of ancillary information.

When you first set out to try a presentation like this, it will be really difficult. "How will I sync up the words to my slides if they automatically switch?" "How will I fit everything I need to say in without sounding like a rambling loon?" And admittedly, it is difficult, which is partially why it is a worthwhile exercise. After you give your first successful Pecha Kucha, you will start to see all of your longer form presentations in a similar light. You will, perhaps subconsciously, get used to editing your content down to only the important bits.

In short, you will become a better presenter.

And if it seems like I repeat mantras over and over again, there is one particular one that is a universal truth for designers: practice makes perfect. Pecha Kucha is one of the most interesting and entertaining ways to practice the art of presentation preparation and delivery. As of this writing there were Pecha Kucha events in over 400 cities worldwide. You can find a nearby event and volunteer to participate by going to http://www.pecha-kucha.org.

---

[45] For a great introduction to this format, see Daniel Pink's Pecha Kucha presentation on signage: http://www.youtube.com/watch?v=9NZOt6BkhUg

Setting Up Auto Advance

In Powerpoint, setting your slideshow to automatically advance for a Pecha Kucha presentation is easy. First, select all of your slides so that these changes apply to every slide:

Figure 23.41 - Select All Slides

Next, on the Transitions tab, locate the Timing section on the far right. Here, click the checkbox next to "After" and change the time to twenty seconds or whatever your limitation is. If you deselect the checkbox next to "On Mouse Click" you won't accidentally click forward in your presentation, but you also won't be able to skip ahead without using the arrow keys.

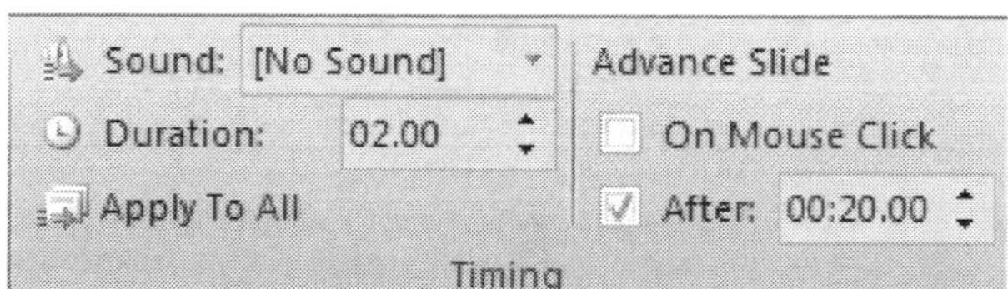

Figure 23.42 - Timing

That's it. Test your slides before you present to make sure that the timings are correct.

Printing Presentations / Handouts

Many presenters will put everything they want to say on their slides. Presenters who see themselves as more savvy will put what they want to say in their notes and hand the slides and notes out to their audience beforehand. Unfortunately, this is just as bad as reading your slides aloud.

Never just print your slides out and give them to your audience.

Again, remember: your audience can read faster than you can talk. If you think there is value to what you are presenting, then you are going against your purpose by handing out slides or notes beforehand. The audience will spend their time flipping ahead in the notes instead of hearing your pitch.

But often handouts are expected. There are three ways to handle this:

1. Buck the trend.

Abstain from giving out handouts at all. This is risky. Do you have a message that you want your audience to take home with them? By not giving handouts, you put a lot of pressure on delivering a message that sticks in their warm, mushy brains. You will only have that one chance to convey your message.

2. Give the standard handouts, but give them after your talk.

In your print settings, you can direct Powerpoint to print out "handouts" that consist of your slides and notes. But this too has caveats. If you are part of a string of presenters, you may not have the audience's attention when you try to give your handouts. Since your slides are useless without your narration and your notes are for you personally, this presentation format will likely be hard to comprehend.

3. Create a separate handout document.

This I consider to be the best solution in cases where handouts are expected. Create a document that effectively gives your argument without you present. Include supporting charts and/or pictures. Write this as if it were a magazine article. It needs to be concerned with flow just like your presentation proper because it needs to sell your ideas just as hard as your presentation. Try your best to fit your argument and support on one page if possible. Include your contact information if your audience has questions or wants to connect. The only major caveat to this system is that it takes more time to create three sets of supporting materials: your slides, your notes and their handouts.

But by going the extra mile with your preparation, you will not only be ensuring that your audience leaves with your idea firmly understood, but also that you will be fully prepared having gone through the idea's presentation in two wholly different ways. Once you finish the handout, you should know your argument inside and out.

Imagine the audience's relief: they have just sat through a presentation that takes forever, they've paged through the speaker's handout five times, checked their phones nine times and are watching the speaker struggle with reading his slides aloud and making his text animations trigger properly. Then you come on stage! Your message is clear and concise and you don't waste the audience's time. Your ideas are presented in a novel way and the key points are enumerated on an attractive handout. Given the same quality of ideas, which one will your audience be more excited about?

Chapter 24 - Powerpoint Case Study

At this point I would like to go over a particular example of slides that could be improved. Unfortunately, the non-interactive nature of the textbook limits me to showing just some of the slides and not the presentation itself, but I will try to make some delivery notes.

The following is part of a real deck from a real presentation from a real company. This was a rushed presentation, so it was not necessarily the lack of skill involved that caused the presentation to be so mediocre but it illustrates common threads that are wrong in many presentations I see. Names and images have been changed or blurred to protect the mostly innocent.

I will show you three slides. Try to write down everything you think is wrong with these slides and then flip forward to find my opinion that is informed by both the slides and the delivery. I'll give you a hint: most of the errors are the twelve don'ts I gave in Chapter 22.

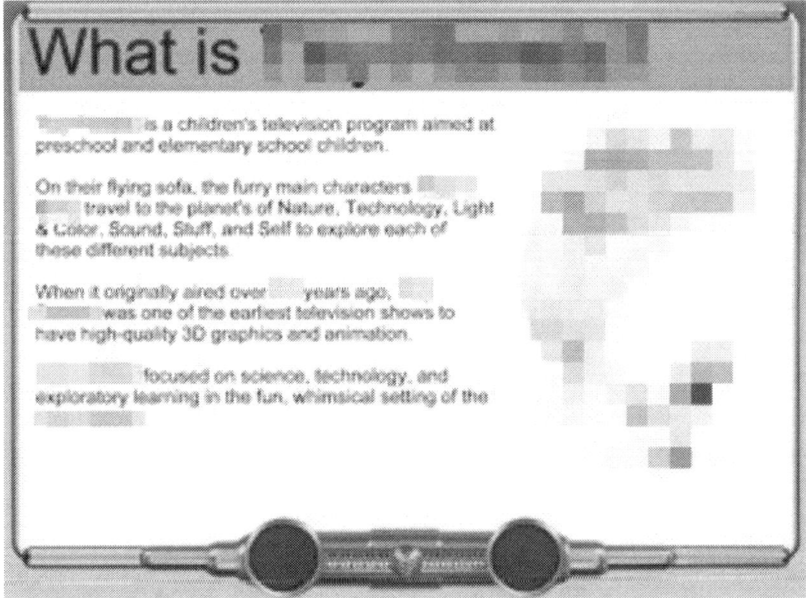

Figure 24.1 - A Redacted Intro Slide

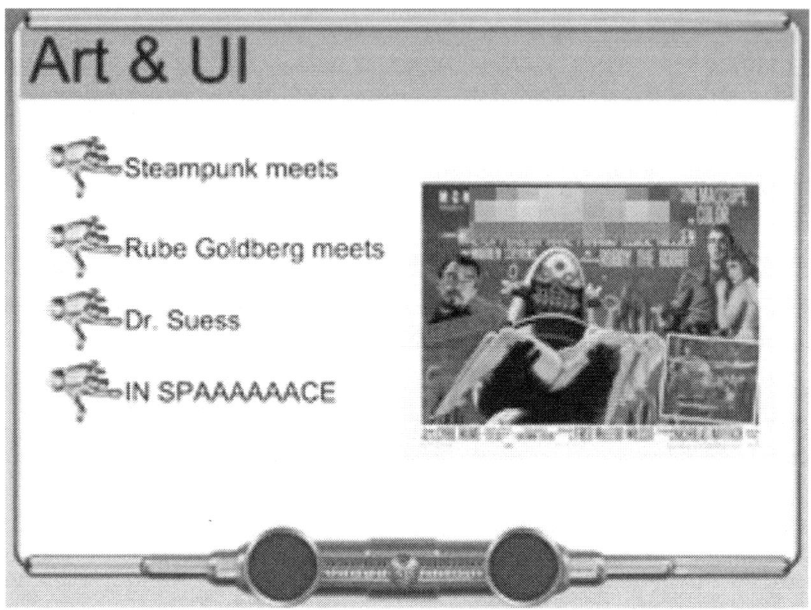

Figure 24.2 - Art Influences, One Per Slide

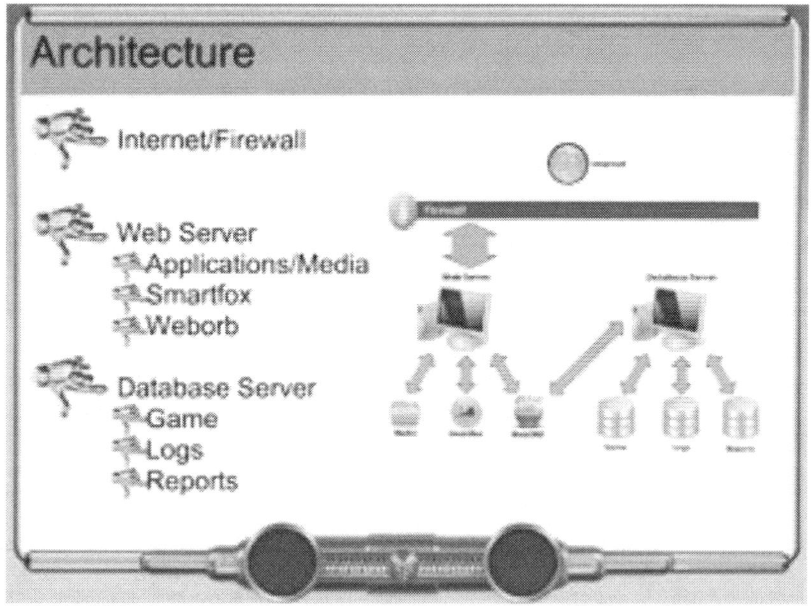

Figure 24.3 - Architecture Slide

What could be better here? Let's look at which of our 12 "Don'ts" were pushed or violated.

1. Don't Read Your Slides Aloud: With so much text on the slides, the presenters just turned around, faced the screen (no!) and read the slides aloud. They didn't have to, but the construction of their slides made it an easy crutch.

2. Don't Make Your Points Through Your Slides, Have Your Slides Reference Your Points: Again, with so much text the presenter was barely needed. With the possible exception of the architecture slide, every slide in the presentation can be grokked without the presenter making the point.

3. Don't Use Text: Already referenced, but text was a primary driver throughout this presentation. What is disappointing is that the property being talked about was based off of a kid's show. The presenters could have easily added video clips to play on the Intro slide while he or she talked about what the property was.

4. Don't Meander, Have a Theme: As is often the case with team presentations, the workload gets split up and so each presenter talks about their silo of the project without ever bringing it back to a wider message. After the presentation, I knew about what they went through, but not what they learned.

6. Don't Make Your Text and Images Hard to Read: This presentation was delivered to a packed room. No one could read the text of the Intro slide in the back. I should know; that's where I was. Look at the Architecture Slide. Would that diagram be easy to read from the back of the room?

10. Don't Act Neutral: This presentation was about a tough project that took the team over two years. You would think that they would be eager to show the best parts and the craziest failures. Yet this presentation is laid out by a template to be just like every other one of its kind. Do the slides reflect excitement to you? How about the template?

11. Don't Waste Ink: Look at the Architecture Slide. Not only is there a bullet point (an overwrought much-too-large one) for every element in the architecture, but also the elements are labeled *again* in the diagram. What is the point of the bulleted list at all?

12. Don't Repeat Boring Information: For the Art Influences Slides, the presenter showed four slides, with one image for each influence along with a bulleted list on the side. Thus, only a small portion of the slide actually showed what the influences were. Most of the slide was white space, accoutrements like the ornate bullets or text. Why not have all four inspiration images on one slide? From there the audience can make connections to how the four are related. Then show how those influences are evident in the game.

Artistically, the color scheme is all over the board with neon greens, blacks, whites, brass tones and big blue circles on the center of each screen bottom for some reason. All these competing colors wrestle for the eye's attention.

But the most glaring problem with the presentation is not on the don'ts list and cannot be seen at all. The team never showed the game. Here is a presentation about a successful game launch in a niche in which the audience is likely unfamiliar, and we never get to see how the game works.

Naturally with more time and experience, some of these issues may have been ironed out. But a well-prepared presentation doesn't necessarily require a big time spend. It only requires planning. By putting yourself in the eyes of the audience and understanding what they may be thinking or how they may wander from your point, you can best plan an effective presentation that keeps them focused and interested.

Chapter 25 - Other Documents

Feature Overviews

We have spent time on creating GDDs that are crafted for the most important folks: those actually making the game. Another group of stakeholders rank right up there: the folks holding the purse strings. These are your executive producers, your studio managers, your publishers, your licensors and so forth. They often ask for design documents when what they really want are **design overviews**.

The distinction is simple: design overviews are meant to be read as one would read an article where design documents are meant to be read as a to-do list. You can supply both to the non-hands-on stakeholders, but they will generally find a design overview more useful.

Why put this in the section about pitching and not in the section about Word? Because you structure a design overview the same way you would structure a verbal pitch, which is often why these are called **feature overviews**.

In a feature overview, you are selling the story of each individual feature or idea. Give the explanation for each feature as you would conversationally. Treat it as if it were a description given in a detailed game review rather than the stark scannable design document.

For instance, take a GDD from an earlier section. For Chili Cookoff, we would not necessarily have the bulleted list of features. A feature overview or design overview might look like this.

Chili Cookoff - This event is part of the design goal of making multiplayer active events available to all classes. (Previous event proposals clearly favored warriors and wizards.) In this case, the event clearly favors herbalists, clerics and cooks.

From 3-5 players start the event and add a number of ingredients that they have found on their journeys to a Chili Recipe. Each event will have a different makeup of NPC judges that favor a particular class of ingredient. By tasting the chili during preparation, the user can deduce if he is going in a correct direction. This adds a puzzle-solving element to the event along with an exploration element where users will hold onto interesting ingredients for their future chili cookoffs.

Winners will receive gold and experience bonuses. These events are watchable by spectators, who can learn what techniques can help them win.

Notice immediate differences between this and the GDD:

- The feature overview does not go into specifics. An engineer could not implement from this. How much does a player win? What screens will he/she see? But someone who cares about the overall scope and goals of the feature (producers, publishers, licensors) will have their questions answered.
- The feature overview is written in a manner that captures goals and reasoning. Engineers don't necessarily care about this, but external groups do. Remember to always write for your audience.
- The feature overview does not answer every question, but lets the readers fill in the blanks. This is important. Go into too much detail and external groups will quarrel with you over values and specifics. These arguments are rarely helpful because by the time the feature is implemented, playtesting will have negated your original guesses of numbers that you placed in the original GDD. Give only enough to satisfy and anticipate arguments, no more.
- The feature overview identifies the what-is, what-could-be gap when applicable. In this example case, the game didn't have events for herbalists. This gives herbalists a chance to participate in something directly related to their skills.

Given these differences, you can see why feature overviews are more informational for groups that do not care about the minutiae of the design but do care about the overall system.

Crafting a careful design overview can save a lot of time wasted by either having to explain a well-crafted GDD to an external stakeholder or having to explain a superfluous feature overview to an engineer that just wants a GDD. If you have external groups that check in often, both need to be vigilantly maintained.

Pitch Documents

We have covered the game design document and the best practices that help it to be created. But we haven't discussed a document that is often called a "game design document" but shares little with what we have been discussing: the "pitch document".

The pitch document is larger than a feature overview. The pitch document is a summary of what the game is about as a whole and is used to show the basics of a game idea to an external group or is just used to have the internal team reach agreement on a direction. It is sometimes called the "high concept". It is not the game design document because it doesn't tell anyone exactly what to design, only a description of what it will look like when it is done. It is the difference between the blueprints to a Camaro and a brochure for the Camaro.

Generally, the pitch document will briefly cover some standard points. Don't use this as a template, however. Tell the story of your game's targeted development in a way that is natural for you and the audience. Here are some of the standard points covered in many pitch documents:

Setting/Genre: What type of game is this? What kind of world is the game set in? This is more of a game mechanics focused question than a story question. If your game is a shooter, is it a military shooter like *Call of Duty*, a simulator like *Arma*, or an arcade shooter like *Bulletstorm*?

Story: In very broad strokes, what does the player do in this game? How is he/she part of a world?

Characters: Who/what do you play as? Who else is in the world?

Hook: What is the unique selling proposition for the game? Is it mechanics? Story? Tech? **There has to be a hook**. This section is not optional. This needs to be in the pitch early and often. Remember when we talked about theme of a presentation? This should be your theme. "We are going to be better than our competitors" is a meaningless theme. That's every team's goal and is not a unique selling proposition.

Major Features: Take your best Feature Overviews and show them in the pitch. Features are what make the game!

Play Example: This is a short walkthrough of what the player will experience. Teams with the resources often do this in the form of a video. It is important to know what the player actually will do.

Comparison to Competitors: This is usually needed when talking to business folk at the studio or publisher level. What games will your game be compared to? How did these games sell? How were they received critically? How will we exploit their successes and mitigate their mistakes?

Development Risks: Don't be a Pollyanna; every project has risks. Be upfront about them. Has a design never been tried before? Are you going up against a behemoth in your industry? Do you have a team inexperienced with the genre or platform? Identify the risks and how your team will handle them. This is the same as in our pitching instructions. Anticipate your enemies and defeat their arguments before they are raised. Your risk management plan must stand up to scrutiny and must be realistic. Have Plan Bs at the ready. Even if you are doing an indie project or a game for a class, these questions are important to answer so that you can plan for unforeseen events. Student projects have risks too: risks of scope, of mastery, of technical events, of life events. How will your team handle them?

Timeline: How long will this project take? When will consumers be able to buy it? What are the major milestones? What is the QA plan? When will extra hiring take place? Anyone interested in the financial side will demand this. You may not be able to answer, so team up with folks that can answer these questions.

A pitch document is different for every team. For instance, characters and setting are irrelevant in sports simulations. But external stakeholders are similar wherever you go. Be able to answer all the questions posed above thoroughly in a pitch document and you will be more prepared than most teams who jump in without looking.

Exercises

1. Go to TED.com and watch some of the presentations there that touch on topics that interest you. Focus on the presentation style. How is the presenter interacting with the audience? What do his or her slides look like, if any? How does his or her presentation flow?

2. Create a presentation on any element of your life story to this point. You may write no more than two words on any one slide and no more than ten in the whole presentation.. Record this presentation. What slides did you choose? Where do you stumble? Why did you structure the presentation the way you did? Does it have a beginning, middle and end? Does it tell a story? What features of Powerpoint did you use to help better tell the story?

3. Create a Pecha Kucha presentation on any topic you wish. Deliver it with the principles outlined in this book. Review it when finished. Did you create something engaging? If not, either go back and try and deliver it again or start over with a new topic. Practice makes perfect.

Summary

- Pitching is about delivering a message to your audience in the most effective means possible.
- If you are spending more time on the flash of your presentation than on the organization of the message of your presentation, you are doing it wrong.
- Limit the number of words you put on screen when presenting.
- Don't read your presentation to your audience.
- You are the focal point, not your slides. The slides are there to augment your presentation not to give it.
- Your slides are not speaker notes.
- Assume that you should never use bullet points, clip art, slide transitions, sound or video in your presentation unless there is no alternative.
- You should create three artifacts for most presentations. In order of importance: your personal speaker notes, your document to hand out afterwards to the audience and then your slides.

Part Five – Get Your Hands Dirty

Chapter 26 – On Being Done

In the opening chapter of *Art of Game Design*, Jesse Schell claims it is easy to become a game designer. He advises to simply say "I'm a game designer" and then let yourself create games. Both aspects are essential.

Many "game designers" I know no longer make games. They talk about games, they manage game projects, they play games but they don't make them. They have been game designers in the past but no longer make games. It is a problem I deal with now that I am an educator as a matter of self-identity.

Some self-styled game designers rarely make games. I ran into a few in my time at EA, but they are in every big company. They make some game-related decisions, but they are really producers, making decisions about teams and feature priority and so forth. They don't make stuff, they make decisions *about* making stuff.

You cannot be a game designer that doesn't actually make stuff.

Some folks are on the other end. They make games all the time, but don't call themselves game designers. Nearly every engineer I have worked with has been a game designer, but refuses to call him or herself one. They make decisions about how the game will play, run and feel. How are they not game designers? They just do not believe that they are.

By reading this book, you are likely okay with calling yourself a game designer. Part one is complete.

Part two is the rub.

Go make games.

In this section, I'll point you to some ways you can get your hands dirty by exploring some tools that let you directly make games. Some require no programming knowledge. Others require a pinch of scripting. Some are so extensible that few developers have tackled all of the intricacies of the platform.

Don't expect to knock it out of the park on your first pitch. You'll make some embarrassingly bad games. Most designers have the insight to see that a game will be bad at some point before the game is finished. What do they do when they reach this point?

Usually, they quit and start something new.

That's one of the biggest mistakes you can make. You have to write a novel to be a novelist. You are not a *novel*ist if you've written a few sentences. You are a *sentence*-ist or a *chapter*-ist at best. If you haven't finished a game, how can you be a game designer?

"Nobody tells this to people who are beginners, I wish someone told me. All of us who do creative work, we get into it because we have good taste. But there is this gap. For the first couple years you make stuff, it's just not that good. It's trying to be good, it has potential, but it's not. But your taste, the thing that got you into the game, is still killer. And your taste is why your work disappoints you. A lot of people never get past this phase, they quit." - Ira Glass

Finish what you start. This will teach you things that no book on design can ever teach you. Release these bad games to the wild. Trust me. You can take them down later if you get famous.[46] In the meanwhile, get comments from friends and strangers. You will grow as a designer.

And when you are at a party and someone asks you what you do, you can say you are a game designer. And when they follow that up by asking you what you've designed, you can give them titles (it doesn't matter that they will never have heard of them) instead of sputtering and saying you've never actually finished anything.

It is very easy to talk about games - what makes them fun, not fun, frustrating, memorable, placid, jovial, stuttering, important, trivial, whatever. It is a whole other level actually making them.

Go forth and create.

---

[46] Although nothing is ever truly deleted from the Internet, the amount of useful feedback you can get on these early games is worth potential future embarrassment. After all, if you don't get better now, you can't be a superstar later!

Unreal Development Kit

The juggernaut in engines at the time of this writing is Epic's Unreal Development Kit (UDK). UDK is based on Unreal Engine 3 that is used in dozens of AAA titles such as the *Gears of War* series, *Bulletstorm*, *Infinity Blade*, the *Tom Clancy's Rainbow Six: Vegas* series, the *Mass Effect* series, and the *Batman: Arkham* series.

At first it can seem a bit daunting that these incredibly complex games are created with UDK. After all, you are just one person without years of complex training behind you (yet). UDK is a deep and complicated tool. But if you want to jump into something that will make your resume stand out, something that is of direct use to industry, UDK is your best bet. The tradeoff comes in the learning curve and the resources needed to complete a full game.

One of the most innovative aspects of UDK is the Kismet visual scripting tool. Kismet requires no code knowledge. Elements and behaviors can be tied together visually to create complicated interactions. While other engines have elements that are drag-and-drop (GameMaker, Unity, &c.,) none are nearly as deeply integrated without the use of code as Kismet. Many other engines are attempting to make integrated (not plug-in) visual scripting editors that are as easy-to-use and comprehensive as Kismet, but time will tell if they meet the high bar set by Epic.

Due to the depth of features, (UDK has detailed animation, physics, terrain, networking, rendering systems and much, much more) Unreal can be a tough nut to crack. Where most open engines and languages have a library of books written about them, Unreal Engine 3 / UDK literature is fairly sparse. Luckily, the online communities do a yeoman's job of providing help and materials, but it does require moderate searching.

At the time of this writing, users can sell their games by paying a small registration fee. Epic will not require any royalties for using UDK as long as your game's revenues are below $50,000. This makes UDK the most powerful tool available for student projects. You have the same tools available to large studios without any of the strings attached. UDK is a free download on Epic's site and an active community supports new users with tutorials and forums (see resources below).

If you are not overwhelmed by the possibilities, UDK is the most professional tool available to students.

Resources

UDK Download - http://www.udk.com/download

3D Buzz UDK Tutorials - http://www.3dbuzz.com/vbforum/sv_videonav.php?fid=292838127fecccd8b151c72003546386

UDK Central (Wiki and Tutorials) - http://udkc.info/

Unreal Game Development - Ashish Amresh, A K Peters (2010)

Unity

One of Unreal's biggest competitors in the student market is Unity. Unity has come out of nowhere in the past few years to gain significant market share on a number of platforms. Like Unreal, Torque, Blender and other popular engines, Unity is fully contained in an integrated graphical environment.

Unlike Unreal, Unity runs on both Windows and Mac systems. One of Unity's strongest features is the ease of making web-embeddable executables using the Unity web player plugin. Unity supports most major platforms including the major consoles, Android and iOS devices.

Unity has significant support for 3D projects for all supported platforms. It lacks a graphical scripting engine similar to Unreal's Kismet and so detailed work in Unity must be done by scripting. Unity supports a number of methods for scripting, from using Unity's own UnityScript language to C# to variations on .NET and Python.

Unity features a softer learning curve than Unreal as long as the user is comfortable with scripting. The interface is generally seen to be more intuitive than UDK's. The Unity development team and community is highly supportive, active and growing every day.

Unfortunately, Unity doesn't play nice with normal free versioning software, so the company does try to sell Unity Asset Server for versioning versus Unreal that builds the technology into every release. 2D games can be made in Unity, but most of the features are designed with 3D in mind. Unreal is the same way but does include some help to 2D game designers.

Students can use the plain version of Unity for free and can publish to any licensed platform with the inclusion of splash screens or watermarks showing the Unity logo. The pro version of Unity removes the splash screens and watermarks and opens up vast libraries of features. Licenses for development on consoles, Android and iOS devices are additional purchases that can make developing a cross-platform game very expensive. Unlike Unreal, Unity does support the Nintendo Wii.

Many professional games use Unity. From the IGF student award winner *FRACT* to the web-based *Tiger Woods PGA Tour Online* to the popular puzzle platformer *Max and the Magic Marker* to advergames reaching millions, Unity has significant use in the industry.

Resources

Download Unity - http://unity3d.com/

3DBuzz Unity Tutorials - http://www.3dbuzz.com/vbforum/sv_videonav.php?fid=1ec1a7be9c0d4cf9e7a31525250a30ff

Unify Community Wiki - http://www.unifycommunity.com/wiki/index.php?title=Main_Page

Unity-Tutorials.com - http://unity-tutorials.com/

GameMaker

GameMaker, created by Mark Overmars and now sold by YoyoGames is an interesting and popular platform for burgeoning game designers due to its ability to make playable and executable games without requiring a single line of code and without the need for the player to download an interpreter of some sort to run the created game.

While not requiring code, GameMaker includes a powerful scripting language called (quite simply) GML or the Game Maker Language. Most games created with GameMaker are 2D in presentation, but GameMaker does support DirectX/OpenGL in-engine allowing for 3D games to be created.

Decidedly not flashy, GameMaker is one of the most polished and well-supported low-cost development engines in existence at the time of this writing. Additionally, it has both low economic and technical barriers to entry. Since it was made originally to teach game making, effort is focused on workflows that make sense to new developers without sacrificing power and flexibility for advanced users.

Unlike using a more professional tool such as the Unreal Development Kit or Unity, there are no restrictions on selling games made using GameMaker. The ability to publish GameMaker games to Sony's Playstation Portable, Apple's iOS devices and Android devices is in development.

The main drawbacks of GameMaker are less-intuitive 3D support and complete lack of any industry buy-in. GameMaker is strictly an indie tool.

Resources

The GameMaker Site - http://www.yoyogames.com/gamemaker/

Official GameMaker Tutorials - http://www.yoyogames.com/make/tutorials/

GameMaker for Beginners -
http://forums.tigsource.com/index.php?topic=3251.0

Video Overview of a Variety of GameMaker Games -
http://www.youtube.com/watch?v=bdgQyOIyWPY

Adobe Flash

Of course, everyone has played Adobe Flash-based games on the web and thus Flash's near-universal support on the web and devices (iOS notwithstanding) makes it one of the more recognized development environments.

But Flash's industry use doesn't stop at Kongregate.com or Facebook "social" games. Flash is used extensively for prototyping purposes in the AAA section of the industry and is even used in shipped titles for user interface. EA Sports' titles have used an interpreted version of Flash for many years. Other studios also still use Flash for HUD and UI elements. With the ascendancy of Autodesk's Scaleform, Flash's hegemony in this area is waning.

Flash was originally developed as an vector-based animation tool. The default view shows a "timeline" with "frames" and much of the nomenclature supports that view. Flash ships with a proprietary scripting language called ActionScript that was originally a barebones way to script animation sequences. This has since evolved into a full gaming-caliber scripting language capable of texture mapping, GPU rendering and other cutting-edge features. With ActionScript 3.0, even basic users never have to touch the timeline and can code a game completely from script.

Students learning ActionScript will be able to publish their games to the web. In order to view Flash games, users need Adobe's Flash Player, which is nearly ubiquitous in modern browsing. The notable exception, of course, is Apple and their iOS devices, which do not have a supported plugin for Flash content. Flash is also generally not used for AAA game development except in limited situations as mentioned above.

For those wishing to avoid scripting, Flash is not the tool for you. It has nothing like Unreal's Kismet or even the 3D integrated editor of Unity. It does have the flexibility to be used in applications beyond games and it is relatively easy to iterate on ideas once developers get over the initial learning curve. The ActionScript language is fully featured and makes it easy to place images, add physics and create user interfaces.

Another major drawback of Flash is price. While the Flash Player is free, the Flash development environment can cost hundreds of dollars for even the student editions. Also, the Flash IDE is notoriously prone to crashes and the debug environment for ActionScript is basic at best leading to long periods of fighting with the system versus evaluating and debugging.

There is a wide library of support manuals and tutorials for learning Flash and ActionScript and the community extends far beyond just game developers to encompass web developers, media developers and animators, allowing for a wide user base and differing perspectives on common problems. Even with the growth of alternatives, Flash is as popular and important as ever.

Resources

Foundation Game Design with Flash, Rex van der Spuy, Friends of ED.

Tutorialized Flash Tutorials -
http://www.tutorialized.com/tutorials/Flash/Games/1

Inform

If you are younger, you may not be acutely aware of the text adventure games that dominated the video game landscape in the 1980s. A text adventure strips down the interface to a written description and a prompt where a user can type text instructions to move the game along. The seminal text adventure, *Zork*, from 1981 starts thusly:

```
West of House
You are standing in an open field west of a white
house, with a boarded front door.
There is a small mailbox here.
```

The player is then presented with a bracket ">" as a prompt to type. He can type anything, but the interpreter will only understand certain commands. These commands generally are not enumerated for the user.

For instance, jump was recognized but in most cases did nothing:

```
>jump
Are you enjoying yourself?
```

Other verbs confound the engine and throw errors:

```
>contemplate philosophy
I don't know the word "contemplate".
```

Figuring out what to do was the main player challenge in these games.

Text adventure games waned in popularity when personal computers got powerful and cheap enough to display different genres of games that were more visually appealing (although the "why" of the decline of text adventures is disputed). But in the 90s and early 2000s, independent developers rekindled the love of text adventures with free and open development of text adventure engines. Competitions and communities have burgeoned development and the adventures coming out today have fantastic depth and are cutting-edge examples of storytelling in games.

While many languages/engines exist today, the premiere language/engine for text adventure development is Inform 7. Inform 7 is unique because it is designed to be programmed in natural language. The source code is very readable.

Here's source code from Emily Short's "Bronze":

```
The Scarlet Tower is southeast of the Scarlet Gallery.
"A little hexagonal room, from whose [narrow window]
you can see the moat, the lawn, and the beginning of
the forest outside."
The narrow window is scenery in the Scarlet Tower.
The outdoors is scenery in the Scarlet Tower.
Understand "moat" and "lawn" and "forest" as the
outdoors.
The description of the outdoors is "Beyond a short
stretch of clear ground, the forest grows thick and
uninhabited for many miles."
Instead of searching the narrow window, try examining
the outdoors.
The description of the narrow window is "It gives a
view of the forest beyond: the way you came from, in
fact."
```

From this, the language interpreter translates our natural language into game code. Inform's natural language source code should make it particularly appealing to designers who balk at programming. Additionally, designers interested in narrative and story should be drawn to Inform for practice.

Inform7.com has riches of tutorials on how to create text adventure games, so we will not cover this. See "Writing with Inform" and "The Inform 7 Handbook." Most interactive fiction works are free and source is available. Check out the entries from The Interactive Fiction Competition (ifcomp.org) and the XYZZY Awards for inspiration and support.

Text adventures provide some of the quickest and easiest ways to experiment with setting, form, dialogue and tone.

Resources

Inform 7 Homepage - http://Inform7.com
Interactive Fiction Competition - http://Ifcomp.org
IF Writer Emily Short's blog - http://emshort.wordpress.com

Ren'Py

If you would like to get a little more visual than text adventures, but still stay in a simple and heavily narrative form, perhaps you should check out the awkwardly named Ren'Py Visual Novel Engine. The "Ren" part come from Ren'ai, the Japanese term for the dating simulation genre and the "Py" part comes from Python, the common scripting language usable in engine.

Dating simulation is a popular genre in Japan where you choose what to say to a number of suitors in the hopes of gaining dates. There's an entire subculture based on these games that I suggest you do not Google. Ren'Py has deeper roots than just this genre and is able (with the help of some Python scripting) to do more in-depth simulation than a standard choose-your-own adventure.

Ren'Py excels at dialogue-heavy games. The main ease of use comes from the simplicity of displaying images and dialogue choices. Look at this simple scene from a Ren'Py script:

```
label sceneatstore:

    scene bg store

    with dissolve

    show zack confused

    "I can't find a game I like."

    clerk "Well, that sounds like a problem of
    taste, doesn't it?"

    show zack angry at right

    clerk "Sorry. Which game do you want?"

    menu:

            "Call of War Game"

                    jump callofwargame

            "Final Quest Warrior XXVII"

                    jump rpg
```

```
            "None. Leave in a rage."
                  jump correctanswer
```

This would require a lot more overhead in a more broad engine like Flash because in Ren'Py the event listeners, menu systems, image display functions, transitions, sound libraries and save/load systems are provided for you.

Images can be tagged like in the above example, all "zack" images are declared at the start to have keywords. Images can be moved by declaring them "at right" or in other keyword positions. Transitions can be called by name. Until you've used an engine without these features, you will not appreciate how useful this can be.

Ren'Py is completely free and there are no licensing agreements necessary to sell your games.

However, documentation and support are sparse due to the small user-base and the integration of native script and Python script can be confusing. Ren'Py has little use outside of its narrow genre.

Resources

Ren'Py Download - http://www.renpy.org/

Ren'Py Documentation - http://www.renpy.org/doc/html/index.html

Ren'Py User Forum - http://lemmasoft.renai.us/forums/viewforum.php?f=8

ZZT

Epic "Megagames" may be known today for *Gears of War*, the Unreal Engine and mind-blogging displays of technical wizardry, but in 1991, Epic released a very primitive-looking game that would inspire a generation of designers (your present author included). That game was called ZZT.

The games included with ZZT were quite primitive. Characters and objects were made out of ANSI characters (essentially just text and symbols) that move around the map and could interact with each other. The player character is always a smiley face symbol.

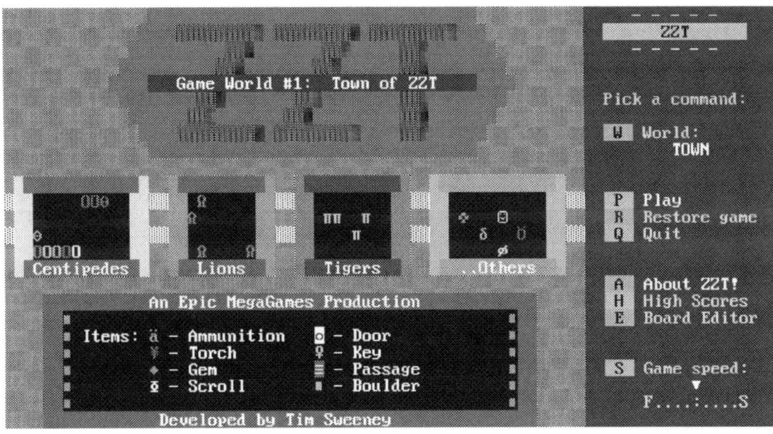

Figure 26.1 - Town of ZZT

ZZT thrived however due to the inclusion of a level creator and a simple scripting language called ZZT-OOP. Using under fifty commands, users have been able to create vastly interesting worlds in different genres. Many are top-down shooters, but RPGs, platformers and puzzle games are possible.

ZZT-OOP is simple to learn.

```
:SHOT

#GO OPP PLAYER

#SET FLAG NPCangry

#PLAY Q3BBB
```

```
Hey, Don't Do That, Jerk!
I'm serious!
```

This is code that would tell an object placed in the world that when it is shot, to run away from the player a step, set a variable that the object is now angry, play a sound effect and then show a text box voicing the NPC's displeasure.

The very nature of its constrained scripting language lets creators bootstrap simple commands into complex behaviors. Nearly every notable ZZT release in a twenty year-old active community of ZZT creators is more complex and interesting than the initial levels packed in by Tim Sweeney in 1991. These serve as a great first start to script programming because it is difficult to be bogged down by complex interface when that interface doesn't exist!

While ZZT is extremely niche, even more so than Inform, it can still be used as an exercise in basic scripting. Some ZZT games ship "unlocked" which means their source code can be viewed and edited. Some are locked, but can be unlocked with external software.

ZZT games require the original ZZT executable to run and are thus rarely packaged as standalone games.

Resources

Z2, a ZZT Community - http://zzt.belsambar.net/

ZZT Heaven -
http://www.autofish.net/video_games/creation/zzt/zgames.html

Indie Developer Auntie Pixelante's Recommended ZZT Games -
http://www.auntiepixelante.com/?p=443

Board Games

Perhaps you were taken aback by this section header? Here we are talking about IDEs with development costs in the millions and yet I bring up board games?

Indeed I do.

Many games are about decision-making, about analysis, about math, statistics, flow, psychology, participation.

Good board games incorporate many of these elements.

As we talked about in the analog prototyping chapter, the bonus to making board games is speed. Without having to learn a new development environment and language, I can use some dice, markers and paper to create an idea for a multiplayer environment in a few minutes versus a few days in digital form. If I want to make changes, I just scratch out some rules instead of having to re-code and track down bugs.

The drawbacks to board games (or analog games) is of course, the lack of scalability and the lack of immersion. Board games need to be physically published to get them into the hands of many, whereas a Flash game can be put on a server and enjoyed by millions overnight. And board games require player imagination whereas digital games can often be quite literal in showing the player what is happening.

Many digital proponents scoff at analog games for being niche partial fulfillments of the spectacle that video games can perform. They downplay their importance. To them I have two words: *Dungeons and Dragons*.

Rare is the game that does not cite *Dungeons and Dragons* among its influences either in feel or in mechanics. We have covered the d20 system earlier, but what is your modern shooter but a twitch-based version of a ranged *Dungeons and Dragons* battle? What is your modern RPG but a DM-less module? *Dungeons and Dragons* did not require million-dollar voice actors or teraflop-processing multi-core CPUs. It required pen, paper, people and books.

Figure 26.2 - Board Games are More Than What You May Think

European Influence

We can thank Klaus Teuber for the innovation in modern board gaming that in recent years has extended to the digital medium. In 1995, his *Settlers of Catan* instantly sparked an international interest in strategic board games with rich dynamic systems.

The explosion of the Internet and board game designer communities allowed for what was largely a European phenomenon to gain traction in the United States and other parts of the world. The central locus of the board gaming world is still in Essen, Germany at the Spiel festival where nearly every new European game is launched and where hundreds of hopeful designers come to have their game picked up by a publisher.

Features in Eurogames

Why are the so-called "eurogames" so popular?

No Player Elimination - Unlike Monopoly, Risk and other traditional board games, most Eurogames do not feature player elimination, keeping players engaged with the game until the end. This shows in a focus towards eliminating positive feedback loops so that even trailing players stay interested.

Minimized Levels of Luck - The hardest of the hardcore eurogamers abhor randomness in all forms, opting to determine victory by strategic and tactical excellence on its own. Most eurogames take a more measured stance but generally attempt to award victory based on the player's decisions rather than on the luck of the card draw or the luck of the die roll. Some games do have a high luck element that can be ameliorated by skilled play. This gives games a sense of learning and progression lost in truly luck-based games.

Systems Thinking - Eurogames often contain a number of interconnected systems. For instance, in *Power Grid* the supply and demand of fuel types affects the bids for power plants in the auction phase. This leads to highly emergent play, where decisions are important enough to have ripple effects across the entire game. Balance is a coveted feature as these games are meant to be highly replayable and not traditionally solvable.

Reverence Towards Design - Designers names are usually on the box of eurogames. Hobbyists can identify the feel of a game based on its designer just as film enthusiasts know what a Quentin Tarantino or Michael Bay movie will feel like. This shows a focus on craftsmanship and that the idea of the game is something personal and important.

But Why?

Most importantly, though. Why are these kinds of games helpful in becoming better designers?

Force Playtesting - In aiming to achieve balance, creating a board game requires the testing of multiple kinds of players. This testing is sometimes ignored in the solo or indie project realm but can mean the difference between an elegant collection of systems and a broken idea that was almost there.

Force Decision Making - In digital games, we can often hide the mechanics behind pretty art assets, cool character design, or impressive sound effects. In board games the systems are front and center and there is no hiding behind a pretty facade. This forces designers to make tough choices about game dynamics that could otherwise be ignored by stuffing them into some milieu that distracts from the game's faults.

Remove Affordances of Platform - When the Wii first came out and low-quality shovelware was selling like hotcakes, many designers were confused. Why was such dreck selling so well? The shovelware was not any better than anything else on the platform!

What they missed was the novelty of the platform itself. It was fun to use the Wii controller whatever game was played. Even if the attached game was bad, if it leveraged what affordances made the Wii itself fun, it could succeed. Phone games for the longest time were crap, but because of the novelty of playing something on your phone, companies could sell millions of dollars in crummy poker and bowling games. Board games can't hide behind the novelty of platform. Their success must hinge on the power of the system itself.

If this sounds hard, it is! Despite record-breaking sales year after year, it is very hard to get a board game to market unless you finance it yourself. This requires your game ideas to be executed flawlessly. The leg up you have on competition is that you can test your ideas quickly and inexpensively where they will have to struggle with code and technical bugaboos.

Where Do I Start?

Many gamers simply do not know this niche of the hobby was out there. In order to get a good start, it can be helpful to know what some of the successes are. Unlike dealing with Unreal or Unity, there is no comprehensive tutorial to learn how to make board games. All you can do is look at other's successes and brainstorm from there. It can be expensive to procure these games as they come in small print runs compared to *Monopoly* and *Operation*.

Here is a short list of my favorite titles to get you started:

Dominion, Donald X. Vaccarino, 2009, Rio Grande Games

If you have ever played *Magic: the Gathering* before, you will be familiar with some of the structure behind *Dominion*. Whereas in *Magic*, you build a deck before the game, in *Dominion* the deck building is the game. Players all start with the same deck of money and victory cards and use them to buy new cards from a common pool to build synergies in their decks that allow them to continually buy bigger and better things. There are a number of clever mechanics in play foremost of which is that the cards needed to win the game (victory point cards) are mostly useless during the game, leading players to determine when to slow growth in exchange for gaining points.

Settlers of Catan, Klaus Teuber, 1995, Kosmos

Mentioned earlier, *Settlers* has all of the hallmarks of the eurogame industry. Players race to control the resources of an island in an attempt to build the most settlements and cities. Trading is a key aspect of Settlers and leads to a number of tactical decisions - should I build somewhere where I can get wood or should I just count on one of my opponents trading me wood? Repeated games can get dull as some decisions can be made on autopilot, but expansions help avoid falling into the same ruts.

Figure 26.3 - Settlers of Catan is © Catan GmbH. Photo by Flickr user "Randy Son of Robert"

Ticket to Ride, Alan Moon, 2004, Days of Wonder

While some games require a heavy dose of tactical know-how, *Ticket to Ride* is at its surface what board gamers call "light". There is little math to the game and little in the ways of negotiation or espionage. Players race to lay their colored trains in a line across the board connecting cities listed on their secret tickets. Only a limited number of trains can be laid on any track, so blocking opponents from getting to where they need to go can be a calculated risk. I received this for Christmas one year and my parents (who cannot be called gamers by any stretch) asked to play it again and again. To use more board gamer nomenclature, *Ticket to Ride* is an excellent "gateway game".

Le Havre, Uwe Rosenberg, 2009, Lookout Games

Rosenberg is known chiefly for his heavy and complex game about 17th Century farming called *Agricola*. I find his more recent game about a shipping harbor, *Le Havre*, much more compelling. In *Le Havre*, players each represent a shipping concern and can choose between using buildings near the harbor or procuring resources from incoming ships. Players take from a number of different resources that can be shipped in and use them to build buildings or ships or they can convert goods into other goods or money. An interesting facet of the game is that once the game has started, there are no random elements. Much like in *Chess*, your success lays in better utilizing the board's state than your opponents. But the biggest success in the game is the feeling of abundance. In *Le Havre*, even players who do not grasp the strategies can still be successful at building and shipping meaning that no one player has the monopoly on fun[47].

There are literally dozens more I could cover and gush about in this space, but if it is a development area that interests you, I will leave it as an exercise for you to discover the innovation going on in cardboard and paper.

Resources

Board Game Designer's Forum, community for new designers - http://bgdf.org

Board Game Geek, community for players and designers alike - http://boardgamegeek.com

The Game Crafter, POD board game printer - http://www.thegamecrafter.com

[47] Forgive me.

Exercises

1. Make some games.
2. Make some more games.
3. Okay, joking aside.
4. Install UDK...
5. Install Unity...
6. Install GameMaker...
7. Play *Zork*. (Google it). Take one of the rooms and deconstruct how you would write the game in natural language. Talk about what surrounds the room, what descriptions are available, what objects are in the room and how those objects react to player actions.
8. Play *Book & Volume*. (Google it). Play it to completion. What themes does it cover? What does this work do that would be difficult in a different genre?
9. Install Inform 7. Create a one-room text adventure using *Inform*. Choose a theme that would be difficult to cover in another genre.
10. Play a "eurogame". It can be one of the ones listed above or any other strategic game. What dynamic systems are present? Come up with a video game idea that could also use a similar dynamic system.
11. Join a game jam like the Global Game Jam or Ludum Dare. (See Game Jams at the end of Chapter 33)

Summary

- The way to become a designer is to design. It is a necessary but not sufficient condition.
- The only way to become a good designer is to make things.
- Unreal Development Kit and Unity provide two great kits for designers to get their feet wet and make games, but both have a lot of overhead.
- GameMaker is a great platform for creating 2-D games independently, but has little industry use.
- By looking in nontraditional places, you may find an engine that allows you to recreate your vision with minimal overhead work. Perhaps your idea works best as a text adventure and Inform is your tool? Maybe your game idea shouldn't be digital at all and a board game is the answer?

Part Six - Personal Promotion

As you know, getting into the industry is notoriously tough. In some cases, there will be a hundred or more applicants for a single entry-level job. How do you make yourself stand out? That is the focus of this section.

First, unless you live in an enclave of developers like in Silicon Valley or Montreal, it can be tough to get to know actual developers. Luckily, we have the tools that can get you noticed no matter where you are.

Your resume will be the first look a human resources department will have as to who you are as a person. How can we get that resume moved into the interview pile instead of into the shredder?

We will also discuss a number of ways to get more involved in the industry that have the bonus impact of helping you to develop your skills.

Unfortunately, we are not in an industry where you can get by on just your resume alone. It requires work to build and maintain an outward-facing persona that shows how truly interesting and special you are. In fact your personal promotion abilities may even be even more important than the quality of your work when it comes to the complex task of getting hired.

Chapter 27 - Broadcasting via Blogging

Thomas Jefferson, John Milton, John Locke, and Jonathan Swift would have been bloggers. They kept a journal of sorts where each recorded aphorisms, quotes and notes they wanted to remember. These were called *commonplace books*. The parallel to modern blogs is not perfect, but there are similarities. In their commonplace books, these great men recorded the things they did not want to forget and many times included comments to remind themselves of these important notes.

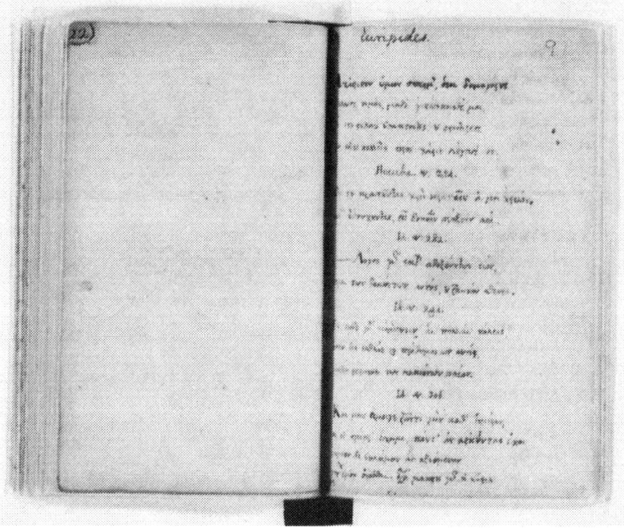

Figure 27.1 - Jefferson's Literary Commonplace Book. Quotes and context from Euripides.

You become a better game designer by designing games. This is true. But remember that design is about *communication*. This is why we have spent so much time on using Word for design documents with a focus on how those documents communicate their message and not on the content. It is why we have spent time on pitching and removing obstacles to communication. Design in an interpersonal environment is about communication and that *is* something you can practice.

One thing that I recommend to all aspiring designers is to start a blog and to take it seriously. Give yourself a posting quota (say, three times a week) and stick to it. Like the commonplace books of old, your blog can be used to store interesting ideas that you want to reflect on in the future. But unlike the commonplace book, your blog can be public. Your blog will become an extension of your **personal brand**.

Now "personal brand" is the kind of thing business hacks throw out there as if it had innate meaning but I think it is something to consider. If someone Googles my name, my blog is the first result. Anyone who clicks on it will see my latest post and will instantly form their opinion of me from that post. This makes every single blog post my first impression to anyone looking me up for the first time. Talk about pressure!

More importantly, blogs get you to practice writing. No matter how well you think you communicate through text, it is likely that you are overestimating your abilities. Writing every day or every other day to a public audience will vastly improve your ability to communicate. And since blogs can allow public comments, you can get instant feedback.

When I was working in the industry, I would start my day by perusing the blogs and news sites to which I subscribed. Most likely something in there would elicit some sort of response: interest, skepticism, anger, something. I would use that as the seed for a morning blog post. It would take no more than a half hour at the most. By time I had published the post, I was in "writing mode" and could tackle my professional design documents at full speed. It worked!

When I look back at my posts from years and years ago, I can see a distinct change in the quality and maturity of my writing. These things happen in baby steps, but they don't happen unless you work at it.

Unlike the commonplace book that was only record keeping, these blogs, journals and diaries can spark comments and discussion. One of their most powerful strengths is their openness and accessibility. I have met numerous people thanks to my blog and it has even lead to some unforeseen opportunities.

When I was laid off from EA in the recession that hit in 2009, I blogged about it. Little did I know my blog was followed by a reporter for the Orlando Sentinel newspaper, who contacted me for some comments for a story he was writing about technology and the recession. Shortly after that was published, I received an email from a producer of the CBS Evening News. They too were doing a story on how the recession was hitting tech workers. They flew a reporter down and had a two-hour interview with me...that they cut into the most trite six seconds they could find.

Figure 27.2 - © CBS News

"Unemployed Game Designer". Great. From that I made contact with people from all over the world. All from a simple blog post. I am not saying that will happen to you, but unforeseen connections happen to those who put themselves out there. I'll mention another time my blog "blew up" for me a little later.

What to Write About

Okay, so I have convinced you. You want to write a blog. Since you are reading this book, I assume you are interested in the games industry. There are a lot of armchair game reviewers out there - people who are interested in playing games and comment on whether certain games are good or not and why. We don't need more of those. Everyone who plays games forms opinions on what they like and do not like. Making posts that are reducible to "I like this" or "I don't like this" does nothing to differentiate you from hundreds of thousands of other blogs.

One way of differentiating yourself is to write about *why* things work for you or not. What design decisions in games worked for you? Why do you think the team made those decisions? What kind of commentary does such-and-such say about the industry as a whole? This provides a more nuanced insight as to who you are as a designer and is much more interesting to read than a review.

Whatever you do, follow the cardinal rule of personal promotion as often as possible: Don't Be Boring.

Temptation

There's a temptation to fight whenever you are providing commentary to a faceless audience. It is astoundingly easy to see what is going on in the world, point fingers and be negative. It is easy to trash games, say they suck, and say that the developers are clearly stupid and subhuman. Why not? You've never met them.

Not only is this potential dangerous for your career, but it is boring to read. You want to increase your readership in the hopes of making connections. Don't be boring. People don't care about whether something sucks. They care about insights and seeing things in different ways. This, of course, is not true for all blogs. For instance, Ben "Yahtzee" Croshaw has made a living slagging games, but he does it in a non-boring way and certainly is not in it to make friends and connections.

Many companies don't know exactly what to do with bloggers. There's this line between the personal and the professional that is quite blurry. It is important to check with the blogging policy of wherever you are applying. You don't want to step on any toes.

But even then, you can run into problems.

I'll try to obfuscate this as much as possible. I got into hot water with one of my former employers by writing a blog post on the balancing act of adjusting player attributes and making it worthwhile. I mentioned it in light of a feature just announced for one of the company's games at another studio. I didn't rip on it, but the conclusions of the post hinted at skepticism.

Apparently, a vice-president of the company was searching for links with his name (I used a quote of his), found my blog and sent it down the chain that I should be punished. Besides being shocked at the narcissism of it all, I was beside myself at how just citing an article in a blog post could get me in trouble, but it did. I removed the post, of course.

Lesson Learned: Anything that can be implied as criticism will be. Don't criticize those you hope to impress.

I was a big fan of the *Splinter Cell* series of games, but found problems with the fifth installment of the series, *Conviction*, and wrote a post about dynamic differences in it versus earlier games in the series. Nearly a year later, I found myself interviewing with a high-ranking member of a studio who had worked on *Conviction*. This could have gone very poorly. But because I was measured in what I had to say and could back it up with examples, we kept the conversation at a high level of respect and I learned quite a bit about their design decisions. Imagine if I had posted something like "*Conviction* sucks and their designers have no clue what they are doing!"

Lesson Learned: Be prepared to back up anything you say. If being negative, always treat it as if you were talking directly to the creator.

In 2010, I crafted my most widely spread post. It was a series of images showing how silly *Super Mario Brothers* would be if it used the tropes of 2010: long tutorials, achievements, Facebook sharing. The post went viral and between my site and the cross posting at Kotaku and other sites, the post itself had over a million hits. Even a year later, I get a large portion of my traffic from links to that post.

The post was inspired by design battles I was having at the time, but was not a commentary on anything specific person or team as it was just meant to be a joke and I mentioned as such in the post.

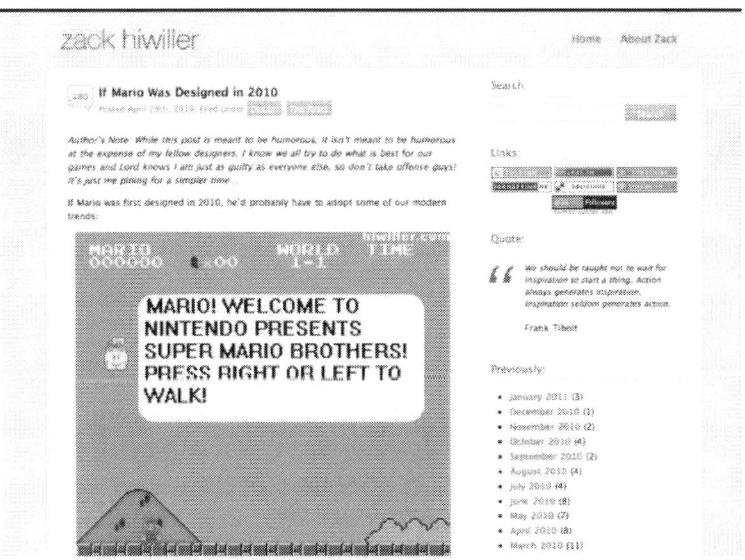

Figure 27.3 - The Go-To Site

Almost immediately when it hit the viral channels (it was #1 on Digg and was all over Reddit, Metafilter and other sites) I got people coming up to my desk asking if that was my post. I said yes. They would lean in and whisper. "That was awesome, but you are going to get fired!" Fired? Why? I checked with HR that I could blog when I was hired and the post was not anything about the company. I didn't even mention I worked there on the blog[48]! Even though I was in the right, I felt nervous.

The lesson above applies—anything that can be implied as criticism will be. But I didn't expect all the fear I heard from nearly everyone I worked with that has since been echoed at other places I have worked.

Lesson Learned: Speak loudly and stand behind what you say. Most people are too afraid to do either because they have nothing to say or because they are too afraid to be truthful about how they feel. Most people are boring. Those "you'll be fired" designers were terminally boring. Don't be boring.

One final lesson on this topic that is a bit of an aside. Because of the nature of the sound-bite based transfer of information that is part of modern culture, we are often given opportunity to comment on wide-ranging topics. While nearly everyone claims humility on topics like astronomy or medicine, nearly no one expresses that humility on two topics that can destroy you professionally: politics and religion. Both can make you inspired or angry, but neither should be broadcast on your blog or (by extension) your social networks. People have insane prejudices when it comes to these two topics. Liberals, conservatives, atheists and believers have these caricatures of each other. You will immediately disqualify yourself from the running of a lot of jobs if you are loud about these topics because people will see you as a caricature. Don't be pigeonholed! Stay away from broadcasting your politics or religion. Nothing good comes of it.

---

[48] Fun fact: Three months later, I'd be gone from the company. I'll never know if the blog post had anything to do with it. Before that post I already knew I wasn't staying at that studio long so the avenues its wide exposure gave me was well worth the stress it caused.

Chapter 28 - Wordpress

Setting up a blog requires almost no technical skill and is something a student can do long before he or she has created his or her first technical project.

Wordpress is my blog software of choice. It has an incredibly easy setup and is extremely flexible.

There are two methods to start a Wordpress blog. If you have your own web hosting service, you can download the Wordpress software and install it yourself. The online guides that Wordpress provides to walk you through this process are excellent and change with the newest versions, so rather than detail it here, just go to the Wordpress Codex[49] to view the latest instructions.

If you don't have your own hosting solution, Wordpress still has you covered. Instead of going to wordpress.org, try wordpress.com where they have a wholly integrated hosting solution for your blog. Again, they have excellent (brilliant, even) tutorials posted for even those a bit petrified by technology at learn.wordpress.com.

The best way to learn this process is to do it. Before continuing, go ahead and get yourself a blog. The rest of this chapter will be based on the wordpress.org installation, but the interface should be similar to wordpress.com users and users of other blogging packages like Tumblr or Posterous will have similar features.

Themes

Part of the ease of use of Wordpress can be attributed to its wide variety of themes and the simplicity of applying and modifying themes. Most blogging packages have the ability to theme the look and feel of the blog.

To find themes, use the Wordpress Free Theme Directory[50] where hundreds of users have uploaded thousands of themes that the community can use. Another popular method of finding themes is to look at the footer of a site that you know uses Wordpress. Most sites will credit the theme maker in

---

[49] http://codex.wordpress.org/Installing_WordPress

the footer. Then you can look up the particular theme in the Wordpress Free Theme Directory. Or you can search for a theme using the tag filter list. Perhaps you have an idea as to what you are looking for in a general layout. In the tag filter you can focus on the number of columns, colors or features.

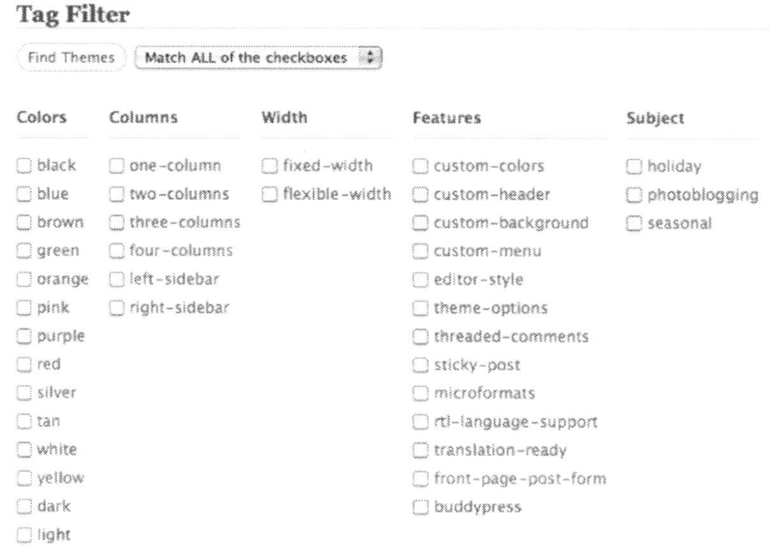

Figure 28.1 - Theme Directory Filter

Once you find a theme and want to apply it, you download the zip file and extract it to the themes directory on the FTP that has your Wordpress install. From there, login to your Wordpress dashboard and find "Themes" under "Appearance". Here all the theme directories you have in your install will be listed. You can click on "Activate" to switch themes painlessly. The "Preview" link will show you what your site will look like with your posts and data in the new theme without actually switching your live site. This only is helpful, of course, if you already have posts live to examine.

[50] http://wordpress.org/extend/themes/

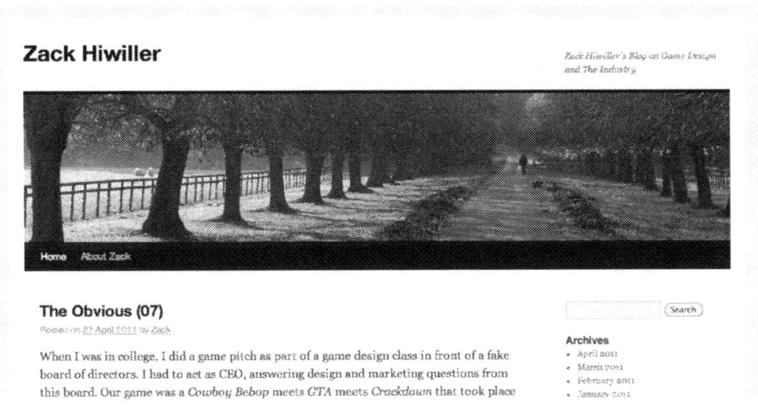

Figure 28.2 - My Blog on the Default Theme

Here is what my site looks like using the default 2010 theme. Snooze. But I was able to check out the theme in just a minute. If you know or learn CSS, you can tweak these themes to make them perfect for your requirements.

Enable Comments

A blog without the ability to comment is mostly useless. If you plan on using your blog as a promotional channel for your career, you will need your blog to help you make connections. There is no easier method of connecting than directly commenting on posts.

Luckily, Wordpress enables commenting by default. I would strongly encourage you to leave this setting alone. Sometimes, however, in a situation where you do not want to encourage commenting or the commenting going on is getting out of hand, you can turn off the comments for that post only by going to the post editing page and deselecting the checkbox in the "Discussion" section.

Akismet

One of the more vexing problems of running a blog that features comments is the prevalence of spam. Mention a keyword of one of these spambots or get a link from a connected site and expect a wave of spam comments drowning out any legitimate conversation.

If you have written one of these spambots, please put this book down and walk into traffic. Otherwise, a popular Wordpress plugin called Akismet can help deflect 95% of the unwanted messages.

Finding and installing plugins uses a very similar workflow to finding and installing themes. Wordpress keeps a plugin directory[51] with thousands of plugins. You can search the directory by keyword or tag. When you find one you want to install, you unzip the folder into your Wordpress installation's plugins directory and then go to the Plugins page on your dashboard. Each plugin that exists in the right directory will be listed. A plugin then has to be *activated* to be used on your site.

There are hundreds of useful plugins, so I will only highlight a few:

Google Analytics allows you to easily tie a Google Analytics account to your blog. Google's tool shows you detailed data and information about your users: where do they come from, what pages do they view, how long do they stay and what search terms do people use to find your site.

WP Super Cache is a plugin that I only learned about after my site became hammered by traffic in the wake of my aforementioned "Mario in 2010" post. Wordpress has a lot of overhead in that it connects to databases to retrieve and present your posts. If you get hammered by a deluge of traffic, it is likely that your server won't be able to handle the simultaneous connections and will lapse into a catatonic state. Using WP Super Cache takes your popular posts and converts them to a static page that is served instead of the high-overhead dynamic version. If you use a hosted solution like wordpress.com this is not needed, but if you host on your own, this can be crucial.

Facebook Comments for Wordpress does exactly what you think it would do - makes it so that people can sign in to post comments on your blog using their Facebook credentials. Whether or not you think that is a good idea is up to the type of site you want to cultivate and whether you think that would be a barrier to entry to some readers.

WP to Twitter allows you to ping your Twitter followers every time you update your blog. There are pros and cons to this, of course. Your page views will go up because your blog posts will be more visible. But you may

---

[51] http://wordpress.org/extend/plugins/

alienate potential followers if you update your blog often and fill users' streams with update notifications.

There are hundreds of useful plugins like ones that make image galleries or others that integrate other social networks. By periodically searching the plugins database, you can always be on top of the quickest ways to add functionality to your blog that you and your users can appreciate.

Chapter 29 - Networking

It is usually assumed that the best way to go about getting a job is to scour listings on web sites and send out a forest's worth of resumes. While that may work sometimes, most jobs are found through connections and that means you need to spend a significant amount of time establishing and maintaining your professional social network.

Strong vs. Weak Ties in Employment

In the study of social networks[52], there is a concept of interpersonal relationships that classifies them as either strong, weak or absent.

A **strong tie** is a relationship that has significant value in your life. These are the folks that you invite to your wedding, that you know everything about, that truly matter in your life.

A **weak tie** is someone whom with you are acquainted. You know the person, maybe you are friendly with them and you may come into contact from time to time. But you are not really in their social circle. These are the friends-of-friends, people you don't necessarily count on but still people you know.

In 1970, a Harvard study attempted to analyze the influence of strong and weak ties on employment opportunities. Surely, since strong ties know you better, they must be the best way to leverage your friends to get jobs?

Actually, the opposite was found. Subjects in the study who found jobs through connections used people they saw "rarely" or "occasionally" almost five times as much as they did for connections they saw "frequently".

What this means is that you are much more likely to land a job via the guy you used to play softball with versus via your best friend.

---

[52] Not the services like Twitter and Facebook, but the actual social relationships between humans.

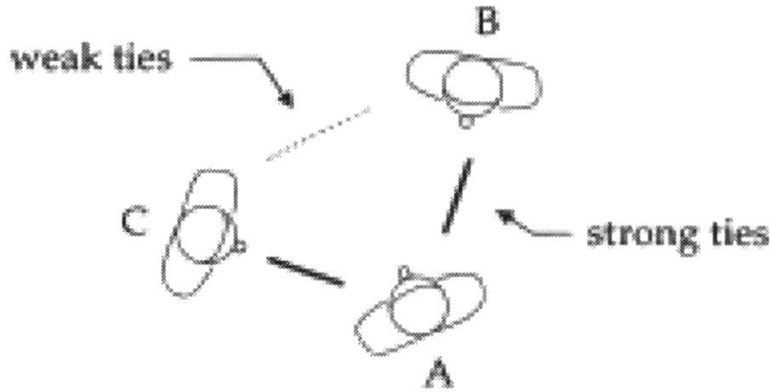

Figure 29.1 - The Weak Tie Hypothesis

It is theorized that this happens because of the distance from one member of the network to another. People tend to know each other (B-C) if they share a strong tie with a third party (A). This is called the **weak tie hypothesis**. For instance, if I am a strong tie with my friend Mark and a strong tie with my friend Erin, it is reasonable to assume that the two would have met at least a few times and established at least a weak tie.

To put it another way, your strong ties all likely know each other. The weak ties truly expand your network's reach. You don't gain exposure to many new individuals (people who have the connections to help you) through strong ties.

Take a look at a portion of my social network as represented by the business social network LinkedIn:

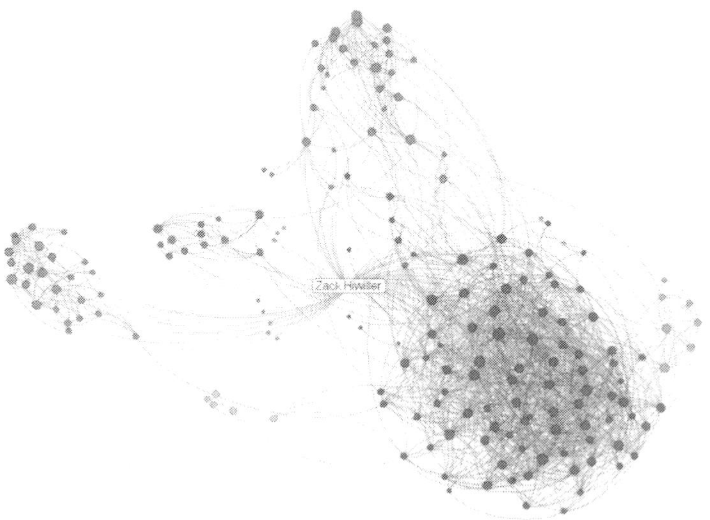

Figure 29.2 - The LinkedIn-Visible Portion of my Social Network

Notice how my connections are "clumped" by color. The clump in the lower right are people I knew when I worked at EA. The clump on the left are people I knew from college. The top clump are industry folks I know through conferences and other events. Notice that in the clumps everyone tends to know each other. If I were to be looking for a new opportunity with just folks in the EA clump, I would probably be pointed back to the same sources. The people that don't fall directly in a clump that are the most useful because they don't necessarily all know the same people.

LinkedIn

Despite the "me-too" feel of it, LinkedIn actually started before Facebook, Twitter, et al. It is a social network based solely on employment history and it is starting to make the paper resume obsolete.

Generally, LinkedIn is used to connect with past business associates to see where they are. One thing that makes LinkedIn interesting is that when you search for people, you find out how many degrees of separation there are between you and that person and (if they are close enough) who you have to connect through to reach them.

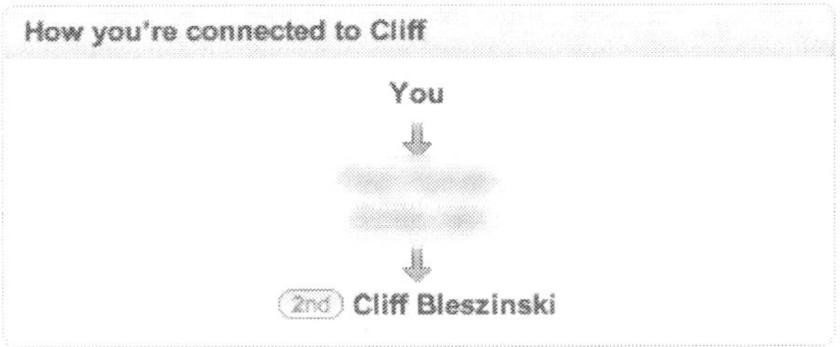

Example 29.3 - Names Blurred to Protect the Innocent

Your personal LinkedIn page is formatted like a web-enabled resume. We will talk about crafting resumes in a later chapter, but it is worth noting here that to many potential employers your LinkedIn profile is just as or more important than your resume. You should treat completing it with the same amount of care you would take in crafting the perfect resume.

Conferences

One of the single best ways to meet people in the game industry is through conferences. Here you can get your business cards into the hands of employers, hobnob with developers and students and generally have a good time and learn a bunch. Here are some of the recommended ones:

Game Developers Conference - San Francisco, CA

The Game Developers Conference or GDC is the Mecca for game developers. Everyone goes, companies spend boatloads to control the press and have the best parties. Many of the major developers give talks and are generally accessible and in the mood to share. There is, frankly, too much to do at a GDC so you will likely miss a lot. Year after year, it is the place to be for both aspiring and established designers.

Every year there is a career expo room where potential employers collect reams of resumes. You can go with the drop-your-resume-off route, but I would recommend going there with a laptop with something playable you made on it. Be interesting.

The first two days of GDC are generally filled with summits and workshops. Some very gifted and friendly designers run the Game Design Workshop annually. Many years ago, I attended one of these workshops and came out with great new friends and renewed vigor for the craft. There's always something to learn.

It can be expensive to go to GDC, especially if you are not on the west coast of the USA. The ticket to the show is also extremely pricey. One of the ways students (and many developers) skirt paying the expensive entry fee is to be a CA. CAs are volunteer conference staff that help with mundane conference jobs like crowd control and gophering. CAs get a pass to explore GDC when they are not scheduled to work.

GDC is generally held in the late winter/early spring.

GDC Online (Formerly Austin GDC) - Austin, Texas

GDC Online used to be a alternate conference held in the fall to broach special topics like audio, writing and online games (Austin is the location for joining an MMO developer in the United States). It has branched into the conference that focuses on online games, virtual worlds and social games as well.

It is not nearly as massive or media-focused as the mothership version of GDC and is more focused on specific topics. You will not find as many big name speeches there but perhaps that is a good thing. If you are looking to work at an Austin developer, there is little reason not to go.

Project Horseshoe - Boerne, Texas

Horseshoe is not so much a conference as it is a small think tank of designers who meets every year to try and tackle some of the big questions facing the industry and have some fun doing it. The Horseshoe group is tight - it is more of a brother/sisterhood. They only accept applicants who are already in the industry and recommended by a current Horseshoe member. So while it is not for students, it is a conference to consider once you are established in the industry.

Electronic Entertainment Expo - Los Angeles, CA

E3 at one time was the center of the gaming universe calendar. Nearly every big announcement in the industry was made during the week of E3. But in order to be heard in the din of announcements that week, you had to be bigger, gaudier and louder than everyone else. This lead to a publisher arms race where everyone was spending their entire marketing budget trying to outspend everyone else at E3. This lead to a armistice between publishers that briefly shut down the show to only retail buyers and other connected individuals.

E3 has since relaunched and grown to share the spotlight with GDC. For students who can get passes (see your school for a vouching letter), it can be an opportunity to meet with some members of the industry. When I worked in the last "big" E3 in 2005, I was always more than happy to discuss life with the few students who trickled in to our booth rather than the tired media and skeptical competition to whom I had to repeat the company line again and again.

Be sure who you are talking to is on the development team and not a hired marketing figure or part-time contractor hired for the show as many of the people on the show floor are not involved in the actual making of the games at all!

Of course there are tons of other conferences worth your time like PAX, Gamescom and DICE. Keep an eye on Gamasutra and other industry sites for the latest.

The One Rule of Conference Going (For Students)

If you are a student, I must address the One Rule:

Do Not Ask For A Job.

That seems counterproductive, doesn't it? You need a job. They might have a job. Why not? (Oh! By the way, this doesn't apply to HR people you meet. Those folks are supposed to field these questions.)

The answer is this: it puts the developer in an awkward situation. He/she doesn't know you personally yet. He/she may not even know what job positions are open or if they are currently being filled. He/she cannot promise anything and cannot stick up for you since he/she does not know you. The most awkward situations have happened when students have asked me straight on to get them a job like I owed them something. Developers you do not know do not owe you a thing.

Here is the alternative: be interesting. Strike up genuine and heartfelt conversations with people. At the very least you will have fun and learn something. Exchange cards. Then, weeks later, you can email him/her and thank them for your talk at GDC and maybe you can hint that you are looking for something. Since he/she is not being blindsided with it and has a chance to ignore the request, it is not uncomfortable. And if you were truly interesting and have a great site and/or portfolio, maybe the developer will pass on your information.

The Other Rule of Conference-Going

I lied. There is another rule. But it is so often broken that it doesn't get as much respect as the one rule. It is this:

Respect Everyone.

At a conference, there will be throngs pushing up to meet with whoever made the hot game that year. In 2008, it was Ken Levine (*Bioshock*). In 2011, it was Notch (*Minecraft*). Their shows will be dominated by people telling them how awesome they are. Not to be selfish, but what does that get you?

Imagine Notch at GDC two years before *Minecraft*. No one knew who he was but a few indies. He certainly was not hiring people. He was just a guy making games like thousands of others at the show.

That's who you want to meet.

The scrub student you meet today could be the director of the Next Big Thing five or ten years down the road. Don't you want to be part of that? Remember the value of weak ties.

Conversely, there are hundreds of grizzled veterans whose best games may be ten years old, who may make nothing but shovelware and who may have never had actual fans. Buddy up to them.

They give the best advice.

At the end of the day this boils down to a directive to be amicable to everyone. Not only is it morally the right thing to do, but it might be the thing to do for your career as well.

Chapter 30 - Twitter

Sean Duncan teaches a class in game studies at Miami University in Ohio. As an experiment, he posted this on Twitter on April 5th, 2011:

> Hey, if you work in games, can you tweet hi to my class (#ims211)? I wanna make a point about Twitter and the game dev world.

The response was nearly instantaneous. Twenty-four hours and thousands of tweets later, the hashtag (the name for the "#ims211" marker put on every post) boasted tweets from some of games' most notable folks: George Broussard, Clint Hocking, Jane McGonigal and many, many others.

The points Dr. Duncan was trying to make are that: the game industry is tightly connected, small, and mostly members of the social network Twitter. The success of the #ims211 conversation quickly proved all three of these assertions.

The key to Twitter is not that it only allows for 140 characters at a time in a post (although that is a very nice feature enforcing brevity) but that you do not need permission to follow someone. As such, with a little searching and effort, you can connect with and message hundreds of movers and shakers in the industry for free.

Look at the positives of Twitter:

- **Know what the industry is up to, what games devs are playing, what their pet issues are**. Think: on an interview you will already know the cultural zeitgeist of developers. You can use that to instantly tap into what they find interesting.
- **Ask questions directly to the creators**. A direct line to people in the industry was before tough to nab.
- **Be connected**. Dr. Duncan didn't have to personally ask every developer he knew. He didn't even have to follow every developer. All he had to do was create a message and ask politely for it to be replicated. Three degrees of separation later and the entire industry had seen it. If you have a need, just ask and ask for your followers to retweet your request. Maybe your followers can't help you, but

maybe your followers' followers can. Or your followers' followers' followers can. You get the idea.

- **Instant review**. Working on a game project on your own? Need someone to put it through its paces? You have a connection to people who generally are interested in what you have to say! Use them!

- **Practicing brevity**. You will rage when you have the perfectly composed tweet that is 141 characters long. But with practice, you will become better and better at expressing yourself in a very short space w/o rsorting 2 cheap trix 2 condense ur text. Remember what we said about brevity in the GDD section?

- **It has a great API**. This might mean nothing to you if you are not a developer, but what it means is that there are apps on nearly every platform imaginable for interfacing with Twitter. There are clever apps for your phone, computer or console and even great aggregation services like ThinkUp that help you analyze your Twitter activity. For instance, ThinkUp tells me that 42% of my tweets are responses to other people. Clearly, I use Twitter for conversations.

- **Lowest barrier to entry**. To fire up Twitter and compose a tweet takes a few seconds. Unlike blogging, which can require research and formatting, tweeting has the lowest overhead of any of what I call "brain primers" - services that help you to start your day being creative.

- **Tons of jokers**. The concise nature of the service makes it great for comedians with short jokes. @Badbanana, @Hodgman, @DarthVader, @StephenAtHome, @TheOnion. The comedy may not always be "safe for work" as they say, but at the very least you can find some daily humor.

Retweets

One of the most valuable features of Twitter came about organically. Twitter was noticing that users were sharing interesting tweets with their stream by reposting the tweet with the prefix RT and the username like so:

RT @zhiwiller: Here's a tweet I said.

It was happening so often that Twitter made it an internal feature.

You can use retweets to share the most interesting tweets in your stream with your followers. Some folks like being *curators* where they rarely post themselves, but follow many and repost their best things.

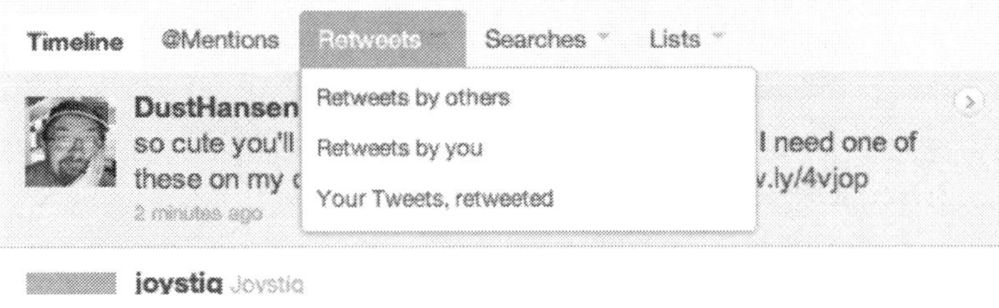

Figure 30.1 - Your Retweets

If you want to see if any of your insightful tweets have been retweeted, go to the retweets tab on the main Twitter page and go down to "Your Tweets, Retweeted". Here you can click on each tweet and see who and how many retweeted it.

Mentions

Twitter works well as a conversation platform. To send a message to someone, regardless of whether they follow you or not, type the @ symbol followed by their username followed by your message. If you would like to send a message to me, you could do it like so:

@Zhiwiller I love your book. Thanks!

Your message would appear in my "Responses" stream. Go ahead and message me. I don't mind.

Hashtags

As mentioned above, hashtags are a way of following specific events or topics rather than people. For instance, during the annual Game Developers Conference, most attendees tweet about it with the #gdc hashtag.

There are two ways you can follow a hashtag. Either you can manually search for them in Twitter's search field or you can use an independent application that allows you to monitor hashtags. In a standalone viewer like Tweetdeck, you can specify columns to return specific hashtags, making a separate feed relating only to that topic.

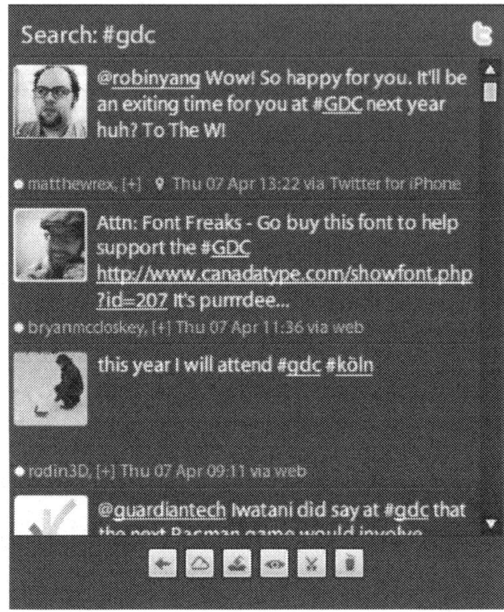

Figure 30.2 - Hashtag Search in TweetDeck

Much like retweets in the early days, hashtags are not actually an internally supported feature of Twitter, but with continued use they may be some day.

Geolocation

In competition with other mobile services like Foursquare and Gowalla, Twitter has added a feature where you can add your location to a tweet. This allows you to search for tweets that are near you, maybe fellow audience members at a concert or conference goers watching the same talk.

Volume

Now a short comment on form. The rules we talked about in blogging hold true for Twitter and other social networking sites. But something else needs mentioning regarding Twitter.

A blog has a very "pull" model of readership. Users who want to read your contact at this moment make an effort to get it. Twitter, on the other hand follows a "push" model—whether users want to hear from you or not at this particular moment, your tweets will show up on their feed.

Some people tweet like a fire hose, twenty or more times a day with whatever comes to mind. These tweets push out the tweets of people who post less often with more meaningful content. Consider a party where one person screams over every conversation. This is the problem.

It is tempting to tweet too much since it is so easy to do, but do try to gauge the "tempo" of your follows and match accordingly. I won't give a hard and fast rule for number of "broadcast" tweets per day, but if you notice less and less people following you, this could be the reason. Lower the volume.

Facebook

Six hundred million users can't be wrong. It is likely that you already have Facebook. Facebook is not as useful for meeting industry folks because it requires confirmation to be connected. Thus, Facebook is a great tool for staying connected with people you already know while Twitter is great for learning new things from new people.

Of course, one realm where Facebook excels is in embedded games. Zynga and others make a multi-billion dollar business on games hosted on Facebook. If you are not familiar with them, you should register a Facebook account just to see what the fuss is about. If you are considering developing Facebook games, these generally require PHP or other server-side scripting experience and many Facebook games use a Flash front-end. The Facebook API is free to access and use and is quite simple.

Since Facebook is more private, it tends to lead users into a false sense of security about what they post. The same rules apply here as everywhere else: post only what you would be comfortable defending in a job interview.

Chapter 31 - Resumes

You would like to think that when you apply for a job, a knowledgeable and qualified team will look at your resume, weigh your pros and cons and then decide to proceed from there. Unfortunately, it does not always work like that. Human resources teams get hundreds of resumes from all over the world for every job. From those hundreds, they are tasked with selecting only a few to follow up on, spending only a few seconds on each resume.

The job of your resume is to get you past that first cull.

Being a student means that you likely do not have any employment experience of note, so you have to be a bit creative in how you present yourself.

First, you want everything on your resume to be either a) **something that makes you stand out** or b) **relevant to the industry**. Bonus points if you have both. For everything on your resume, keep those two points in mind.

Many resume help sites tell you to start with a summary paragraph that explains your strengths and weaknesses. These are almost never read. If you must include one, limit it to two or three lines.

My scolding about brevity even makes it into this chapter. A resume should be one page only. You would be surprised how many people violate this. A multi-page resume doesn't make you seem qualified, it makes you seem loquacious. And if you are padding your resume with fluff for length, that just makes you look naive.

Never, ever, ever, ever lie on a resume. If it is important enough to lie about, it is important enough for an interviewer to ask about. If the interviewer asks about it and sniffs out the lie, not only will you be disqualified for that position but since the game industry is small, it is likely that your reputation will be besmirched farther than just the one company.

I am going to assume you have no resume and walk you through step by step on how to draft one. The embellishments you make on this are your own responsibility as there really is no formula to an effective resume.

Step 1 - Contact Info

Your name and contact info go at the top of the resume. This includes your full given name (no nicknames), address, telephone number, email address and website. Simple enough.

Step 2 - (Optional) Summary

Next you may put a very short summary. Only do this if you think it is important to frame something about yourself early. Maybe you are a level designer first and foremost and you want to frame that with something like "Level Designer with Over 12 Level Design Contest Awards". This is fine. "Dedicated Hard Worker" or "Enthusiastic About Games" is generic and avoidable.

Steps 3/4 - Work Experience and Education

If you have any industry work experience, put it here first. If your work experience is entirely outside the industry, start with your education.

For education, put the name of the institution, degree and concentration (if applicable). If your degree is in progress, put a projected graduation date, otherwise put your graduation date. Include your GPA if it is excellent. Include any significant honors you have received. If you took any classes particularly relevant to the jobs you are applying for, make a note of them. You may include your high school in this list, if you think it is important to mention[53].

For work experience, include only what is a) interesting and/or b) relevant to industry. Dog walking, babysitting, selling hot dogs at the fair may be your most recent work experience, but if it is not applicable to industry, then why should an employer care? Write a short description of your responsibilities under each role. List your roles in reverse chronological order. This is the most important section of the resume, so be impressive.

---

[53] Especially if you were valedictorian/salutatorian and can make a note of that.

Step 5 - Any Interesting Game Projects

Shortly list and describe any game projects you've be a part of as a hobbyist or student. In any other industry, making *Halo* Forge levels is not particularly something you would want to include on your resume, but here it is recommended especially if your resume is lacking professional experience.

Step 6 - Technical Skills

Do you know any programming languages? What software are you familiar with? If you toyed around with the tools in this book, you should be able to fill out this section nicely. Few things make a student candidate more impressive than a wide variety of tools listed. It shows he/she is willing to learn and experiment. But be willing to answer questions in an interview about whatever you list!

Step 7 - Something Interesting

Mention something about you that makes you interesting and stand out beyond what you do in work and school. In my resume, I mention my blog and writing (over a million hits) and the fact that I officiate varsity high school football games. While these things are not necessarily relevant to industry, it sticks with readers so they remember "Oh, that's the referee guy" or whatever your interesting factoid is.

Step 8 - What to Leave Off

For an entire generation, putting "References: Available Upon Request" was standard. It is now generally frowned upon because *of course* your references are available upon request. Why wouldn't they be? The statement is pretty much a waste of space that could be filled with something interesting. If you read a resume guide that tells you to include that, ignore it.

Do not include a picture of yourself. In many jurisdictions this raises legal issues since there could be a possibility of discrimination based on gender or race, even if these are patently obvious from your name. There is no reason to include your picture and it makes HR offices uncomfortable, so don't.

Do not be cheeky or cute. Some resume writers like to stand out by using crazy fonts or odd forms like writing their resume as a dialogue. The form should not stand out; the content should. Remember the HR folks have to go through hundreds of resumes. If yours is hard to read for any reason, they will likely just pass it over.

Step 9 - Cull to One Page

Now you have all this great stuff on your resume and you can start cutting off the weakest bits until you get to one page. Resist the urge to mess with the margins to fit more on a page. That just makes your resume look cluttered. White space is okay. Remember that it is likely that your resume will be printed at some point if you make it past the first pass. Make sure it is something that can be read when printed (meaning reasonable margins and black-and-white with no watermarks).

Step 10 - Review

Have someone review it like a teacher or friend. They will likely see mistakes that you have missed or phrases that don't make sense. Everyone who has gotten a job pretty much considers themselves a resume expert. You do not have to do all of their suggestions, but consider every one. They might have the same reaction an HR person would, even if the reaction is unfounded.

Now that you have a beautiful resume, you can send it out to every company that may take you. Don't be discouraged. Even for developers with loads of experience, sending out fifty resumes and only hearing back from three companies (even if they say 'no') is quite common. Follow-ups are important. But most applications will just disappear into the aether. You can't fret over them. Instead move onto the next. Be confident! You are working hard on your skills, making games in any spare time you can find, you don't have time to fret!

Chapter 32 - Business Cards

Business cards have an awkward name as they aren't just for hurried businessmen and women. Students and unemployed developers need business cards even more than developers with steady jobs. A business card is an advertisement, one that potential connections and employers will readily accept.

I'll give you a simple formula for making a business card:

- It should have your name and an email address.
- It should have something that defines you, even vaguely.
- It should have links to find out more.
- It should be creative in some way.

That's it. Let's discuss each in detail (except for the first one, because... come on):

It should have something that defines you. What are you most interested in? Story? Put "Storytelling Designer" on your card. Levels? Social? What defines you? Enthusiasm? Curiosity? Mine says "Professional Game Designer" to insist that I have experience and credibility. No one is really going to take your card's word for it, but plant that idea early and often.

It should have links to find out more. You should have a website by now. Put the address on your card. Make sure your work is visible if you have a portfolio. Now your site is just as much a part of your card as anything else. I put links to my personal blog and Twitter account on my card because those show what kind of person I am and how I think. When I see a card without a website link, I pretty much assume there's not much to know about the guy/girl.

It should be creative in some way. There are two ways this can go wrong. On one end of the spectrum, you can have the most boring card in the world that no one remembers. On the other end, your card can be so wacky and out-there that it outshines your message.

The point of having a business card is communication. And what do you know? The main skill of game design is communication. Like it or not many game designers put a lot of weight into what goes on that business card as a barometer of the person's ability to communicate.

Here are some mistakes you can make and what someone receiving a card containing that mistake might think about you:

The Irregularly Sized Card says: "It's about me, not you."

Figure 32.1 - © Ninja BTL Advertising Agency, Lithuania

Everyone complains about the designer with the monster ego and then we ooh and ahh at Kevin Mitnick's lock pick business card. A designer that gives out an irregularly-shaped business card is saying: "I know you can't file this with your other business cards, but I'm so important that you will need a special place to put my contact info." Uh, no.

Corollary: If your card is made of titanium or hemp or souls of the damned, it better well be important to your business proposition. Otherwise, you are essentially broadcasting that you are all style, no substance.

The Glossy Card or No Space to Write says: "I don't think ahead."

If I am at a conference and I collect fifty business cards, I like to put a little note on each saying what we talked about or where we met. Nearly everyone I met does the same. If you don't make your card easy to write on, you are essentially putting all of your eggs in the "I'm so memorable that he won't have to take notes" basket. For someone as forgetful as me, that's dangerous. For me, the back of my card is completely white. Everything I need to tell people I would give the card to is on the front. They can fill in the back with what they need.

There is no reason for a shiny card that resists scribbles!

For game designers, a card that can't be written on says that you plan systems that don't make affordances to how the user will actually need to use them!

Bonus: you can take notes on your own business cards when you need to remember something and have no other means nearby.

The Hard to Read Card says: "I don't communicate well."

Figure 32.2 - © Unmana Datta

If your card is hard to read, what kind of screens will you design? I violated this on my first business cards by accident as the final product didn't have the same contrast as my screen proof. Your card should attempt to be easy to read at a glance, right? Contrast. Repetition. Alignment. Proximity. Yes, it spells crap. That's what makes it easy to remember.

The Focal Clip Art Card says: "I am not creative."

If I see a piece of MS Paint clip art like in the example above, you better be the best designer in the world and be using it ironically. Luckily, I don't see this much in games, but I do see it often in just about every other industry that hands out cards. Luckily, in many of those industries, you don't have to be creative. In games, you must be. If you even think for a second of putting clip art as a focal point in your card, give yourself twenty lashes and start over.

There's a corollary to this: images are not bad. If the image is evocative of something and if it blends well with the other content on your card, then go for it. But do not make it the focal point and make sure it is related to what you do and used in an attractive manner. My card has a lot of black space on the front. I have filled that with some line art reminiscent of *Asteroids*. It is evocative of my style and it is not a focal point. It breaks up the visual field. I'm not making a Spinal Tap album.

The Contains-a-Game Card: "I like games so much that I don't care if they are terrible."

I haven't seen one out in the wild, but I have heard about many instances of these. If you are putting a game on your card, it better be: 1) fantastic in design, 2) playable in no time at all with no extra effort or materials, and 3) memorable. Just putting a game on your card is of no use unless it is spectacular, otherwise you are showing people that you don't know how to design games. An at-least-we-tried is not particularly wowing.

I am sure there is a memorable business card game out there somewhere, but I have never seen it. How about just putting a link to your game that's on the web that is already awesome?

The Printed on Your Home Ink-Jet Printer Card: "I'm not doing so well."

My parents have instilled in me very powerful lessons on saving money for the lean times. Nonetheless, there have been times when I have been broke as a joke. You may desire to print some cards on whatever thick paper you have in the apartment. Stop. These cards generally bend and crease and fall apart in people's pockets. There are usually coupons for Overnightprints.com or Vistaprint where you can get professional weight cards for very little cost. (Don't get the free Vistaprint ones). If you go the cheap route, you end up looking kind of pathetic, even if you *are* kind of pathetic (and we have all been there).

Too Much Text: "My design documents will be impossible to parse."

If you have no negative space on your card, if you try to cram as much info as possible into those few square inches, I am just going to assume that you put five hundred words on each Powerpoint slide and fill your design documents with meandering asides. There's a place for additional information. That would be your website.

Doesn't Have a Website: "I'm All Talk and Have Nothing to Contribute"

If you don't have a website that has some sort of content that gives me an idea of who you are as a person and/or as a designer, then what do I have to go on? If you are a student, the link to your portfolio should be up front and highlighted.

My card contains in order: my email address (where you can ask less public questions), my blog (longer-form writing and other content), Twitter (something where we can talk publicly and you can see my personality). If your information is easy to find or if you tell everyone within earshot of your website that is easily Googleable, then maybe you can leave that out. Err on the side of caution.

These snap judgments I listed leads you to a very simple card: name, sparse but evocative presentation and links to additional information/communication channels. Every other statement you make about yourself should be in the conversation you have with the guy or lady you are giving your card to! Be memorable there! How much time are you spending designing your card versus actually being interesting so people will want to keep your information?

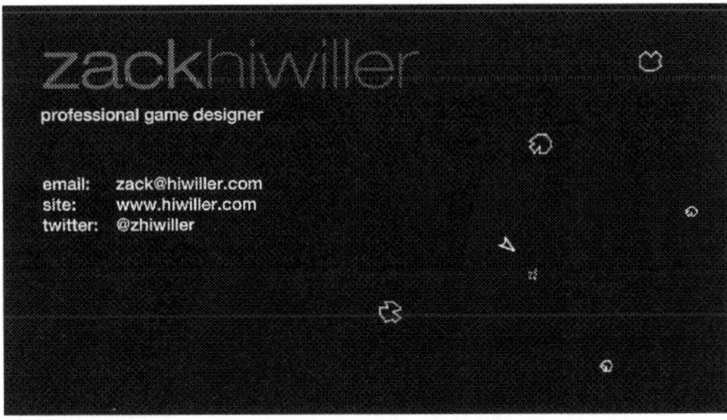

Figure 32.3 - Mmm, Look at That Card

Chapter 33 - Interviewing

You have found a position in which you are interested. You have submitted your resume and passed the eye test. You have survived the first cull. You are in the top ten percent. Congrats! Now you face the next step: the interview.

Having been on both ends of the process, both being interviewed and being the interviewer, I can tell you a number of things that may help you vault over that brick wall and get you deeper into the hiring process.

Pre-Interview

Your work starts long before the call or on-site.

The very first thing most interviewers will tell you is a disqualifying attribute is for the interviewee to know nothing about the company or the position. Sometimes that is tough—maybe the studio is new or maybe the position is inadequately defined. Know what the studio makes. Know what platforms they service. Know what the type of job is at the very least. It helps to have played their games. If you are on a short schedule, at least read the reviews of their games and know where they succeeded and where they failed.

Interviews are two-way streets. Think of questions you can ask them. If you know the name of the person you are interviewing with, find out on what titles he or she worked. Have questions prepared. These should be honest questions—things you are really curious about. Interviewers can see through the veneer of falsely looking interested.

If there is anything on Facebook, Twitter, MySpace or whatever that would embarrass you, get rid of it. Most interviewers will do a casual Internet search of their candidates.

Work on your introduction. The way most interviews open is with the interviewer saying, "Tell me/us about yourself". Have a good overview that is about thirty seconds long that is not just a rehash of your resume. They've seen the resume. They know what is on it. That's why you got this far.

At the very least have answers to these questions:

- Why do you want to work at XYZ?

- What makes you more interesting than all the other people we will interview?
- What are your weaknesses? (Be honest. "I work too hard" can be smelled out as a non-answer a million miles away.)
- Talk about your biggest success.
- Talk about your biggest failure.

The Interview

Even though we live in the future, cell phones still drop calls. If you cannot find a landline to have the phone interview, be sure to let them know and get a callback number in case the call drops.

If you are doing an on-site, be fifteen minutes early. Any earlier and you will impose on them to see you sooner than they had wished. Any later and you run the risk of being tardy. If you show up late, count yourself out. Your interviewer's time is more important than your own no matter if they are an HR drone or the head of the company.

If you are on-site, turn your phone off. Even on vibrate it can be distracting. If on a phone interview, make sure you will be in a place with few distractions. Dogs decide to bark at the wind at the most inopportune times. Landscapers start up their mowers when you need peace and quiet. Find a room insulated from those distractions. If you are a pacer (I am), find a place where you can walk around untethered but still without disruption.

Speak slowly. However slowly you think you speak, you likely run your words together when in the excitement of an interview. If you must, learn relaxation techniques. You should be relaxed during an interview. It shouldn't be a stressful event.

Most people over-present. They ramble on well after answering the question. But at the same time there is the danger of saying too little. If you are introverted, be mindful that you are doing more than just giving simple yes or nos.

Focus on how you will fit for the position. If they mention something in which you are interested, tell them so. "Oh, it's interesting you have narrative designers on your team because I have always been interested in how story and mechanics are joined." But be honest. Interviewers can see fake a mile away.

If you have previous experience, the interviewer will ask you about it. You could have the baddest blood of all for a previous employer, but do not bad-mouth them. It makes you look petty and you risk the danger of bad-mouthing a friend of the interviewer.

If you are on-site, dress comfortably but professionally. The games industry is sort of unique in that dressing overly formally paints you as a boring stuffed shirt. Most game developers have an extremely liberal dress code, but you still want to dress on the more professional end of that scale. It is best to ask HR what is appropriate for that studio.

If you are on-site, make eye contact when you give answers and ask questions. It shows confidence. Even if you are not confident, forcing yourself to do this will fake it pretty well.

This may be TMI for some people, but avoid eating too soon before your interview. Do not eat too much and do not eat anything that will make your breath smell bad. Some people, when nervous, will pass gas. You want to be focusing on the questions, not straining to hold back the urge to fart. Silly, yes, but important.

Most importantly: be yourself. You do not want to get a job for which you are a bad fit. It will be bad for them and bad for you. Every interview in the future will ask: "I see on your resume that you were only at your first job for four months. Tell us about that." Is that a question you want to answer for the rest of your days?

Never **ever** ask about the remunerative aspects of the job such as salary, benefits or vacation during the interview. There will be a time for that, but the interview is not the time.

At the end of the interview, always ask what the next steps are. Ask who you should contact for the follow-up. Thank each and every interviewer. In a week, follow up with your contact. It shows you are committed.

The Wait

Then comes the interminable waiting period. Keep busy. Don't stress over how the interview went as it is in the past. Don't bug the interviewer or your HR contact. Give it some time. It is likely that they will be interviewing other candidates and will not make a decision until they have interviewed everyone. If you start bugging them before they are ready to make a decision, it will reflect poorly on you.

If you have waited a week or two and heard nothing, give them a call and ask them what your status is. If they say they are still evaluating, find out when would be appropriate to call back.

Find something to fill your time. Maybe you have other places to send resumes? Maybe you are working on a project? Maybe you should just go see a movie?

You may get called for a second interview. In that case, there was something in the first interview that they didn't get answered. Try and figure out what that is. Are they asking a lot about a certain area of your experience? Maybe they want to know about your programming experience. Be honest but sell yourself to whatever they are asking. They wouldn't be giving a follow-up if they were not interested.

Sometimes you will get the standard "We're sorry but you don't fit what we are looking for at this time." Be gracious in defeat. Do not ask them why you are not being hired. They cannot tell you without the possibility of being open to litigation, so you will almost always receive a stock answer. Thank them for their time and move on.

Sometimes it is as simple as not being a good fit for the position. But if you keep in contact and keep a positive relationship, when the right opportunity comes by, they will think of you. In the end, that is better for the both of you.

Aside: More Ways To Connect

Obviously, there are more ways to connect with other aspiring developers and employers than what I can enumerate in this book, but here are some more:

IGDA

The International Game Developers Association is the largest advocacy group in the world for game developers. It consists of a board of directors and special interest groups at the global level and hundreds of distinct chapters at the local level. IGDA local chapter meetings can be a good way of finding out what is going on in the employment market in your particular area and is a cheap alternative to schmoozing at a conference.

Game Jams

The Global Game Jam was an initiative of the IGDA started in 2008. The idea is to bring together game developers of all walks of life into impromptu teams, present them with a prompt and have them feverishly work to create a game in forty-eight hours. The jams foster creativity, allow students and developers to practice their skills and serve as a way to meet fellow enthusiasts and professionals. Tens of thousands of jammers have participated since the start of the program yielding over a thousand finished games.

It is easier to participate in the Global Game Jam if you live in an area with a lot of students or developers, but jammers can even participate remotely in many cases. For more information, go to the Global Game Jam site at globalgamejam.org

Contests

Much like the idea behind the Global Game Jam, contests can be a great way to create real material that can be shown to potential employers. Finding contests can take a little more work. The Independent Game Source forums at TIGsource.com often run contests for independent game developers.

Often engine and toolmakers sponsor contests. Epic previously ran the "Make Something Unreal" contest, which asked developers to create a full game mod in the Unreal Engine 3 for a million dollar prize.

The Interactive Fiction Competition has been running for seventeen years and provides great competition. The XYZZY awards is another venerable competition for interactive fiction having been run since 1996.

Kongregate.com runs a weekly and monthly contest to encourage developers to submit their games to the service.

Since contests come and go, any list here is impossible. Be on the lookout as these can provide real incentives to finish projects.

Exercises

1. Join Twitter. Follow @zhiwiller.

2. Set up a blog on a popular blogging site such as Posterous, Wordpress.com, or Tumblr. Every weekday for a month, look through the gaming-related sites you like to peruse and find an article you either disagree with or on which you feel you can elaborate. Make a blog post about your comments. At the end of the month, you will have twenty posts with insights as to how you think as a designer. If you keep up with it, you can promote your blog and use it to connect with others in the industry.

3. Many schools and professional development centers offer resume writing and interviewing seminars. Some will even record your mock interviews so you can see how you unconsciously act. Search around for these opportunities. If you cannot find a mock interview opportunity near you, use your webcam and record yourself for three minutes explaining who you are and your qualifications. When you watch it back, notice any cues in body language that may look bad to an interviewer: lack of eye contact, slouching, tics. Have someone who has interviewed before review it. Like anything, practice makes perfect.

4. Search to find your local IGDA chapter. Attend their next meeting. If your local chapter is the Orlando chapter, find me and say 'hi'.

Summary

- Blogging is a simple way to create a voice that can serve as your personal identity in a sea of applicants. But be careful as what you say can reflect either positively or poorly on how employers may view you.
- Weak ties are the key to extending your network for the purpose of finding new opportunities.
- Thanks to Twitter, your favorite developers are easier than ever to find in order to ask questions.
- The standard resume and business cards will make you seem standard. Given the high degree of competition for entry-level game industry jobs, you have to better than standard. While not enough on their own, a solid website, resume and business card can only help in the pursuit of an entry job.
- Once you land an interview, you've survived the hard part of the process. But the odds are still stacked against you. Be interesting and try to rise to the top.

Conclusion - Life As a Designer

I saved this for the end of the book. I pose this question to you:

Why do you want to be a designer?

The answer I hear all the time is: "because I have grown up playing games and I don't know what to do with my life so games sound cool."

I have grown up eating burgers, but I don't want to be a cowboy.

The industry is not an easy place to be. Jobs are limited. Often, you are stuck on poorly managed projects that force you to work sixty, eighty, one hundred hour weeks for months on end. Ideas are tied to your identity and, to some, their self-worth. These ideas are eviscerated regularly and it is easy to take that personally. The stress level is high. The pay is low compared to similar fields. You may need to move every few years as studios are born and die and with 'seasonal rolloffs' becoming accepted practice. And you are competing with everyone else out there for the small handful of positions.

So again, I ask: why do you want to be a designer?

You have the opportunity to say something, to have ideas that matter. To craft the pastime and culture of a new generation.

If you are in it because you like to play games, quit. Find something else to do. Make room for the people who want to change the world.

If you are in it to change the world, prove it. As a student you have a choice to make. You can be ordinary. You can pitch the same types of ideas as everyone else: rip-offs on *Star Wars* or *Halo* or *Blade Runner*. Or you can use this time to really spread your wings and be interesting. Make something that is not what everyone else is doing. Take risks. If you fail now, it is not on a multimillion-dollar project. The time is now.

Are you ready to change the world?

Index

Made in the USA
Charleston, SC
05 March 2012